FURTHER PRAISE FOR *BELIEVING BULLSHIT*

"How many times have you found yourself taking part in frustrating arguments in which you are confident that the available evidence strongly supports your position, and yet your opponents somehow keep on managing to come up with superficially plausible but spurious reasons why they should not accept that evidence? Stephen Law has done us all the great favor of presenting a systematic analysis that will allow you to spot such slippery tactics and to counter them with good old-fashioned reason and common sense. What is more, he has done so in a very readable (and often amusing) way. Nice one, Stephen!"

Chris French
Professor and head of the
Anomalistic Psychology Research Unit, Goldsmiths,
University of London, and editor of *Skeptic* magazine

"If you want to escape being sucked into black holes of absurdity, this timely and necessary book offers eight great strategies to keep you safe."

A. C. Grayling
Professor of philosophy,
Birkbeck College, University of London

"One mightn't end up agreeing with all of Law's examples of how we fall short of the ideal of appropriately guarding ourselves against false belief, but his general account of the manners in which we do fall short convinces and it cannot but help one in raising one's guard."

T. J. Mawson
Fellow and tutor in philosophy,
St. Peter's College, University of Oxford

BELIEVING
BULLSHIT

BELIEVING BULLSHIT

*How Not to Get Sucked
into an Intellectual
Black Hole*

STEPHEN LAW

 **Prometheus Books**

59 John Glenn Drive
Amherst, New York 14228–2119

Published 2011 by Prometheus Books

Cover image © 2011 Media Bakery.
Cover design by Jacqueline Nasso-Cooke.

Inquiries should be addressed to
Prometheus Books
59 John Glenn Drive
Amherst, New York 14228–2119
VOICE: 716–691–0133
FAX: 716–691–0137
WWW.PROMETHEUSBOOKS.COM

15 14 13 12 11   5 4 3 2 1

Library of Congress Cataloging-in-Publication Data

Law, Stephen.
    Believing bullshit : how not to get sucked into an intellectual black hole / by Stephen Law.
        p. cm.
    Includes bibliographical references and index.
    ISBN 978–1–61614–411–1
    ISBN 978–1–61614–412–8 (e-book)
    1. Fallacies (Logic) I. Title.

BC175.L39 2011
165—dc22

                                                                    2010049343

Printed in the United States of America

Contents

Acknowledgments

My thanks to Luke Tracey, Jim Hamlyn, Jon and Adele Wainwright, Tom Pilling, Taryn Storey, Bill Law, Tim Mawson, Jon Cohen, John Sandford O'Neill, and Mick O'Neill. My thanks also to those who commented on earlier drafts posted on my blog stephenlaw.org.

Introduction

INTELLECTUAL BLACK HOLES

Even among the world's most educated and scientifically literate populations, ridiculous belief systems abound. Huge numbers believe in such things as astrology, the amazing powers of TV psychics, crystal divination, the healing powers of magnets, and the prophecies of Nostradamus. Many suppose the pyramids were built by aliens, or that the Holocaust never happened, or that the World Trade Center was brought down by the US government. A few would have us believe that the earth is ruled by a secret cabal of lizardlike aliens. Even mainstream religions have people believing absurdities. Preachers have promised seventy-two heavenly virgins to suicide bombers. Others insist the entire universe is only a few thousand years old.

How do intelligent, college-educated people end up the willing slaves of claptrap? How, in particular, do the true believers manage to convince themselves and others that *they* are the rational, reasonable ones and *everyone else* is deluded?

This book identifies eight key mechanisms that can transform a set of ideas into a psychological fly trap—a bubble of belief that, while seductively easy to enter, can then be almost impossible to think your way out of again.

Cosmologists talk about black holes, objects so gravitationally powerful that nothing, not even light, can break away from them. Unwary space travelers passing too close to a black hole will find themselves sucked in. An increasingly powerful motor is required to resist its pull, until eventually one passes the "event horizon" and escape becomes impossible.

My suggestion is that our contemporary cultural landscape contains, if you like, numerous *Intellectual Black Holes*—belief systems constructed in such a way that unwary passersby can find themselves similarly drawn in. While those of us lacking robust intellectual and other psychological defenses are most easily trapped, we're all potentially vulnerable. If you find yourself encountering a belief system in which one or more of these mechanisms features prominently, be wary. Alarm bells should be going off and warning lights flashing. For you may now be approaching the event horizon of an Intellectual Black Hole.

FAKE REASONABLENESS

Note that the mere fact that a set of beliefs is attractive doesn't make it an Intellectual Black Hole. Take a set of beliefs about water, such as that it freezes at 0 degrees centigrade and boils at 100. People are also powerfully wedded to these beliefs too, but that's because they are *genuinely* reasonable. The seductive draw of the beliefs that lie at the heart of an Intellectual Black Hole, by contrast, has nothing to do with whether they're reasonable or true. To those trapped inside, the core beliefs may *appear* quite sensible. But that appearance is illusory—a product of the belief system's ability to disable the truth-detecting power of reason and get its victims to embrace instead habits of thought that are deceptive and unreliable.

AIM OF THIS BOOK

The central aim of this book is to help immunize readers against the wiles of conspiracy theorists, cultists, political zealots, religious nutcases, and promoters of flaky alternative medicines by setting out some key tricks of the trade by which such self-sealing bubbles of belief are maintained. We'll see how an impregnable fortress can be constructed around even a ridiculous set of beliefs, rendering them immune to rational criticism and creating a veneer of faux reasonableness.

Most of us will have had at some point the frustrating experience of trying to hold a reasonable conversation with someone powerfully committed to some ludicrous system of belief, and so will have come up against at least some of the strategies documented in this book. My aim here is to unpack and explain in some detail *eight key strategies*, which I call:

1. Playing the Mystery Card
2. "But It Fits!" and The Blunderbuss
3. Going Nuclear
4. Moving the Semantic Goalposts
5. "I Just Know!"
6. Pseudoprofundity
7. Piling Up the Anecdotes
8. Pressing Your Buttons

In each case I (1) set out the strategy, (2) explain what is wrong with it, and (3) provide illustrations of how it is applied.

DANGERS POSED BY INTELLECTUAL BLACK HOLES

Why worry about Intellectual Black Holes? What does it matter if some people happen to believe absurd things?

There's no doubt that Intellectual Black Holes can exist

without causing any great harm. They remain dangerous, however. In some cases, the dangers are obvious. The hazards posed by an extreme cult, such as the Reverend Jim Jones's (which ended in the mass suicide of his followers in the Guyanan jungle), are abundantly clear. Once our minds have been captured by such a belief system, we become vulnerable to the wiles of those who control it. Victims have even been led into committing terrorist attacks.

There are less dramatic but still significant dangers. Every year, millions of dollars are spent on alternative medicines that, in many cases, just don't work. Not only do these medicines not work, people relying on them may expose themselves to serious risk as a result. For example, people may die as a consequence of relying on homeopathic treatment rather than conventional immunizations to protect them against malaria. Belief in the efficacy of homeopathy to protect against malaria, or that homeopathy has any kind of genuinely medicinal effect, is not supported by the evidence. So why do people believe it works? In large measure because of the kind of belief-inducing mechanisms examined in this book—particularly *Piling Up the Anecdotes* and *Playing the Mystery Cards.* As promoted and defended by at least some of its practitioners, homeopathy is an Intellectual Black Hole.

Each year vast sums are also spent on astrologers, psychics, and others claiming extraordinary powers. Vulnerable people waste both cash and emotional energy seeking out reassurances about lost loved ones that are, in reality, worthless. Again, many of these people have become convinced, or have convinced themselves, about the reasonableness of their belief in psychics and spirit mediums by the mechanisms described in this book.

So Intellectual Black Holes can allow people to be taken advantage of financially. Indeed, they are big business. But victims can be taken advantage of in other ways too.

Intellectual Black Holes can also lead people to waste their lives. In some cases, true believers may be led to abandon friends and family and throw away real opportunities, all for the sake of furthering their belief system's hypnotically attractive, if bogus, cause.

A SLIDING SCALE

We should acknowledge that Intellectual Black Holes lie at the end of a sliding scale. The fact is, almost all of us engage in these eight strategies to *some* extent, particularly when beliefs to which we are strongly committed are faced with a rational threat. And in fact, under certain circumstances, there may be little wrong in using some of them *in moderation* (as I will explain). What transforms even a belief system into a Black Hole is the *extent* to which such mechanisms are relied upon in dealing with intellectual threats and generating an appearance of reasonableness. The more we start to rely on these kinds of strategies to prop up and defend what we believe, the more Black Hole–like our belief system becomes, until a Black Hole is clearly what we have got.

ON RELIGION

This book includes several religious examples of Intellectual Black Holes—including Young Earth Creationism and Christian Science. However, it's worth emphasizing at the outset that I'm certainly *not* suggesting that every religious belief system is an Intellectual Black Hole, or that every person of faith is a victim.

True, I illustrate how even core mainstream religious beliefs are sometimes promoted and defended by means of strategies covered in this book. But that's not meant to show that beliefs in question are false, or that they *couldn't* be given a proper, robust defense. Just because some religious people choose to defend what they believe by dubious means doesn't entail that no one can reasonably hold those same beliefs.

ON BULLSHIT

So, to be clear, when I talk as I do about an Intellectual Black Hole being a *bullshit belief system*, it's not the *content* I'm suggesting is bullshit but *the manner in which its core beliefs are defended and promoted.*

According to philosopher Harry Frankfurt, whose essay *On Bullshit* has become a minor philosophical classic, bullshit involves a kind of fakery. A bullshitter, says Frankfurt, is not the same thing as a liar. The bullshitter does not knowingly tell a fib. He does not assert something he knows to be false. Rather he just says things to suit his purposes—to get away with something—without any care as to whether what he says is true.[1]

I don't entirely agree with Frankfurt's analysis of bullshit. Frankfurt's definition, it seems to me, is in at least one respect too narrow. People regularly talk about the latest self-help fad, astrology, feng shui, and Christian Science as being bullshit, and their practitioners as bullshit artists, even while acknowledging that those who promote these beliefs typically do so in all sincerity. Not only do they believe what they say, it matters to them that what they say is true.

What nevertheless marks out practitioners of astrology, feng shui, and Christian Science as bullshit artists, I'd suggest, is the kind of faux reasonableness that they manage to generate—the pseudoscientific gloss that they are able to apply to their core beliefs. They create the *illusion* that what they believe is reasonable, while not recognizing themselves that it's only an illusion. They typically manage to fool not only others, but themselves too.

ON STUPIDITY

Victims of Intellectual Black Holes need be neither dim nor foolish. The sophistication of some of the strategies examined in this book demonstrates that those who use them are often smart. Nor need those who fall foul of Intellectual Black Holes be *generally* gullible. Victims may, in other areas of their lives, be models of caution, subjecting claims to close critical scrutiny, weighing evidence scrupulously, and tailoring their beliefs according to robust, rational standards. They are able to, as it were, *compartmentalize* their application of these strategies.

So if, after reading this book, you begin to suspect that maybe you have become trapped inside an Intellectual Black Hole, there's no need to feel foolish. People far cleverer than either you or me have fallen victim.

APPENDIX A TO THE INTRODUCTION

Why Do We Believe What We Do?

This book does not attempt to provide an overarching theory of why we are drawn to particular belief systems in the first place, or why we are drawn to using the kind of mechanisms described in this book in their defense.

Why, for example, is belief in supernatural beings—such as ghosts, angels, dead ancestors, and gods—so widespread? Belief in such supernatural agents appears to be a near-universal feature of human societies. There is some evidence that a predisposition toward beliefs of this kind may actually be innate—part of our natural evolutionary heritage. Psychologist Justin Barrett has suggested that the prevalence of beliefs of this kind may in part be explained by our possessing a *Hypersensitive Agent Detection Device*, or H.A.D.D.[2]

The H.A.D.D. Hypothesis

Human beings explain features of the world around them in two very different ways. For example, we sometimes appeal to natural *causes* or *laws* in order to account for an event. Why did that apple fall from the tree? Because the wind blew and shook the branch, causing the apple to fall. Why did the water freeze in the pipes last night? Because the temperature of the water fell below zero, and it is a law that water freezes below zero.

However, we also explain by appealing to *agents*—beings who *act* on the basis of their *beliefs* and *desires* in a more or less rational way. Why did the apple fall from the tree? Because Ted wanted to eat it, believed that shaking the tree would make it fall, and so shook the tree. Why are Mary's car keys on the mantelpiece? Because she wanted to remind herself not to forget them, so she put them where she thought she would spot them.

Barrett suggests we have evolved to be overly sensitive to agency. We evolved in an environment containing many agents—family members, friends, rivals, predators, prey, and so on. Spotting and understanding other agents helps us survive and reproduce. So we evolved to be sensitive to them—oversensitive, in fact. Hear a rustle in the bushes behind you, and you instinctively spin round, looking for an agent. Most times, there's no one there—just the wind in the leaves. But, in the environment in which we evolved, on those few occasions when there is an agent present, detecting it might well have saved your life. Far better to avoid several imaginary predators than be eaten by a real one. Thus evolution will select for an inheritable tendency to not just detect—but *over*detect—agency. We have evolved to possess (or, if you prefer, to *be*) hyperactive agency detectors.

If we do have a H.A.D.D., that would at least partly explain the human tendency to feel there is "someone there" even when no one is observed, and so may at least partly explain our tendency to believe in the existence of invisible agents—in spirits, ghosts, angels, or gods.

For example, in his book *Illusion of Conscious Will*, Daniel Wegner points out what he considers to be the most remarkable characteristic of those using a Ouija board (in which the planchette—often an upturned shot glass—on which the subjects' index fingers are gently resting appears to wander independently around the board, spelling out messages from "beyond"):

> People using the board seem irresistibly drawn to the conclusion that some sort of unseen agent . . . is guiding the planchette movement. Not only is there a breakdown in the perception of one's own contribution to the talking board effect but a theory immediately arises to account for this breakdown: the theory of outside agency. In addition to spirits of the dead, people seem willing at times to adduce the influence of demons, angels, and even entities from the future or from outer space, depending on their personal contact with cultural theories about such effects.[3]

Because the movement of the planchette seems odd, it is quickly put down to the influence of an invisible agent (although notice the kind of agent invoked varies from group to group depending on their own particular, culturally led expectations— see *Piling Up the Anecdotes*).

However, I am not here endorsing the H.A.D.D. explanation for widespread belief in such invisible agents (although I suspect there's some truth to it). Also, notice that, even if we do possess a H.A.D.D., that at best explains the attractiveness of only *some* of the belief systems discussed in this book. Many wacky belief systems—such as those involving crystal healing, palmistry, or numerology—involve no invisible agents. I mention the H.A.D.D. hypothesis only to illustrate the point that the mechanisms identified in this book are not intended to rival such psychological and evolutionary accounts of why we believe what we do. My claim is that *once* we find ourselves drawn to a belief system, for whatever reason, *then* these eight mechanisms may come into play to bolster and defend it.

Note that the H.A.D.D. hypothesis does not say that there are no invisible agents. Perhaps at least some of the invisible agents people suppose exist are real. Perhaps there really are ghosts, or spirits, or gods. However, if we suppose the H.A.D.D. hypothesis does correctly explain why it is that so many people believe in the existence of invisible agents, then the fact that large numbers hold such beliefs can no longer be considered good evidence that any such agents exist. It will no longer do to say, "Surely not *all* these people can be so *very* deluded? Surely there must be *some* truth to these beliefs, otherwise they would not be so widespread." The fact is, if the H.A.D.D. hypothesis is correct, we're likely to believe in the existence of such invisible agents anyway, whether or not such agents exist. But then the popularity of these beliefs is not good evidence such agents exist.

There was already good reason to be skeptical about appeals to what many people believe when it comes to justifying beliefs in invisible agents, as well as many other beliefs of a religious or supernatural character. The fact that around 45 percent of the citizens of one of the richest and best-educated populations on the planet believe the entire universe is only about six thousand years old is testament to the fact that, whatever else may be said about religion, it undoubtedly possesses a quite astonishing power to get large numbers of people—even smart, college-educated people—to believe downright ridiculous things. Nevertheless, *if* the H.A.D.D. hypothesis is correct, it adds yet another nail to the coffin lid of the suggestion: "Lots of people believe it so there must be *something* to it!"

The Theory of Cognitive Dissonance

The H.A.D.D. hypothesis may partly explain why we are drawn to certain belief systems in the first place—those involving invisible agents. Another psychological theory that may play a role in explaining our propensity to use the kind of strategies described in this book to defend such theories is the *theory of cognitive dissonance*. Dissonance is the psychological discomfort we feel when we hold beliefs or attitudes that conflict. The theory says we are motivated to reduce dissonance by either adjusting our beliefs and attitudes or rationalizing them.

The example of the "sour grapes" in Aesop's story of "The Fox and the Grapes" is often used to illustrate cognitive dissonance. The fox desires those juicy-looking grapes, but then, when he realizes he will never attain them, he adjusts his belief accordingly to make himself feel better: he decides the grapes are sour.

How might the theory of cognitive dissonance play a role in explaining why we are drawn to using the kind of belief-immunizing strategies described in this book? Suppose, for the sake of argument, that our evolutionary history has predisposed us toward a belief in supernatural agents, but also toward wanting to hold beliefs that are, broadly speaking, rational, or at the very least, not downright irrational. That might put us in a psychological bind. On the one hand, we may find ourselves unwilling or even unable to give up our belief in certain invisible agents. On the other hand, we may find ourselves confronted by overwhelming evidence that what we believe is downright unreasonable. Under these circumstances, strategies promising to disarm rational threats and give our beliefs at least the illusion of reasonableness are likely to seem increasingly attractive. Such strategies can provide us with a way of dealing with the intellectual discomfort such innate tendencies might otherwise produce. They allow true believers to reassure themselves that they are not being nearly as irrational as reason might otherwise suggest—to convince themselves and others that their belief in ghosts or spirits or whatever, even if not well confirmed, is at least not *contrary* to reason.

So we can speculate about why certain belief systems are attractive, and also why such strategies are employed to immunize them against rational criticism and provide a veneer of "reasonableness." Both the H.A.D.D. hypothesis and the theory of cognitive dissonance may have a role to play.

APPENDIX B TO THE INTRODUCTION

Two Threats to the Rationality of Theism

Our discussions will include examples of how strategies described in this book are sometimes used to deal with intellectual challenges to Theism—belief in God. I focus on two intellectual challenges in particular: (1) the evidential problem of evil, and (2) the problem of nontemporal agency. Because people often misunderstand these objections, it's worth spending a little time clarifying them at the outset.

The Logical and Evidential Problems of Evil

Perhaps the best-known challenge to Theism is the so-called *problem of evil*. In fact there are at least two versions of the problem—the logical problem and the evidential problem.

The logical problem is essentially simple. It's a challenge to belief in the traditional God of monotheism—a god that is (1) all-powerful, (2) all-knowing, and (3) all-good, or supremely benevolent. To indicate when it's this particular god that is being discussed, I use a capital "G." And to indicate that I am referring to those who believe in specifically this God, I call them Theists with a capital "T" (otherwise using a lowercase "t").

The challenge is: if there is such a God, why does evil exist? "Evil" in this context means either *moral* evil—agents doing things that are morally wrong, such as killing, stealing, torture, and so on—and/or *natural* evil, such as the diseases and disasters that cause very great suffering. Surely, the argument runs, an all-powerful God would have the ability to create a world without such depravity and suffering. Being all-knowing, he would know whether a world he created would contain evil, and being all-good, he would not desire the existence of a world containing evil. But the world does contain evil. Therefore there is no such God.

Notice that this particular argument against the existence of

God requires only that *some* evil exist. It matters not how little there is. The claim is that the existence of any evil at all logically entails that there is no God.

One standard theistic response to the logical problem is to say that God might create a world containing *some* evil, if that evil allowed greater goods. For example, war is a result of our exercising our free will. We humans choose to start wars. God could have made us mere puppet beings. He could have had full control of our actions and prevented us from starting wars. But such puppets are not morally responsible for what they do, so they can't be morally virtuous. So a world of puppet beings would lack a particularly important variety of goodness—moral goodness, which requires free agents doing good of their own volition. In order for the world to contain that kind of good, God had to cut our strings. As a result, some evil exists—that caused by our freely choosing to do wrong. But this evil is more than outweighed by the good that free will allows.

Interesting though the logical problem of evil is, it is not the problem I'm going to focus on here. My concern is with a different problem—the *evidential* problem of evil. The evidential problem starts not by noting that the world contains *some* evil but with the observation that it contains an *enormous amount* of both moral evil and pain and suffering. Even if God had to allow some evil for the sake of certain greater goods, surely he could have no reason to allow quite so much. We can sharpen this problem by noting that God will presumably not allow any *gratuitous* evil to exist. God, if he exists, must have good reason for allowing every last ounce of it.

Yes, for an affluent Westerner, life can be pretty good. However, for much of humanity, life is lived out in grinding poverty, frustration, misery, sickness, and horror. Parents watch as their children starve, waste away with terminal cancer, or become the abrupt victims of natural disasters such as the 2005 Pakistan earthquake that buried thousands of them alive. Enormous numbers of humans are struck down or killed in an appallingly slow and cruel way. Many are left so physically and psychologically crippled by their experiences that they bow out in despair. Such human suffering has been the rule for several million years, long before the development of antibiotics and anesthetics capable of reducing it a little. In ancient times and during the Middle Ages, almost one in three children died before they reached the age of five. Even before we humans made an appearance, other sentient inhabitants of this planet—including our own forerunners—had to endure unimaginable quantities of pain and suffering doled out over hundreds of millions of years. And of course such animal suffering continues today. A recent episode of a BBC wildlife documentary concluded by interviewing a cameraman new to the team. He had been filming komodo dragons poisoning then slowly tracking their water buffalo victim over a period of weeks, until it become so weak they could eat it alive. It was an episode of such cruelty and horror that the cameraman confessed he was now considering giving up wildlife photography as it was too much to stomach. We inhabit a beautiful but staggeringly cruel world.

Surely, if there is a God, he would not unleash such vast quantities of appalling suffering. *Some* suffering perhaps. But nothing like this much. Isn't the existence of so much seemingly pointless suffering excellent *evidence* that, even if there is some sort of creator or intelligence behind the universe—perhaps even a god—it isn't the Judeo-Christian God? While the existence of such a being might remain a possibility, it is surely a very unlikely one.

Theodicies

So runs the evidential problem of evil. Theists have developed a range of responses to the problem. One type of response is to construct a *theodicy*—an explanation for why God would, after all, create or allow such quantities of suffering. Here are three popular examples:

Free will theodicy. Free will may be invoked to deal with not just the logical problem but also the evidential problem. Here's an example. God could have made us puppet beings that always did the right thing. But then the world would have lacked the most important form of goodness—moral goodness. So God cut our strings and set us free. Unfortunately, as a result, we sometimes choose to do wrong—we start wars, steal, kill, and so on. But these evils are still outweighed by the good that free will allows. That's why God allows them.

Character-building theodicy. This is, in the words of theologian John Hick, a "vale of soul making." Someone who has suffered will often say they don't regret it. They may learn from the experience. The suffering we experience is not pointless. It is there to give us opportunities. For example, parents watching their child learn to ride a bike will inevitably have to watch their child fall and hurt themselves a few times. But of course, when the child finally masters their bike and shouts, "Look at me! I can do it!" the pain they experienced in the process becomes worthwhile—their sense of achievement at having persevered through the pain and learned to ride would not be possible otherwise. Yes, we suffer, but there's good reason for it.

Laws of nature theodicy. In order for us to have the opportunity to act on our environment, and interact with each other in it, the universe must be law governed. There must be a predictability to what will happen if, say, I strike this match. I need to know a flame will result. If, when a match is struck, it sometimes results in a flame, but sometimes a cherry, sometimes disappears, sometimes causes my eyebrows to grow very fast, and so on—if, in short, the behavior of the physical world were random and chaotic—there would be no point in my trying to do anything. So laws are required for the very great good of our being able to perform actions, such as the action of helping our fellow humans. However, there is a downside to such laws. The laws that allow us to walk around and interact with each other on this planet have other consequences—such as tidal waves and earthquakes. These, in turn, cause pain and suffering. However, that pain and suffering is outweighed by goods such laws allow, such as goods done of our free will. And there are other benefits too, as Reverend Dr. John Polkinghorne, both a physicist and theologian, points out. About earthquakes, Polkinghorne says:

> Earthquakes occur, and if they are under the sea they generate tsunamis, because there are tectonic plates that sometimes slip. Would it not have been better, therefore, for God to arrange the earth to have a solid crust all over? The answer is, No, it wouldn't. The gaps between the plates enable mineral resources to well up from deeper down and replenish the face of the earth. Without this happening, life would not be able to keep going very long.[4]

So the very great good of life on earth actually requires that there be earthquakes.

These three theodicies are merely examples. Many more have been devised. Of course, all three have obvious limitations. The free will theodicy, for example, explains, at best, only the evils caused by our own free actions. It fails to explain natural evils, such as the pain and suffering caused by diseases and natural disasters. However, despite their individual limitations, many theists believe that such theodicies can collectively, if not entirely solve the evidential problem of evil, then at least bring it down to manageable proportions, so that it can no longer be supposed to deal a fatal blow to traditional Theism.

The Evil God Hypothesis

But is this true? Consider a rather different god hypothesis. Suppose there is a maximally powerful, all-knowing creator. Only this creator is not maximally good but maximally evil. His cruelty and malice know no bounds. Call this the evil god hypothesis.

How plausible is the evil god hypothesis? Almost everyone dismisses it out of hand, of course. It's a patently ridiculous suggestion. But why? Many of the standard arguments for the existence of God, such as that the universe must have a designer, or that it must have a first cause, or be the product of a necessary being, actually have nothing to say about the moral properties of this cosmic designer/creator/necessary being. They support the evil god hypothesis just as much as they support the good God hypothesis. So why dismiss the evil god hypothesis out of hand?

There is an obvious reason, of course: the evidential problem of good. Yes, the world contains much evil. But it also contains a great deal of good. Far too much good, in fact, for this world to be the creation of a maximally powerful and supremely evil being. Why, for example, would an evil god:

- Bestow upon some individuals immense health, wealth, and happiness (surely he'd rather, say, torture them for all eternity with a red-hot poker)?
- Put natural beauty into the world, which gives us pleasure?
- Allow us to perform selfless deeds, which are both a moral good and reduce the amount of suffering that exists?
- Give us children to love who love us unconditionally in return (for an evil god despises love)?
- Give us beautiful, healthy, young bodies (rather than say, ugly, painful, arthritic bodies)?

Notice how the evidential problem of good mirrors the evidential problem of evil. If you believe in a good god, you face the challenge of explaining why there is so much evil in the world; if you believe in an evil god, you face the challenge of explaining why there is so much good.

Notice that, just as theodicies can be constructed to try to explain away the problem of evil, mirror theodicies can be constructed to try to explain away the problem of good. Here are three examples:

Reverse free will theodicy. Evil god could have made us puppet beings that always did the wrong thing, so that we always acted to maximize pain and suffering. But then the world would have lacked one of the most profound and important forms of evil—moral evil: evil freely done of our own volition for which we can be held morally responsible. For an evil god, a world lacking moral evil is seriously deficient. So evil god cut our strings and set us free. As a result, we sometimes choose to do good— we sometimes selflessly help each other, for example. But such goods are outweighed by the moral evils free will allows. Which is why evil god allows them.

Character-destroying theodicy. This is a vale, not of soul making, but of soul destruction. Evil god wants us to suffer, do evil, and despair. Why does evil god create natural beauty? To provide some *contrast*. To make what is ugly seem even more so. If everything were uniformly ugly, we wouldn't be tormented by it half as much as if it contained some beauty. Contrast also explains why a few enjoy lavish lifestyles and success. Their happiness is designed to make the rest of us suffer even more: from jealousy, resentment, and frustration. No one can rest content (and remember, too, that deep down, even the few on which these gifts are bestowed not *really* happy). Why does evil god allow us to have children to love and who love us unconditionally in return? Because it's only if we really care about someone that we can really be made to worry agonizingly about them. Only parents know the depths of anguish and suffering that children bring. Why does an evil god give us healthy young bodies? Because we know that our health and vitality will be short-lived, that we will either die young or else slowly wither. By giving us something wonderful for a moment, and then gradually pulling it away, an evil god can make us suffer even more than if we had never had it in the first place.

Reverse laws of nature theodicy. In order for us to have the opportunity to act on our environment, and interact with each other in it, the universe must be regular and law governed. It must be predictable what will happen if, say, I strike this match. I need to know a flame will result. If, when a match is struck, it sometimes results in a flame, but sometimes a cherry, sometimes disappears, sometimes causes my eyebrows to grow very fast, and so on—if, in short, the behavior of the physical world were random and chaotic—then there would be no point in my trying to do anything. Laws are required for the possibility of my being able to perform morally evil actions, such as the action of my deliberately lighting a match and burning down a family's house while they are sleeping inside it. True, these same laws have some good consequences—they allow us to do good deeds, for example. Moreover, as Polkinghorne reminds us, the tectonic plates that produce the evil of earthquakes also produce certain goods, such as minerals that help replenish life. However, the pain, suffering, and, most important, the moral evil the laws of nature allow more than outweighs such goods.

How effective are these reverse theodicies? Most of us recognize that they are not effective at all. The fact is, the amount of good that exists clearly *is* sufficient to place beyond reasonable doubt the conclusion that there is no evil god, notwithstanding such ingenious and convoluted attempts to try to explain it away. But if it remains fairly obvious that there is no evil god, given the available evidence, why isn't it equally obvious that there is no good God either? If belief in an evil deity remains patently ridiculous given the amount of good there is in the world, why should we consider the good god hypothesis to be significantly more reasonable—at the very least not unreasonable—given the staggering amounts of evil the world contains? I consider this to be one of the most serious challenges facing belief in God.

I don't claim the challenge cannot be met. However, personally, I cannot see how. While there are some interesting asymmetries between the good and evil god hypotheses,[5] they are not, it seems to me, anything like enough to render one hypothesis significantly more reasonable than the other. Perhaps there is some sort of intelligence behind the universe—a first cause, fine-tuner, necessary being of some sort. But surely we have overwhelming evidence that, even if there is, it is not an evil god. Ditto a good God.

Two Misconceptions about the Problem of Evil

It's worth dealing with two common misconceptions about the problem of evil.

First, some theists dismiss the evidential problem of evil on the grounds that it is too "impressionistic." Precisely this response was made to my presentation of the problem of evil in a contribution to a recent book. The reviewer, David Hart, said that such objections to Theism were "incorrigibly impressionistic."[6] Similarly, in a radio conversation with me, scientist Denis Alexander responded to the evidential problem of evil by saying, regarding the huge amounts of seemingly pointless suffering we observe, that "we simply are not in a position to measure those kind of things [quantities of evil], we can measure certain things in science and so forth."[7] Alexander's suggestion seemed to be that *if we cannot scientifically measure suffering, it cannot constitute strong evidence against a hypothesis.*

Now, it is true that pain and suffering are hard to measure and quantify with great precision. There is no calibrated scale on which we can place pain to measure exactly how much there is, for example. It is undeniable that estimations of quantities must, to *some* extent, be "impressionistic."

But does it follow that there isn't clearly enough of it to rule out the hypothesis that there exists a good God? Surely not. After all, notice that good cannot be weighed on a calibrated scale either. Our assessment of how much good there is must be no less "impressionistic." Yet, despite that, we know there is more than enough to establish beyond reasonable doubt that there's no evil god. So why can't we know that there's more than enough evil to rule out the good god hypothesis as well?

In fact, if it were true that quantities of pain and suffering inflicted cannot be used as good evidence because they cannot be "scientifically" measured, then we would not be able to convict someone of, say, inflicting great pain and suffering on a defenseless animal. Suppose that in response to compelling evidence of the appalling torture the accused inflicted over a long period of time, the judge said: "Ah, but we can't *scientifically measure* this pain and suffering, can we? In which case, the prosecution's evidence is hopelessly impressionistic and thus inadmissible. Case dismissed!" Clearly, that would be a perverse verdict. The same is true of the verdict that hundreds of millions of years of appalling suffering can't count as good evidence against the existence of God just because it, too, can't be "scientifically" measured.

A second common misconception about the evidential problem of evil as an argument against the existence of God is that it somehow *presupposes* that there is a God. Why? Because talk of things being "good" and "evil" requires that God exist. Such talk only makes sense if there is some objective standard against which good and evil might be gauged—and the only possible standard is God.

This objection is easily dealt with. First of all, note that the problem can be rephrased without using the word *evil*. We can just ask those who believe in God, "If there is a God of the sort you believe in, why does he unleash so much pain and suffering? Surely such a God would not unleash gratuitous pain and suffering, correct?" Second, the objection, as it stands, simply *assumes* that moral talk about "good" and "evil" only makes sense if there's a God. This would need to be shown, and I very much doubt it can. Third, and most important, whether the problem of evil presupposes God is irrelevant, for what the problem of evil reveals is an *internal* inconsistency in Theism. So suppose, for the sake of argument, that there is a God. In that case, there are moral properties, good and evil. Actually, there's quite a lot of evil: far too much, arguably, for there to be a God. So, Theism leads us to the problem of evil, and the problem of evil leads us to see that God doesn't exist. So Theism, if true, is false. And, obviously, if it is false, it is false. So it's false.

The Problem of Nontemporal Agency

Here's a second, rather different objection to belief in *any* sort of creator god, let alone a good one.

Human beings are naturally drawn to explanations in terms of agency (and of course, the H.A.D.D., if it exists, would partly explain why). This is particularly true when we are faced with features of the universe that we cannot otherwise explain (remember the Ouija board example). When we could not explain the movement of certain heavenly bodies across the sky, such as the planets, we supposed they must be, or must be guided by, agents of some sort. Only not mere humans (we are incapable of such feats) but *supernatural* agents. When we could not explain what made plants and flowers grow, we supposed they must be forced up by supernatural agents—fairies or sprites or whatever. When we could not explain why diseases and natural disasters occurred, we supposed they must be the actions of more supernatural agents—witches and demons. When explanations in terms of natural causes and laws are not available, our default setting, as it were, is to switch over to explanation in terms of agency, and, if the situation demands it, *supernatural* agency.

Of course, as science has progressed, many of the phenomena such supernatural agents were invoked to explain have received plausible naturalistic explanations. But there will always be questions science cannot answer (as we'll see in chapter 2), including: *Why is there anything at all?* And so, with respect to such questions, it's always tempting to invoke some sort of supernatural agent to do the explaining. God is of course the ultimate supernatural agent.

However, when we invoke a supernatural agent to explain why the universe as a whole exists (and of course, an H.A.D.D. would, again, at least partly explain this powerful temptation), we run into a problem that does not plague the suggestions that there are fairies, witches, and ghosts at work within the universe. The problem is that God, as creator of the spatiotemporal universe—as the instigator of the big bang (which, remember, marks *the beginning of time itself*—there is supposedly no "before" the big bang, only an "after")—is not himself a temporal being. God did not exist in time prior to the universe, as there was no time for him to exist in. But then the suggestion that there exists such a *nontemporal* agent doesn't make sense.

Compare an analogous case. Suppose I claim there exists a nonspatial mountain. I might think I know what I am talking about. But a little reflection reveals that I don't. The concept of a mountain is the concept of a physical object that has parts that stand in certain spatial relations to each other. A mountain must have a summit that is *higher* than the rest of it, and valleys that are *lower*. It must have *sides*, and so on. The concept of a mountain has its home with a spatial framework. Strip that framework away, and we end up talking nonsense.

We run into a similar problem with talk of a "nontemporal agent" that is the creator of space and time. For the concept of an agent is the concept of a being that can perform more or less rational *actions* on the basis of their *beliefs* and *desires*. But beliefs and desires are psychological states, and states require temporal duration. Actions also require a temporal setting. Surely God can only perform the act of creation if there *already* exists time for him to perform the action in. On closer examination, the idea of a nontemporal agent seems to make scarcely more sense than the idea of a nonspatial mountain.

Notice that, unlike the evidential problem of evil, the problem of nontemporal agency is not dependent on our observations of what the world is like. It is not based on empirical evidence. Rather, it is a conceptual objection generated purely by a little armchair reflection and unpacking of the concept of agency. The conclusion is not that the claim that such a God exists is false, but that it is *nonsensical*. But if the concept of a nontemporal agent doesn't even make sense, then *we cannot explain the existence of the universe by appealing to such an agent*.

These two intellectual threats to belief in God—the evidential problem of evil and the problem of nontemporal agency—are set out here as examples of the kind of powerful-looking objections that can and have been raised against it. I don't argue here that these objections cannot be properly dealt with. Many Theists have of course attempted to offer such a response. Perhaps some have succeeded. However, these two objections certainly can't properly be dealt with by means of the kind of strategies examined in this book. Rather than address such problems in an intellectually rigorous way, these strategies involve attempting to immunize belief in God against such threats by means of obfuscation, evasion, and intellectual sleight of hand.

Chapter 1

Playing the Mystery Card

S uppose critics point out that not only do you have little in the way of argument to support your particular belief system, there also seems to be powerful evidence against it. If you want, nevertheless, to convince both yourself and others that your beliefs are not nearly as ridiculous as your critics suggest, what might you do?

Perhaps you might *Play the Mystery Card*. As we'll see, this strategy is particularly popular when it comes to defending beliefs in the supernatural—beliefs in ghosts, angels, psychic powers, gods, and so on. By far the most popular version of the strategy—the version on which I focus here—is to say, "Ah, but of course *this is beyond the ability of science/reason to decide*! We must acknowledge that science and reason have their limits. It is *sheer arrogance* to suppose they can explain everything!" As we'll see, those who trot out this line are often as not conjuring up little more than a smoke screen.

the (bad) argument

"BUT IT'S BEYOND SCIENCE/REASON TO DECIDE"

Scientism

The view that science can ultimately explain everything—can answer every legitimate question—is called *scientism*. Actually, few scientists embrace scientism. Most accept that there may well be questions science cannot answer.

Take *moral* questions, for example. Is killing always wrong? Is it morally acceptable to design a baby? Science can make new technologies possible, including weapons of mass destruction and genetic engineering. But even most scientists agree that science cannot tell us whether it is ever morally permissible to use such technologies. It seems, as the philosopher David Hume famously noted, that science ultimately reveals only what *is* the case; it cannot tell us what we morally *ought* or *ought not* to do.

Nor, it would seem, can science explain why the universe itself exists—why there is anything at all. Scientific explanations involve appealing to natural causes or laws. For example, if you ask a scientist why the water froze in the pipes last night, he might explain by pointing out that the temperature of the water fell below 0 degrees Celsius, and that it is a *law of nature* that water freezes below zero. That would explain why the water froze. But what explains why there are any natural laws or causes in the first place? What explains why there is a natural world *at all*? Here, it seems, science cannot provide the answers.

So, scientism is probably false. There probably are questions science can't answer, questions that extend beyond its proper domain. But then, if the credibility of what you believe is under scientific threat, why not *protect it by suggesting that it, too, is something science cannot adjudicate*. Indeed, accuse your critics of scientism!

things Science will probably never be able to explain

The Veil Analogy

Such appeals to mystery can be particularly effective if combined with a *veil analogy*. Suggest that the observable, scientifically investigable world is not all there is—there is a further mysterious reality hidden from us, as if behind a veil. Maintain that some of us—those lucky enough to be equipped with the right sort of transcendent faculty or insight—can glimpse this mysterious reality (and of course it's terribly important that we listen to these "experts"—psychics, say, or "spiritual" people). Suggest that, even if we are not fortunate enough to be equipped with such a transcendental sense ourselves, we can all discover *suggestive clues* about the character of what lies beyond (at this point, you might wish to reach for a generous helping of supporting *anecdotes* to bolster your conviction that, say, angels or psychic powers exist—see *Piling Up the Anecdotes*). But insist that science, as a discipline, with its overly rigid and restrictive conception of what counts as "evidence," is pretty useless when it comes to establishing anything about what lies behind the veil. Yes, science is a remarkably powerful tool when it comes to discovering how things are on *this* side of the veil. The natural, physical world is its proper domain. But maintain that only a fool would suppose science can reveal what lies beyond the natural, physical realm.

So what does lie beyond the veil? Some would begin with the dead. Spiritualists often use the veil analogy, describing the deceased as having "passed over to the other side." While science is unable to penetrate the veil, the spiritualist, luckily, has the ability to glimpse, if only dimly, what lies on the far side. If the spiritualist's abilities fail to show up when subjected to some rigorous scientific testing, well, you wouldn't expect them to—such gifts are just not the kind of thing science is equipped to investigate.

Of course, it's not just our dead loved ones who are supposed to reside behind the cosmic divide. Angels, fairies, demonic beings, and trans-dimensional aliens do as well. Supernatural powers or energies, such as those that account for the miraculous abilities of psychics, spoon benders, and dowsers also operate behind the veil. And of course God, the ultimate agent, resides in large measure beyond the divide. "God," as the philosopher G. W. F. Hegel once put it: "does not offer himself for observation."[1]

Because all these phenomena lie beyond the cosmic curtain, it's widely supposed that belief in such things cannot be discredited by rational or scientific means. Such beliefs are all *immune to rational or scientific refutation*.

Character Assassination

This kind of immunizing strategy is often combined with an implicit, or not-so-implicit, attack on the character of the critic. A quotation from Shakespeare's *Hamlet* (after the appearance of the ghost of Hamlet's father) can be used to lend the ad hominem attacks a little gravitas: "There are more things in heaven and earth, Horatio, than are dreamt of in your philosophy."

See? *Your* philosophy is rather foolish. It fails to acknowledge that reality is far richer than your narrow, naturalistic, scientistic worldview can appreciate. You're an arrogant know-it-all who thinks that you—or at least science—can supply all the answers. Show a little humility!

Nowadays, the accusation that someone is unfairly discriminating against others is one of the most potent you can make. No one likes to think of themselves as a bigot, or to be associated with bigots. So dressing up your charge of scientism as an accusation of unjust discrimination is likely to be doubly effective. If someone persists in presenting what looks like a credible scientific threat against what you believe, try asserting, or, better, implying that they are an intellectual bigot—that their scientistic worldview manifests nothing more than a nasty, unimaginative, and irrational bias against people who hold beliefs such as your own. Try claiming that, just like women or ethnic minorities, you're being victimized.

You, by contrast, will now appear wonderfully humble, modest,

(handwritten margin note: Same argument can be made both ways)

and open to new ideas and perspectives. Clearly, you are also far
wiser and more "spiritual" than your narrow-minded critics, for
you appreciate that the world extends far beyond your own, or even
science's, limited horizon. Who would want to side with such arrogant, scientistic oppressors against the humble and wise?

haha

NONSCIENTIFIC REFUTATIONS

Is it true that beliefs about supernatural agents, gods, powers,
and other phenomena are essentially immune to scientific refutation? Might they be immune to *any* sort of rational refutation?

Before we look at the specific question of whether *science*
might settle certain supernatural claims—including the claim that
God does or does not exist—I want to first make two important
preliminary points.

It's often assumed that if supernatural claims are to be
refuted, then they will be refuted *by science*. Only science has
that capability. But actually, some supernatural claims may be
refutable—even *empirically* refutable—even if they're not, properly speaking, *scientifically* refutable. The two preliminary points
I'll now explain are:

1) not all refutations are scientific, and
2) not all *empirical* refutations are scientific.

The Scientific Method

"Science," as the term is most commonly understood today,
refers to a certain sort of activity involving, and/or body of
knowledge produced by, the application of something called the
scientific method—a human invention not much more than four
hundred years old, the emergence of which owes much to
thinkers such as the philosopher Francis Bacon (1561–1626).

Scientists collect data by observation and experiment. They

formulate theories to explain what they observe and, where possible, subject those theories to *tests*. Scientists derive from their theories predictions that can be independently checked. For example, an astronomer's theory that predicts the planet Mars will be in a certain place at a certain time can be checked by other astronomers. Tests can also take the form of controlled experiments carefully designed to be repeatable (other scientists should be able to repeat the experiment and obtain the same result). A scientific approach to testing theories emphasizes the importance of formulating theories and predictions with clarity and precision, focusing, wherever possible, on mathematically quantifiable phenomena that can be reliably measured, for example, by using a calibrated instrument.

Through the application of the scientific method, various hypotheses and theories can be, and have been, refuted. The point I want to stress here, however, is that people have been producing powerful refutations of beliefs for much longer than the four hundred years or so that the refined tool known as the "scientific method" has existed. Even today, beliefs are refuted by other means. The following are two examples.

Conceptual Refutation

Suppose an explorer claims that, on her travels, she discovered a four-sided triangle. We ask her what she means. "Was it really a *triangle*?" we ask. "You are using the word 'triangle' with its *normal meaning*?" "Oh, yes," she replies. "Only, the one I discovered has four sides." It's clear that, with just a bit of elementary reasoning, we can show that our explorer has discovered no such thing. A triangle, by definition, has exactly three sides. So a triangle with four sides involves a straightforward logical contradiction—it would have to have exactly three sides but not have three sides. This is something reason alone can establish. We don't have to bother mounting our own expedition to trace our explorer's footsteps and check whether there's a four-sided triangle where she claims. We can know, *just by thinking about it*, that there's no such thing. This refutation of the explorer's can hardly be classed as "scientific." It's certainly not an exercise in empirical science. No observation was required. Some straight-forward reflection on certain *concepts*—those of triangularity and four-sidedness—is sufficient to refute her claim.

This raises the possibility that various claims about the super-natural might also be refuted without any appeal to science. Indeed, my introduction (appendix B) provided a possible example. If we understand God to be, literally, an *agent*—a person who acts in a rational way on the basis of his beliefs and desires, but God is (or was?) also a nontemporal being, capable of existing outside of a temporal setting, then we run into similar conceptual obstacles. The concepts of agency, action, belief, desire, and so on, are, it seems, essentially temporal concepts. Talk about a nontemporal agent or person seems, on closer inspection, to make little more sense than talk of a four-sided tri-angle. But if that is true, then we can refute the claim that the time is itself the creation of such an agent without any appeal to empirical science. A simple conceptual argument does the trick.

So here's one way in which a rational refutation of a claim need not be a *scientific* refutation. It might be a conceptual refu-tation. These are, of course, the kind of arguments in which philosophers specialize.

Empirical but Non-"Scientific" Refutation

It also seems to me that even an *empirically based* refutation—that is to say, a refutation based, at least in part, on observation of the world around us—need not be "scientific." Suppose Jim claims to have a cat stuffed inside his shirt. We carefully go around him, visually inspecting and patting every part of his shirt. We hear no "meows" and find no out-of-place bumps that might be a cat. So we conclude, reasonably, despite not having actually looked inside Jim's shirt, that there's no cat there. We have pretty clearly refuted Jim's claim, and have done so on the basis of empirical observation. Were there really a cat inside Jim's shirt, we would surely expect to detect some signs of its presence. If, even after careful checking, we find no such signs, we are justified in supposing there's no cat there.

I extract two morals from this example. The first is that, while this refutation is empirically based, it would surely be odd to class it as a *scientific* refutation. Were we really doing *science* when we noted the absence of bumps and "meows" and concluded there was no cat present? Surely, this is an example of the common or garden-variety empirical refutation people have been conducting for millennia, long before the development of the rather refined and specialized tool known as the scientific method. If we conclude that it's not raining because the ground outside is not wet, or that the chicken is not cooked because the juices are not running clear, or that it can't be 8 p.m. yet because the sun is still up, those are perfectly acceptable empirically based inferences to draw, despite the fact that these inferences are not ordinarily classed as scientific. Indeed, such common or garden-variety, everyday refutations can be just as devastatingly effective as their laboratory-based counterparts. Call them "scientific" if you like, but, given that such refutations aren't typically performed by scientists and don't involve the "scientific method," it seems to me less misleading to describe them as empirical but nonscientific.

The second moral I draw is that the effectiveness of such everyday refutations is not threatened by the fact that we could yet turn out to be mistaken about there being a cat in Jim's shirt. This refutation, like any empirical refutation (even of the properly scientific variety), is open to the *possibility of error*. It is possible, for example, that Jim has secretly been producing mute microcats. Perhaps, by a program of selective breeding, Jim has managed to get them down to just an inch or two in size, and he has one of these microcats hidden under his left armpit, where we have failed to detect it. This is a possibility. But the mere fact that we *might* be mistaken doesn't entail that we do not, on the basis of the available evidence, have excellent grounds for believing there's no cat present.

Might such an empirical, if not properly scientific, refutation of certain supernatural claims be possible? Again, I don't see why not. Suppose Mary claims she has a supernaturally aided ability to predict the toss of a coin. She says an angel whispers into her ear whether the next toss will be heads or tails. Because Mary's claim concerns the supernatural—concerns what is behind the veil dividing the natural from the supernatural realm—does that entail that the claim is not amenable to empirical investigation and refutation? Obviously not. Mary's supposed angel may be on the other side of the veil. But its activities, if real, have consequences that can be observed on this side. If there really is an angel whispering in Mary's ear, Mary will able to predict correctly the next ten tosses of the coin. If she fails to predict all ten tosses correctly, it's reasonable for us to conclude that Mary is either lying or deluded. While not terribly "scientific," this would constitute a straightforward and effective refutation of a supernatural claim.

What about belief in God? Might that also be open to an empirically based, if not properly scientific, refutation? Again, I can't see why not. In fact, as we saw in my introduction (appendix B), the evidential problem of evil does appear to constitute just such a refutation. If there really is such a maximally benevolent and powerful being, then surely, while the universe might contain some pain and suffering and moral evil, it wouldn't contain anything like the amounts we observe. It certainly wouldn't contain any gratuitous suffering. But surely there is so much suffering, including nonhuman suffering, that it's implausible that it can all be explained as the unavoidable price paid for certain greater goods. Notice this argument is obviously *empirically based*—it relies on our observation of the world and the vast quantities of suffering it contains. Science might make a contribution toward the argument's effectiveness, of course, by revealing, for example, that the suffering we observe has also been going on for hundreds of millions of years (*that's* a properly scientific discovery). But the evidential problem of evil is not ordinarily classed as a "scientific" argument, despite being empirically based. It's a common or garden-variety type empirical refutation. Which is not, of course, to diminish its effectiveness.

To sum up, even *if* we cannot, strictly speaking, provide a scientific refutation of belief in God, it does not follow that we cannot refute belief in God. I'd suggest that anyone who supposes that *only* science is capable of refuting god beliefs is seriously underestimating what other approaches—including more philosophical or conceptual approaches—might be capable of.

SCIENCE AND THE SUPERNATURAL

Let's now turn to the suggestion that no *scientific* refutation of a supernatural claim is possible. I see no reason to accept this.

Samantha's Supernaturally Empowered Spit

Consider a hypothetical case. Suppose Samantha claims her saliva has miraculous healing powers. She supposes that if she rubs her saliva over wounds, skin complaints, diseased organs, and so on, this has a miraculous curative effect. Samantha's friends and relatives swear to the amazing restorative powers of her spit. Samantha doesn't know exactly how it works, but she does claim to know that it has something to do with the spirit realm. By some supernatural means, people are cured.

Does that fact that Samantha's claims that her spit has some sort of *supernatural* power—that the cures it produces are of a supernatural origin—mean that her claims are not scientifically refutable? Obviously not. It's not difficult to think up some properly scientific tests. For example, suppose we provide Samantha with three vials, one of her own saliva, one of a stranger's, and one of something that is not saliva at all, but just looks and feels like it. We have Samantha rub her miraculous spit on a number of subjects with various medical conditions: cuts, skin complaints, and so on. This trial is "double-blind": neither the subjects to whom the substances are applied nor Samantha know who are getting Samantha's saliva and who are getting something else. We then monitor the subjects to see if those with a certain sort of skin condition, cut, and so on recover more effectively than those who do not. If Samantha's spit really does have the miraculous power she claims, we should expect those who receive it to get better quicker than those who don't.

Such a test might provide strong evidence that Samantha's spit does, indeed, have such extraordinary powers. However, suppose those who receive Samantha's saliva treatment fail to get better any quicker than those who don't. Surely this would provide us with a strong piece of scientific evidence that Samantha's claim is false. Suppose a variety of further tests are conducted, all of which produce a negative result. And suppose that we have (which, of course, we do) credible scientific evidence that people are highly prone to the power of suggestion (merely telling someone that something will make them better can be surprisingly effective—see *Piling Up the Anecdotes*). Surely the reasonable conclusion to draw, now, would be that Samantha is mistaken, and that the testimony of her friends and relatives concerning the miraculous powers of her saliva is in large part a result of the power of suggestion.

It's worth emphasizing that in the above example, science would not just have failed to find evidence that a certain supernatural power *does* exist. It would have established pretty conclusively that it *doesn't* exist. We would have not just an *absence of evidence* but *evidence of absence*. When supernatural claims are tested, and we get a negative result, true believers often insist that this "proves nothing"—we may not have found evidence for what they believe, but we haven't shown what they believe is false. In some cases, that's true. But "prove" is a slippery word (as we'll see later in this chapter), and it may be that the tests have established beyond reasonable doubt that their belief is false.

So *science can pretty conclusively refute at least some claims of a supernatural nature.* This is because such claims, if true, often have *empirically observable consequences.* They are, in this respect, no different to claims about other "hidden" phenomena, such as claims about tiny, unobservable particles, or about the distant past. Such claims may be about phenomena to which we don't have direct observational access. But that's not to say that they cannot be pretty conclusively refuted by the methods of science.

Of course, it will always remain possible that Samantha's spit does, sometimes, have miraculously restorative powers. We might still be mistaken. But that's not to say we're not justified in supposing Samantha's claim is false. It's *possible* that my attic is inhabited by invisible space gerbils, that George Bush was a robot, and that the French are Martian imposters and the Eiffel Tower is a transmitter for secretly sending reports back to Mars. Any nutty belief about the world can always claim to be *possibly* true, for we can never prove beyond all possible doubt that it's false (as we'll see in *"But It Fits!"*). That's not to say we can't prove beyond *reasonable* doubt that it's false.

Samantha and her miraculous spit was a hypothetical example. However, many claims of a supernatural nature have been scientifically investigated in some depth. Scientists have tested the claims of remote viewers, psychics, crystal healers, and so forth and others claiming to have some sort of supernatural ability. Such investigations have failed to provide good evidence that any of these abilities actually exist, and, in many cases, they have provided overwhelming evidence that they don't.

Let's look at an actual example of such an investigation—an investigation that prompted a believer in the amazing powers of crystals to *Play the Mystery Card.*

Professor Christopher French and colleagues Lyn Williams and Hayley O'Donnell at the Anomalistic Psychology Research Unit at Goldsmiths, University of London, conducted a study into the claim that crystals have unusual powers that can be detected when they are held. The resulting paper was presented to the British Psychological Society Centenary Annual Conference in Glasgow in 2001. The study compared the reactions of a group of volunteers who were told to meditate while clutching real crystals bought from "New Age" shops with a control group given fake crystals. Those given real crystals reported higher concentration powers, heightened energy levels, and better spiritual well-being. However, exactly the same feelings were reported by those holding fake crystals. This experiment repeated an earlier one in which the experimenter, Williams, knew which crystals were real and which were fake, and so it was not "double-blind." This second study was double-blind. The result? Neither experiment found any difference in the effects reported between real and fake crystals. Richard Wiseman, a colleague of French's, commented on the results: "The suggestion is that the power of crystals is in the mind rather than in the crystals themselves."[2]

Let's suppose you believe in the miraculous powers of crystals and, in particular, in the ability of people to sense the power of crystals that they physically handle. But you're now presented with these experimental results that strongly suggest, as Wiseman notes, that the experiences people have as a result of handling crystals are a product of the power of suggestion, rather than anything in the crystals themselves. Oh, dear. What do you do? One commentator on a blog reporting the experiments responded like so:

> There is much that exists beyond the visible spectrum of light, and beyond the five senses. Not being able to prove the existence of something does not disprove its existence. Much is yet to be discovered. You would do better to discover it by looking outside your narrow frame of reference.[3]

This is a curious collection of sentences.[4] The first three are, of course, all true—indeed they are truisms. Yes, there's much that exists beyond the visible spectrum of light and beyond the five senses. X-rays, for example. It is undeniable that not proving the existence of something does not disprove its existence. And of course, who would want to deny that "much is yet to be discovered"?

However, while the first three sentences are truisms, they fail to engage with the experimental results. What the experiment produced is some rather compelling evidence that some of the effects people typically report on handling crystals—increased concentration, spiritual well-being, heightened energy levels—are *not* a result of some special feature of the crystals themselves but rather of the power of suggestion. It is important to stress that what we are looking at here is not a *mere absence of evidence for* the claim that crystals have such effects, but rather that it is some *positive evidence of the absence* of any such effects. Yet notice how, in response to this experimental evidence, our commentator says "not being able to prove the existence of something is not to disprove its existence," thus misrepresenting the results of this investigation as a mere absence of evidence.

What of the suggestion that there's much that is "beyond the senses" (whether it's a supernatural realm or merely more of the natural world is left open) that the methods of science are not well suited to discover (being too "narrow"). The thought seems to be that if we want to discover more about this undiscovered realm, we need to open ourselves up to other ways of knowing. But what other ways of knowing? A survey of crystal healing literature and websites suggests a combination of gut feeling and intuition (see *"I Just Know!"*) and heavy reliance on various anecdotes about the effects of crystals, such as people being supposedly cured, and so on (see *Piling Up the Anecdotes*).

This is a fairly typical example of how people *Play the Mystery Card* in order to deal with compelling scientific evidence against their beliefs in miraculous or supernatural phenomena. The scientific method has a fantastic track record when it comes to revealing what lies beyond the visible spectrum of light and is hidden from our ordinary five senses. As I say, scientists have discovered not only X-rays, but also subatomic particles, distant galaxies, and so on. We are given no reason to think the scientific method is not suitable when it comes to investigating the alleged powers of crystals. Indeed, many of the claims made about crystals clearly *are* scientifically investigable because they have observable, empirically testable consequences. Moreover, science has produced good evidence that at least some of these claims are false.

Still, our commentator sweepingly dismisses such scientific findings, misrepresenting them as a mere "absence of evidence." On no grounds whatsoever, and in the teeth of evidence to the contrary, our commentator insists that scientific methods are far too "narrow" to refute the various claims made about crystals. And of course, his dismissal of such scientific evidence is delivered with an air of humility and superior wisdom in contrast to the implied know-it-all attitude of the scientific critics.

THE SKEPTIC DAMPING EFFECT

A version of "it's beyond science to decide" that often crops up in defense of supernatural claims is an appeal to the so-called *skeptic damping effect*. When those claiming to have extrasensory perception (ESP)—for example, a supernatural ability to psychically read minds, to view things remotely—are tested under rigorous, experimental conditions, their claimed abilities tend to mysteriously vanish. Why is this? Those who insist ESP is real sometimes claim that the presence of skeptical observers has a damping effect on ESP, as Geoffrey Munroe, a psychologist working in this field, notes in his paper "The Scientific Impotence Excuse: Discounting Belief-Threatening Scientific Abstracts":

> Proponents of extrasensory perception (ESP) sometimes discount failed attempts to support the existence of ESP by claiming that the phenomenon disappears when placed "under the microscope," especially the cold microscope of ESP non-

believers. That is, there is a kind of observer effect where ESP is changed or eliminated when attempts to observe and measure it are taken. Thus, scientific methods, including careful observation and measurement, are impotent to reveal answers to the question of whether or not ESP exists.[5]

The skeptic damping effect provides a convenient excuse for the failure of experimental studies to produce convincing evidence of such abilities. But does the suggestion that the presence of skeptical observers somehow suppresses ESP really succeed in immunizing the claim that it exists against scientific refutation? Not necessarily. In fact, if it is merely the presence of skeptical observers that supposedly has the damping effect, then, interestingly, a controlled scientific experiment could be conducted to establish this. Those claiming ESP could be tested, sometimes with a hidden skeptic observing them, and sometimes not, to see if their ability varied in the way they claim (as my friend Jon Cohen pointed out to me). If, on the other hand, it is the involvement of controlled laboratory conditions designed to minimize the chances of trickery, and so on (whether or not a skeptic happens to be present) that supposedly produces the damping effect, well, that excuse would then place ESP beyond the ability of such laboratory-based studies to either confirm or refute. However, we could still have good empirical grounds for being highly skeptical about the reality of ESP if, for example, we know that (1) all the claimed effects can be faked by trained magicians, (2) several of those claiming such powers have actually been caught faking them, (3) the evidence for the existence of such powers is almost entirely anecdotal (see *Piling Up the Anecdotes* for more on this), (4) there are also several known, nonfraudulent mechanisms by which individuals might become convinced that people have ESP when in truth they don't, (5) there is no known mechanism that would account for ESP, and so on.

A similar move is sometimes made in defense of certain religious claims. When a scientific study into the efficacy of, say, petitionary prayer on heart patients (see *Piling Up the Anecdotes*) reveals that prayer has had no effect, defenders of belief in the effect of prayer will sometimes say, "God will not be tested." God does answer petitionary prayers, just not under controlled experimental conditions.

SCIENTIFIC REFUTATION OF GOD CLAIMS?

Let's now turn to the claim that God exists. Might this claim be scientifically confirmed or refuted? We have already seen that the belief that there exists an all-powerful, all-knowing, supremely benevolent creator God faces a serious empirical challenge—that raised by the evidential problem of evil. However, I suggested it would be odd to describe the evidential problem of evil as a *scientific* argument against the existence of God.

Still, why shouldn't a scientific refutation of a god claim at least be possible? The extent to which god claims are refutable depends largely on which particular god is under consideration. If, by "god," I mean nothing more than a mysterious, transcendent something-or-other, then the claim that "god exists" is certainly difficult to refute scientifically. That's because, in order for science to have a chance of refuting it, a hypothesis must have observable consequences, and it's not clear what observable consequences, if any, this particular god claim has.

However, as we begin to add more to our concept of god, there's potentially more for critics—including scientific critics—to get their teeth into. We have seen, for example, that if you claim god is a nontemporal person or agent, then you run up against certain conceptual objections. If you claim there's a God-with-a-capital-G (an all-powerful, all-knowing, all-good creator God), then you run up against empirical evidence—such as that involved in the evidential problem of evil. Go further still and claim, as many do, that your God created the entire universe about six thousand years ago, and science can establish beyond reasonable doubt that no God of that sort exists.

The claim that science can indeed establish beyond reasonable doubt that "there is no god" is a view currently most closely associated with Professor Richard Dawkins, author of *The God Delusion*. Let's take a closer look at his central argument.

The God Delusion

The God Delusion was a worldwide best seller that provoked a huge storm of criticism from many religious people. Dawkins was, and continues to be, accused of all sorts of confusions, muddles, and bad arguments. One of *The God Delusions'* central contentions is that what Dawkins calls the *god hypothesis*—the hypothesis that there exists a superhuman, supernatural intelligence who deliberately designed and created the universe and everything in it, including us—is very probably false.

Dawkins notes how some theists attempt to bolster their belief in the god hypothesis by insisting that it appears to neatly explain features of the universe that, they suggest, would otherwise be deeply and puzzlingly *improbable*. For example, it seems the laws of nature and starting conditions of the universe have the Goldilocks property of being "just right" to produce life. Had those starting conditions been only slightly different, life would have been impossible. That the universe does appear to have such "fine-tuned" properties has been noted by many eminent scientists, including, for example, astronomer Royal Martin Rees, who says:

> A degree of fine tuning—in the expansion speed, the material content of the universe, and the strengths of the basic forces—seems to have been a prerequisite for the emergence of the hospitable cosmic habitat in which we live.[6]

Some theists, noting the universe has such fine-tuned properties, then argue like so: Surely the probability of the universe having such Goldilocks features *by chance* must be extraordinarily low. So low, in fact, that it's much more likely that some sort of intelligence deliberately designed the universe this way. That intelligence, many suggest, is not just a god, but God (with a capital "G"). This kind of fine-tuning argument is not typically supposed to constitute a conclusive proof of God's existence, but it is held to be, in the words of John Polkinghorne, "strongly suggestive."[7]

Actually, before we proceed, it's worth noting that this fine-tuning argument, by itself, is no more "strongly suggestive" that John Polkinghorne's God exists than it is "strongly suggestive" that there is, say, an evil god. The argument, as it stands, is entirely neutral so far as the moral properties of the designing intelligence are concerned. The fine-tuning argument faces all sorts of serious objections (including, for example, the conceptual objection raised in my introduction: that the very idea of a nontemporal, intelligent agent that designed the universe makes no more sense than a nonspatial mountain), but perhaps the most obvious objection is that even if the universe does show signs of having been produced by some sort of intelligence, it is a huge and, as it stands, unwarranted further leap to the conclusion that this intelligence is even a god, let alone the very specific God love that Christians like Polkinghorne believe in. As the physicist Paul Davies notes at the end of his book *The Goldilocks Enigma*:

> The other main problem with intelligent design is that the identity of the designer need bear no relation at all to the God of traditional monotheism. The "designing agency" can be a committee of gods, for example. The designer can be a natural being or beings, such as an evolved super-mind or super-civilization existing in a previous universe, or in another section of our universe, which made our universe using super-technology. The designer can also be some sort of superdupercomputer simulating this universe.[8]

However, let's set this problem to one side and get back to the issue at hand, which is Dawkins's criticism of such arguments. Dawkins argues that, when theists appeal to god to explain such otherwise supposedly improbable features of the universe, they overlook the fact that the god to which they appeal *must be at least as complex, and thus at least as improbable, as that which he is invoked to explain*:

> A designer god cannot be used to explain organized complexity because any god capable of designing anything would have to be complex enough to demand the same kind of explanation in his own right. God presents an infinite regress from which he cannot help us escape.[9]

If the existence of the universe having such organized complexity is highly improbable, then, says Dawkins, the existence of any god having the kind of complexity to account for it must be even more improbable. So postulating a God doesn't solve the problem of the complexity of the universe. Rather, with god, we merely postpone the problem of accounting for such complexity. But then the complexity we observe in the universe provides no justification for introducing god. Worse still, if the theist is right and the probability of such complexity just happening to exist is very low, then surely *the probability of god existing must be even lower*.

Dawkins's argument is intriguing and worthy of closer study. However, I won't assess its cogency here. My focus is not on whether Dawkins's argument is any good (I'm not sure it is) but on some of the dubious moves some theists have made in response to it. While there are theists who have responded to Dawkins's argument in a fairly intellectually rigorous and straightforward way, others have instead reached for the usual bag of immunizing tricks, in particular "Ah, but this is beyond the ability of reason and/or science to decide!"

Alister McGrath's Response to The God Delusion

Theologian Alister McGrath is a long-standing critic of Dawkins. In his article "The Questions Science Cannot Answer—The Ideological Fanaticism of Richard Dawkins's Attack on Belief Is Unreasonable to Religion—and Science,"[10] McGrath attempts to defend religion against Dawkins's attack. He begins by pointing out that even scientists like Peter Medawar acknowledge there are questions science cannot answer:

> In *The Limits of Science*, Medawar reflected on how science, despite being "the most successful enterprise human beings have ever engaged upon," had limits to its scope. Science is superb when it comes to showing that the chemical formula for water is H_2O. Or, more significantly, that DNA has a double helix. But what of that greater question: what's life all about? This, and others like it, Medawar insisted, were "questions that science cannot answer, and that no conceivable advance of science would empower it to answer." They could not be dismissed as "non-questions or pseudoquestions such as only simpletons ask and only charlatans profess to be able to answer." This is not to criticise science, but simply to calibrate its capacities.

McGrath then goes on to do several things. First of all, he accuses Dawkins of being *ideologically wedded to scientism*. Dawkins, claims McGrath, simply assumes that "science has all the answers." But of course, scientists need to show a little humility. There are "questions science cannot answer."

This first line of attack on Dawkins, though popular with his critics, entirely misses its mark. Even within the book McGrath is here attacking, Dawkins quite unambiguously acknowledges, "Perhaps there are some genuinely profound and meaningful questions that are forever beyond the reach of science."[11] Indeed, Dawkins seems happy to concede that moral questions may well fall into this category. Dawkins says, "We can all agree that science's entitlement to advise us on moral values is problematic to say the least."[12] McGrath is attacking a position Dawkins does not hold.

In fact, not only is McGrath's charge of scientism unwarranted, it is in any case irrelevant. For, suppose we can show that scientism is false—that there are indeed certain questions science cannot answer. Does it follow that Dawkins's argument fails? Obviously not. Science might still be able to show there's no god. Perhaps Dawkins has.

McGrath then proceeds to attack Dawkins's argument against the god hypothesis, not by identifying any flaw in it, but by simply insisting we can't "prove there is no god." Now, interestingly, Dawkins himself points out in *The God Delusion* that in McGrath's earlier attack on Dawkins, McGrath's point seemed to boil down to "the undeniable but ignominiously weak point that you cannot disprove the existence of God."[13] Dawkins actually *agrees* that we can't conclusively prove the nonexistence of god, but he points out that that doesn't entail that belief in god is immune to scientific skepticism. For, Dawkins suggests, the god hypothesis has *observable consequences*: "A universe with a creative superintendent would be a very different kind of universe from one without. Why is that not a scientific matter?"[14] Dawkins maintains that, in response to this question, McGrath previously offered no real answer. It's ironic, then, that in the *Times* article in which McGrath attacks Dawkins, McGrath still offers no answer.

In short, *McGrath entirely fails to engage with Dawkins's argument*. McGrath merely levels at Dawkins the inaccurate and irrelevant charge of scientism, and makes the inaccurate claim that Dawkins is trying conclusively to "prove" there's no God, which Dawkins explicitly is not.

Still, it's worth spending a moment to consider *why* McGrath supposes there can be no conclusive proof or disproof of the existence of god. In his book *The Dawkins Delusion—Atheist Fundamentalism and the Denial of the Divine*, McGrath presents an argument of sorts:

> Any given set of observations can be explained by a number of theories. To use the jargon of the philosophy of science: theories are underdetermined by the evidence. The question then

arises: What criterion be used to decide between them, especially when they are "empirically equivalent." Simplicity? Beauty? The debate rages, unresolved. And its outcome is entirely to be expected: the great questions remain unanswered. There can be no scientific "proof" of ultimate questions. Either we cannot answer them, or we must answer them on grounds other than the sciences.[15]

McGrath's point seems to be that, when it comes to such worldviews as "god exists" and "god does not exist," the two theories fit the observational evidence. They are, McGrath supposes, "empirically equivalent." But then neither theory can be proved or disproved by appeals to the evidence.

But is it true that the two theories fit the observational evidence equally well? Actually, as we'll see later in *"But It Fits!"* any theory, no matter how nuts, can be made to "fit"—be *consistent with*—the evidence, given sufficient ingenuity. It doesn't follow that all theories are equally reasonable, or that we can never fairly conclusively settle the question of which among competing theories are true on the basis of observational evidence. In effect, McGrath here just *asserts* that the god question cannot be fairly conclusively settled on the basis of observational evidence. Again, he has no argument at all. But he does have insults. He peppers his responses to Dawkins with numerous ad hominem attacks, variously describing Dawkins's approach as "aggressive," "embittered," "fanatical," and so on.

Say "Ah, but of course this is beyond the ability of science and reason to decide" often enough, and there's a good chance people will start to accept it without even thinking about it. It will become an immunizing "factoid" that can be conveniently wheeled out whenever any rational threat to the credibility of your belief crops up. Perhaps this is why, rather than respond to Dawkins's arguments, McGrath just starts chanting the "Ah, but of course this beyond the ability of reason/science to decide" mantra, recognizing that many readers, even if momentarily stung by Dawkins into entertaining a serious doubt, can quickly be lulled back to sleep: "Oh, yes, I remember, it's beyond the ability of science . . . scientism . . . zzzzz."

Despite its intellectual trappings, McGrath's response to Dawkins, in essence, has no more substance to it than does that of the commentator who defended his belief in the amazing powers of crystals by insisting, without any justification at all, that the scientific method is far too "narrow" to refute such beliefs.

"YOU CAN'T PROVE A NEGATIVE"

Let's now turn to a variant of "it's beyond science/reason to decide." One reason why some suppose science and reason are incapable of establishing beyond reasonable doubt that certain supernatural claims—for example, that fairies or angels or spirit beings exist— are false is that they assume *you can't prove a negative*. Indeed this is widely supposed to be some sort of "law of logic."

For example, Georgia minister Dr. Nelson L. Price asserts on his website that "one of the laws of logic is that you can't prove a negative."[16] If Price is correct and this is indeed a law of logic, then of course it immediately follows that we can't prove that there are no fairies, angels, or spirit beings, or, indeed, that there is no god. We will have established that the nonexistence of God *is* indeed beyond the ability of reason and/or science to establish!

The fact is, however, that this supposed "law of logic" is no such thing. As Steven D. Hales points in his paper "You *Can* Prove a Negative,"[17] "You can't prove a negative" is a principle of folk logic, not actual logic.

Notice, for a start, that "You cannot prove a negative" *is itself a negative*. So, if it were true, it would itself be unprovable. Notice that *any* claim can be transformed into a negative by a little rephrasing—most obviously, by negating the claim and then negating it again. "I exist" is logically equivalent to "I do not *not* exist," which is a negative. Yet here is a negative it seems I might perhaps be able to prove (in the style of Descartes—I think, there-fore I do not *not* exist!).

Of course, those who say "You can't prove a negative" will insist that I have misunderstood their point. As Hales notes, when people say, "You can't prove a negative," what they *really* mean is that you cannot prove that something does *not* exist. If this point were correct, it would apply not just to supernatural beings lying beyond the cosmic veil but also to things that might be supposed to exist on this side of the veil, such as unicorns, Martians, rabbits with twenty heads, and so on. We would not be able to prove the nonexistence of any of these things either.

But *is* the point correct? Is it true that we can never prove that something does not exist? Again, it depends. If John claims there's a unicorn in the tool shed, I can quickly establish he is mistaken by going and taking a look. We could similarly estab-lish there's no Loch Ness monster by draining the loch. But what of the claim that unicorns *once existed*? We can't travel back in time and directly observe all of the past as we can every corner of the tool shed or Loch Ness. Does it follow that we can't prove unicorns never existed?

It depends in part on what you mean by "prove." The word has a variety of meanings. By saying something is "proved," I might mean that it is established beyond *all possible* doubt. Or I might mean it has been established beyond *reasonable* doubt (this is the kind of proof required in a court of law). Can we establish beyond reasonable doubt that unicorns have never inhabited the earth? True, the history of our planet has been and gone, so we can no longer directly inspect it. But surely, if unicorns did roam the earth, we would expect to find some evidence of their pres-ence, such as fossils of unicorns or at least of closely related ani-mals from which unicorns might plausibly have evolved. There is none. We also have plenty of evidence that unicorns are a fic-tional creation, in which case, it's surely reasonable for us to con-clude that there never were any unicorns. Indeed, I'd suggest we can prove this beyond *reasonable* doubt.

In response, it might be said "But you can't prove *conclusively*, beyond all *possible* doubt, that unicorns never roamed the earth." This is undeniably true. However, *this point is not peculiar to negatives*. It can be made about any claim about the unobserved, and thus *any scientific theory at all*, including scientific theories about what *does* exist. We *can* prove beyond reasonable doubt that dinosaurs existed, but not beyond all possible doubt. Despite the mountain of evidence that dinosaurs roamed the earth, it's still possible that, say, all those dinosaur fossils are fakes placed there by alien pranksters long ago.

Let's sum up. If "you can't prove a negative" means you can't prove beyond *reasonable* doubt that certain things don't exist, then the claim is just false. We prove the nonexistence of things on a regular basis. If, on the other hand, "you can't prove a negative" means you cannot prove beyond all *possible* doubt that something does not exist, well, that may, arguably, be true. But so what? That point is irrelevant so far as defending beliefs in supernatural entities against the charge that science and/or reason have established beyond *reasonable* doubt that they don't exist.

PLAYING THE MYSTERY CARD IN RESPONSE TO THE PROBLEM OF EVIL

As we have seen, the evidential problem of evil constitutes one of the best-known and most powerful-looking threats to the rationality of Theism (that's to say, belief in God with a capital "G"). Theists respond in a variety of ways, by, for example, constructing theodicies. However, many Theists acknowledge that, while many such theodicies have been developed, the evidential problem of evil does still appear to constitute a significant problem. How else might they try to deal with it?

One popular response is to appeal to *mystery*. In some mysterious fashion, the suffering we and other creatures experience is all for the best. In some incomprehensible way, this is the kind of world a good God would create, despite the fact that it contains enormous quantities of horrendous suffering.

Of course, as it stands, this is not terribly convincing. After all, we could deal with evidence against any belief by making a similar move. Suppose you are a juror at a murder trial. You are presented with abundant evidence that the accused is a serial killer—including independent eyewitness testimony, excellent forensic evidence, and so on. It appears to be an open-and-shut case. In response to this wealth of evidence, the defense simply says, "In some mysterious way we can't understand, all this evidence was concocted. The accused is, in fact, innocent." If that's the best the defense can come up with, it's clearly still reasonable for you to find the accused guilty. In effect, the defense is admitting defeat—acknowledging that the evidence against the accused really is compelling. They're right, of course, that there remains the *possibility* of error—of some sort of elaborate conspiracy to frame the accused—but that possibility exists in every legal case. It doesn't prevent prosecutions establishing guilt beyond reasonable doubt.

The philosopher Quentin Smith expresses his frustration with this kind of appeal to mystery:

> So how do theists respond to arguments like [the problem of evil]? They say there is a reason for evil, but it is a mystery. Well, let me tell you this: I'm actually one hundred feet tall even though I only appear to be six feet tall. You ask me for proof of this. I have a simple answer: it's a mystery. Just accept my word for it on faith. And that's just the logic theists use in their discussions of evil.[18]

Smith is surely right to condemn such crude and evasive appeals to mystery. However, it's worth taking a quick detour at this point to consider a rather more sophisticated and, I think, intellectually respectable way in which Theists sometimes appeal to mystery in order to deal with the problem of evil. For example, they also often say something like this:

God, let's not forget, is not only limitlessly benevolent and powerful, but also infinitely intelligent and wise. Just as a toddler cannot be expected to grasp the good reasons why its loving parents sometimes do things that cause the toddler to suffer (e.g., give them immunizing injections) so we should not expect to understand everything a loving God does. God's reasons for allowing suffering are often likely to be beyond our grasp. Yes, we cannot understand why such a being would produce hundreds of millions of years of animal suffering, or bury thousands of children alive, but that does not mean such suffering provides us with good evidence that there is no such God.

The philosopher Stephen Wykstra, for example, suggests that "if we think carefully about the sort of being theism proposes for our belief, it is entirely expectable—given what we know of our cognitive limits—that the goods by virtue of which this Being allows known suffering should very often be beyond our ken."[19]

Notice that Wykstra is *not* here making an entirely gratuitous and unjustified appeal to mystery, as in Quentin Smith's example. Wykstra's suggestion is that, if there is a God, then we should *expect* there to be many things we cannot understand. In particular, we should *expect* there to exist many evils for which God's reasons remain mysterious. In which case, *the fact that there exist such evils is not good evidence that there's no such God.*

While this sort of appeal to mystery to deal with the evidential problem of evil may be intellectually rather more sophisticated and respectable than that considered by Smith, I can't see that it ultimately fares much better than the cruder version. First, notice that when loving parents inflict suffering on the child for that child's good, the parents will do their very best to explain to their child that they do care for them and that this suffering is for their own good. They will even make *some* sort of attempt to explain why they are causing this suffering, even if only in the kind of oversimplified terms a child might understand. A parent that did not do these things would rightly be considered callous and uncaring. Yet our cosmic parent figure, if he exists, fails to make himself clearly known, fails to provide any such reassurance to those he makes suffer appallingly, and fails to provide any kind of explanation at all for the horror he unleashes. Surely we do, then, have excellent evidence that even if there is an all-powerful god, he is not particularly caring or benevolent.

In reply, some may insist God does provide these kinds of reassurances and explanations—they are all in the Bible. But it's hardly clear to me, or indeed to the majority of humans currently suffering on this planet, that such explanations and reassurances are to be found there—why didn't God make them clearer? In any case, what about the countless generations of humans that suffered before the Bible was written? Why did God unleash millions of years of agony before finally getting around to providing us with some reassurance that, actually, it is all, in some mysterious way, for the best?

Second, notice that there are presumably *limits* to how much evil can be put down to God's mysterious ways. Suppose the world contained even more evil and hardly any good at all. Suppose it resembled a vast Hieronymus Bosch–like vision of hell: a landscape of endless torture and despair with not a jot of beauty or happiness. Would it still be reasonable to say, "There's no compelling evidence here that the world was not created by a supremely powerful and benevolent creator. It's still entirely reasonable for us to believe in an all-powerful, all-good God!"? Surely, as the level of evil increases, we do eventually reach a point where we can justifiably say, "There may be *a* creator god, but it's not *that* one."

Third, and most significantly, notice that *precisely the same immunizing strategy can be employed to defend belief in an evil god against the evidential problem of good.* Someone who believes in an evil god can say: "Evil god's fiendish intelligence is boundless. So we should *expect* there to be many goods his evil reasons for which lie beyond our ken. In which case, the amount of good that exists is not good evidence that there is no such evil god!"

Clearly, this won't wash. We know we are justified in supposing there is no evil god on the basis of the amount of good we observe. There are limits to the amount of good that can be put down to an evil god's mysterious ways, and those limits are clearly exceeded by what we see around us. There are vast amounts of good in the world, far too much for it to be the creation of an evil god. But then there are also, very obviously, vast quantities of evil—seemingly far too much for this to be creation of a good God.

THE MORAL OF THE UNSOLVED CASE

An example of one last dodgy "appeal to mystery" worth nailing before we end this chapter runs as follows:

> *Why does the universe exist? You cannot answer this question. You must admit that it is a mystery that has not been solved. But if you do not know the answer to this question, then you cannot know that my answer—that it was created by God—is incorrect. You must admit that, for all you know, I'm right!*

This is a bad argument. Suppose Sherlock Holmes is having a bad day. He just can't figure out whodunit. Does it follow that he cannot reasonably rule out certain suspects?

Of course not. Holmes may not know who did it, but he might still know who didn't. He might be able to pretty conclusively rule out certain suspects (the butler, for example, who has a cast-iron alibi). Similarly, someone unable to explain why the universe exists may nevertheless be able to use their powers of reason to rule out certain answers. Even a religious person will typically admit that there is overwhelming evidence the world was not created by an *evil* God. But then they must admit there *could be* overwhelming evidence that it was not created by a good God either.

This point is by no means restricted to religious beliefs. Many belief systems often start with a mystery—they offer to explain what might otherwise seem rather baffling. Those who believe there's a family of plesiosaurs (snake-necked dinosaurs that went extinct sixty-five million years ago) living in Loch Ness, that the world was once ruled by aliens who still visit occasionally, or that there's a ghost in their attic will point to peculiar shapes on the surface of the loch, or the extraordinary ancient Nazca drawings in Peru (huge images visible only from high in the sky—some say they were created for the benefit of passing aliens), or exquisitely constructed crop circles, or the weird rattling sound coming from the attic, and say, "Explain *that*!" They challenge us to explain how such things were formed, or how or why they were made. When we can't, they conclude their beliefs, which we may be forced to concede *do* explain these things (even if rather badly), can't be so unreasonable after all. But of course, whether or not we can explain such things, we may still have excellent evidence that there is no family of plesiosaurs in living in Loch Ness (for a start, the loch has been frozen solid top to bottom many times over during the ice ages that separate us from the age of the plesiosaurs).

CONCLUSION

Mystery, as such, is no bad thing. Pointing out mysteries can be a valuable exercise—firing up our curiosity and getting us to engage our intellects. Nor is there anything wrong with acknowledging that some things may forever remain a mystery, and might even be *in principle* unknowable.

Sometimes it's also reasonable, when faced with a problem case for an otherwise well-established theory, to put it down as a mysterious anomaly. If on countless occasions an experiment has confirmed water boils at 100 degrees C, the fact that on one occasion it appeared not to may quite reasonably be put down to some unknown factor. If we can't discover what went wrong, it can be reasonable to just shrug and move on—putting the freak result down to some mysterious problem with the set up (a faulty thermometer, perhaps).

It's also often reasonable, when we have a theory that works but we don't fully understand why it works, to say, "*Why* this happens remains, for the moment, a mystery. But we know it does." We might have strong evidence that smoking causes cancer, say, long before we understand why it does so.

So the appeal to mystery has its proper place, even in science. What I object to is the way in which the appeal to mystery is increasingly relied on to deal with what would otherwise appear to be powerful evidence or arguments against certain beliefs, particularly beliefs in the supernatural. Whenever mystery is erected as a barrier to rational inquiry, a barrier that says, "You scientists and philosophers may come *this* far armed with the power of reason, but *no further*—turn back now!" we should be concerned, particularly if no good reason is given for supposing science and reason cannot, in fact, take us further. The more we appeal to mystery to get ourselves out of intellectual trouble—the more we use it as a carpet under which to sweep inconvenient facts or discoveries—the more vulnerable we become to deceit: deceit by both others and by ourselves.

Chapter 2

"But It Fits!"
and The Blunderbuss

"*B*ut It Fits!*"* is a popular strategy for dealing with powerful evidence against what you believe. In fact, *"But It Fits!"* does double duty. Not only is it a great immunizing strategy, it can also be used to create the illusion that a ridiculous belief system is not, after all, ridiculous, but *at least as well confirmed as its rivals.* I'll explain how *"But It Fits!"* works by means of a particularly impressive example: Young Earth Creationism.

YOUNG EARTH CREATIONISM

Young Earth Creationism is a theory based on a literal reading of the Old Testament. Young Earth Creationists maintain that the entire universe is less than ten thousand years old (a typical estimate is about six thousand years). They claim that the universe, the earth, and every living species were created literally as described in Genesis, over a period of six days.

So, according to Young Earth Creationists, the theory of evolution, which says that new species have evolved over many millions of years, is false. So are current cosmological theories that say that the universe came into existence several billions of years ago (between thirteen and fourteen billion years ago).

Young Earth Creationism is popular. Polls fairly consistently indicate that about 45 percent of US citizens believe it.[1] Nor is it restricted to the uneducated. A 1972 Gallup poll suggested that about a third of US graduates believe we are all descendents of Adam and Eve. For many, creationism is a moral crusade. According to H. M. Morris, a leading proponent, "Evolution is the root of atheism, of communism, nazism, behaviourism, economic imperialism, militarism, libertinism, anarchism, and all manner of anti-Christian systems of belief and practice."[2] Young Earth Creationists typically see themselves fighting a battle over the souls of coming generations, and are particular keen to have their beliefs taught in schools.

Extraordinarily, not only do many millions of Americans believe the universe is only about six thousand years old, many also believe that Young Earth Creationism is good science. They consider the biblical account of creation to be *at least as scientifically well confirmed as the theories of evolution and a billions-of-years-old universe.*

How, you may be wondering, can any sane, reasonably well-educated person believe that Young Earth Creationism is just as scientifically credible and well confirmed as its more orthodox scientific rivals? After all, isn't there overwhelming empirical evidence against Young Earth Creationism? What about the fossil record, which reveals that the species currently living on this planet have evolved from common ancestors over many millions of years? And of course, we might add that the fossil record is merely one piece of evidence for the theory of evolution. The theory is also powerfully confirmed by, for example, discoveries in genetics (indeed, an overwhelming case for evolution can now be made without appealing to the fossil record at all).[3]

Surely there's also a mountain of evidence that the universe is much older than ten thousand years. For example: What of the light from distant galaxies, which, given the speed of light, would have taken hundreds of millions of years to get here (and even that from stars within our own galaxy can take tens of thousands of years to arrive)?

What of the movement of tectonic plates, which we know to be very slow but that also have succeeded in separating the Atlantic coasts by thousands of miles?

What of the seasonal layers of ice found at the poles, the drilled-out cores of which reveal a seasonal history dating back hundreds of thousands of years?

What of radio-carbon and other forms of dating that reliably date objects to be much older than Young Earth Creationists claim they must be?

What of the chalk beds revealed by the White Cliffs of Dover, which are over hundreds of meters deep? Under a microscope, chalk is revealed to be made of the compressed shells of tiny microorganisms. They died, and their shells sank to the bottom producing a sediment that finally solidified into the chalk beds we see today. At current rates of deposit, the deepest beds would have taken tens of millions of years to produce. According to Young Earth Creationists, the entire universe is less than *one-thousandth* as old as that.

We might go on and on. There's hardly a branch of science that doesn't supply us with evidence that the universe is vastly older than Young Earth Creationists claim it to be. These sciences together provide a consistent, coherent, and increasingly detailed history of life, the earth, and the universe that is almost entirely at odds with the biblical account.

How, then, do so many Young Earth Creationists convince themselves that their theory is not falsified by the empirical evidence? How are they persuaded that it is in fact scientifically confirmed? Let's begin by looking at how they approach the fossil record.

THE FLOOD THEORY

Most Young Earth Creationists appeal to one or more catastrophes to explain geological features—mountain ranges, sedimentary layers, and so on—that might otherwise seem far older. There's nothing wrong with catastrophe theories as such. Even orthodox scientists suppose catastrophes—comet strikes, volcanic eruptions, floods, and so on—have played an important role in shaping this planet and the life on it. According to most contemporary Young Earth Creationists, the key catastrophe involved in shaping our contemporary landscape was the biblical flood: the flood on which Noah famously floated his ark. They believe that Old Testament story is literally true: Noah really did build an ark onto which he was instructed by God to put seven mated pairs of every clean kind of animal and every kind of bird (Genesis 7:2). The waters then rose, drowning the rest. The current inhabitants of the land and sky are descendents of those who boarded the ark.

So how is the flood supposed to account for various geological features, such as the fossil record? It's claimed that, when the waters rose, they produced huge amounts of silt and mud. This material settled and solidified, eventually forming many of the sedimentary rock layers we find today. Many of the fossils we find within these layers are fossils of creatures drowned by the flood. The flood supposedly also explains other geological features, such as the Grand Canyon, which was carved out when the flood waters subsided.

Perhaps you are wondering why creatures are not buried randomly within the sedimentary layers but are arranged in a very specific order? Why, if the flood theory is true, do we never find the fossils of large mammals within the same layers as dinosaurs? Why do the lower layers contain fossils of only simple sea creatures? Why do humans only appear in only the very topmost layers? Why, if they were all buried by the same catastrophic flood, aren't their remains jumbled up together?

Young Earth Creationists have their answers. They say we should expect the simple sea creatures living at the bottom of the ocean to have been buried first. Birds would be restricted to the higher layers, as they would be able to fly from the rising waters. Humankind, being the smartest, would probably have found ways to avoid being drowned until the last moment, so it is not surprising we find human remains only in the top layers. We should also expect to see some order in the fossil record due, for example, to the fact that different ecological zones were submerged at different times, and also because of the different rates at which the corpses of different species bloat and then sink. "So you see?" say Young Earth Creationists. "The fossil record *is*, after all, consistent with our theory! It all fits!"

We might say in reply, "But these moves made by Creationists only postpone their difficulties, as they generate a myriad of further puzzles. What about flightless birds, such as penguins and ostriches, which would not have been able to delay being drowned? Why do their fossils never show up in layers lower than other birds? Why do we find sharks, but no dolphins in the lower sedimentary layers, given they occupy similar ecological zones? Surely both would have been buried in the early stages of the flood? In fact we could go on and on and on, citing a mountain of fossil evidence that contradicts the flood theory." Still, Young Earth Creationists continue to work on developing flood-friendly explanations for these observations.

Of course, it's not just the fossil record that generates puzzles for Young Earth Creationism. Let's think for a moment about the logistics of Noah's expedition. Genesis 16:2 says the ark was 300 × 50 × 30 cubits—that's about 460 × 75 × 44 feet. Not a particularly large vessel (a cross section of 75 by 44 feet is, coincidentally, not very much greater than that of my four-bedroom Victorian terraced house). How did at least two of every kind of animal fit aboard this comparatively small vessel? Remember, Noah didn't just need specimens of today's creatures such as African elephants, rhinos, and giraffes. If dinosaurs were drowned in the flood, then Noah must also have put dinosaurs on board his ark. Young Earth Creationists accept this. But then how did Noah get two T. rexes, two stegosauruses, two bronto-sauruses, and so on, safely aboard? These aren't even the very largest dinosaurs. What about, for example, two argentino-sauruses, at 120 feet long and 100 tons each?

Other questions arise. What did Noah feed his creatures during their voyage? How did Noah round up the known 900,000 insect species from around the planet, and how did he ensure they weren't trodden on during the voyage? Also, how did Noah acquire polar bears from the Arctic and possums from Australia—how did they cross the vast oceans and continents to reach the ark?

But Young Earth Creationists don't give up easily. They have constructed answers to all these and other obvious questions about Noah's voyage. For example, the website of Christian Information Ministries suggests that Noah did not need at least two of every named species of dinosaur, merely two of every "kind" (whatever that is, exactly): "Some creationists believe there may have been far fewer animals if Noah only took on board pairs of 'kinds' as the word is used in Genesis 1. God created these 'kinds' with potential for rich genetic diversity."[4] Creation Ministries International endorses this explanation, adding, "Although there are about 668 names of dinosaurs, there are perhaps only 55 different 'kinds' of dinosaurs."[5]

The same source also suggests that Noah did not need full-sized adult specimens—young examples would do:

> Furthermore, not all dinosaurs were huge like the *Brachio-saurus*, and even those dinosaurs on the Ark were probably "teenagers" or young adults. Indeed, dinosaurs were recently discovered to go through a growth spurt, so God could have brought dinosaurs of the right age to start this spurt as soon as they disembarked.[6]

So how did Noah feed all his creatures while they were at sea? Christian Information Ministries suggests they hibernated:

> How Noah and his small family could have cared for this large menagerie is unknown, not to mention the sanitation problem! What we must remember is that this event, i.e., the Flood, had supernatural elements. For instance, the animals came to the Ark against their natural instincts (Gen. 6:20). It is therefore reasonable to assume, as some creationists do, that the animals' metabolism may have been slowed down during their confinement, even to the point where some of the animals may have gone into a state of hibernation.[7]

Of course, once we allow "supernatural elements" to play a role, we could just say that God *shrank* the dinosaurs to pocket size during their journey. That would deal with many of these problems.

How do Young Earth Creationists explain how polar bears and possums made it all the way to Noah's Ark across the great oceans? According to Ken Ham and Tim Lovett at Answers in Genesis, there were no separate continents at that time. There was a single continent that the flood subsequently broke apart, as they here explain: "As even secular geologists observe, it does appear that the continents were at one time 'together' and not separated by the vast oceans of today. The forces involved in the Flood were certainly sufficient to change all of this."[8] Really? The forces were sufficient to push vast continents around the face of the planet, but not enough to sink a wooden vessel with a cross section of 75 by 44 feet? I guess God must have somehow protected the ark from these extraordinary forces.

Even setting aside ark logistics, the flood theory raises a host of other questions, such as, where did all the water sufficient to cover the earth's great mountain ranges go? Answer: there were no great ranges at that time—they were created by the flood. Because the surface of the earth was relatively flat, there was, and still is, more than enough water to cover the land, as Ham and Lovett also explain: "Simply put, the water from the Flood is in the oceans and seas we see today. Three-quarters of the earth's surface is covered with water."[9]

So how did creatures get back to their respective newly created continents after the ark was finally deposited on the mountains of Ararat (Genesis 8:4)? The marmosets could hardly have walked and swum halfway around the world, across the Atlantic Ocean, to the Amazonian rain forests where they now dwell. I guess Noah must have dropped off the marmosets in South America and the possums in Australia as the waters receded (but how, then, did the ark end up deposited high on the mountains of Ararat?). Or perhaps Noah built them rafts.

So you see: Young Earth Creationists insist they *can* deal with many of these questions! Admittedly, they don't have *all* the answers—and don't claim to. But, as they correctly point out, *who does*? Even orthodox science faces questions it is not currently able to answer, and perhaps never will.

Explanations such as those outlined above are continuously being developed and refined by people describing themselves as "scientists" in multimillion-dollar "research institutes" dedicated to the pursuit of something called "creation science." These "scientists" insist that, far from falsifying Young Earth Creationism, the empirical evidence is broadly consistent with it. Young Earth Creationism, they maintain, fits the evidence at least as well as its orthodox scientific rivals. Surely, they add, good science is all about developing theories to fit the evidence. But then, because they are developing their theory to make it fit the evidence, what they are practicing is *good science*. Moreover, if theories are confirmed to the extent that they fit the evidence, then Young Earth Creationism, developed and refined in these ways, *is as well confirmed as its rivals*.

DOGS ARE SPIES FROM THE PLANET VENUS

To summarize: Young Earth Creationism is supposedly:

1) *not falsified* by the empirical evidence but actually *consistent with it,*
2) at least as well *confirmed* as the theory of evolution, etc.,
3) *good science.*

Let's start with claim 2, which is false. To begin to see why, let's start with an analogy.

Dave believes dogs are spies from the planet Venus. He views any canine with great suspicion, for he believes they are here from Venus to do reconnaissance work. Dogs, Dave supposes, secretly send their reports back to Venus, where the rest of their fiendishly cunning alien species are meticulously planning their invasion of the earth. Their spaceships will shortly arrive from Venus to enslave the human race and take over the world.

Unsurprisingly, Dave's friends think he has a screw loose and try to convince him that dogs are comparatively benign pets, not cunning alien spies. Here's a typical example of how their conversations with Dave go.

> DAVE: It's only a matter of weeks now! The spaceships will arrive and *then* you'll wish you'd listened to me. We must act now—let the government know!
>
> MARY: Look, Dave, dogs are pretty obviously not space invaders, they're just dumb pets. Dogs can't even speak, for goodness sake, let alone communicate with Venus!
>
> DAVE: They *can* speak—they just choose to hide their linguistic ability from us. They wait till we leave the room before they talk to each other.
>
> PETE: But Venus is a dead planet, Dave. It's horrifically hot and swathed in clouds of acid. Nothing could live there, certainly not a dog!

DAVE: Dogs don't live on the *surface* of Venus, you fool—they live below, in deep underground bunkers.

MARY: But then how do earth-bound dogs communicate with their allies on Venus? I've got a dog, and I've never found an alien transmitter hidden in his basket.

DAVE: They don't use technology we can observe. Their transmitters are hidden inside their brains!

MARY: But Pete is a vet, and he's X-rayed several dog's heads, and he's never found anything in there!

PETE: In fact, I once chopped up a dog's brain in veterinary school—let me assure you, Dave, there was no transmitter in there!

DAVE: You're assuming their transmitters would be recognizable as such. They are actually made of organic material indistinguishable from brain stuff. That's why they don't show up on X-rays. This is *advanced alien technology*, remember—*of course* we cannot detect it!

MARY: But we don't detect any weird signals being directed at Venus from the earth.

DAVE: Of course, we don't—like I said, remember, this is *advanced alien technology* beyond our limited understanding!

PETE: How do dogs fly spaceships? They don't even have hands. So they can't hold things like steering wheels and joysticks.

DAVE: Really, Pete. Think about it. You are assuming that their spacecraft will be designed to be operated by human hands. Obviously they won't. They'll be designed to be maneuvered by a dog's limbs, mouth, tongue, and so on.

You can see how this conversation might continue ad nauseum. Mary and Pete can keep coming up with evidence against Dave's belief that dogs are Venusian spies. But, given sufficient ingenuity, Dave can always salvage his core theory. He can continually adjust and develop it so that it continues to "fit" the evidence.

CONFIRMATION—THE "FIT" MODEL

Clearly, Dave's theory about dogs is not well confirmed by the available evidence. The first moral we can extract from this example is that, whatever is required in order for a theory to be well confirmed, rather more is required than achieving mere *consistency* with that evidence.

As Dave illustrates, *any* belief, no matter how ludicrous, can be made consistent with the available evidence, given a little patience and ingenuity. Believe that the earth is flat, that the moon is made of cheese, that the World Trade Center was brought down by the US government, or that George W. Bush is really Elvis Presley in disguise? All these theories can be endlessly adjusted and developed so that they remain consistent with the available evidence. Yet they are obviously not well confirmed.

The claim that Young Earth Creationism is at least as well confirmed as its scientific rivals relies crucially on what we might call the *"fit" model of confirmation*. According to the "fit" model, confirmation is all about "fitting" the evidence. But more is required for genuine confirmation than mere "fit," which any theory, no matter how absurd, can in principle achieve. So what else is required?

GENUINE CONFIRMATION

While scientists and philosophers of science may disagree on the details, most would sign up to something like the following.

In order for a theory to be strongly confirmed by the evidence, at least three conditions must be met. The theory must make *predictions* that are:

1) *clear and precise,*
2) *surprising,* and
3) *true.*

Let's unpack these conditions.

Prediction

First off, let's say a little more about predictions. To be strongly confirmed, your theory must allow for the derivation of predictions about the observable. So, for example, from the theory that water freezes below 0 degrees centigrade, we can derive the prediction that if the temperature of this particular sample of water is reduced to below 0, it will freeze. From the theory that all swans are white, we can derive the prediction that the next swan we observe will be white. As a slightly more complex example, from Newton's theory of universal gravitation we can derive the prediction that the planet Uranus will move in a smooth, elliptical orbit around the sun.

Notice that, very often, the derivation of a prediction from a theory involves the use of certain *auxiliary hypotheses*. The reason the above example involving Newton's theory is more complex is that the theory does not by itself directly entail that Uranus will have a smooth, elliptical orbit. In order to derive that particular prediction, we have to help ourselves to certain auxiliary hypotheses, including the auxiliary hypothesis that there are no *other* bodies exerting a gravitational pull on that planet (which might distort Uranus's elliptical orbit).

The fact that we can derive from a theory a prediction about the observable means that the theory can, in principle, be *tested*. We can check to see whether the prediction is true. Let's suppose the prediction is true. What follows?

Notice that confirmation is a *matter of degree*: theories can be *more or less* well confirmed by a piece of evidence. For example, observing a single white swan provides *some* confirmation that all swans are white, but not very much. So what is required for *strong* confirmation?

Clarity and Precision

Suppose the prediction I derive from my theory is ambiguous and vague. Then it won't be difficult to interpret it in such a way that, whatever is observed, I can say, "Hey, my prediction came true!"

Predictions made by psychics often have this quality. Take the claim that you will "soon meet a tall, dark, and handsome stranger." What does "soon" mean? Today? This week? This year? Is five feet eleven inches "tall"? Does brown hair qualify someone as "dark"? What is considered "handsome"? Because of the usually rather ambiguous nature of a psychic's prediction, it's easy to interpret it in such a way that it comes out as "true." This ambiguity is also a factor in the prophecies of Nostradamus, the medieval seer whose cryptic prose supposedly predicted all sorts of dramatic events, such as the rise of Hitler and 9/11. Nostradamus's writing is so vague that, when some major event occurs, it's not difficult to find a passage that "predicts" it. (I look more closely at the work of Nostradamus in the conclusion to this book.)

For strong confirmation, we need to be able to derive from our theory predictions that are clear and precise, and one very obvious way in which we can do this is if our predictions concern mathematically quantifiable and objectively measurable phenomena. The claim that every dog will be "heavy-ish" is so vague as to be unfalsifiable, while the claim that every dog weighs more than ten pounds can easily be falsified with the aid of a scale.

Surprisingness

However, even a clear, precise, and true prediction is not enough to guarantee strong confirmation. A further, key ingredient is required. The prediction must also exhibit a certain kind of *surprisingness*.

Suppose I believe fairies cause trees to grow more quickly during the summer months. From this theory we can derive the fairly clear and precise prediction that this copse of trees will grow more during the summer months. The prediction, it turns out, is true. Does that strongly confirm my theory that fairies cause trees to grow more in the summer months? Clearly not. For, although it is true that my theory predicts just such a growth pattern, that pattern is to be *expected anyway*, even on more orthodox scientific theories about why trees grow.

Similarly, from Dave's theory that dogs are Venusian spies so ingenious that their devious activities will remain undetected, we can derive the prediction that dogs will be observed to behave like harmless pets. This prediction is true. But while *consistent* with Dave's theory, the observed behavior of dogs in no way *confirms* his theory, as this is just the sort of behavior we'd expect from dogs anyway, even if they *are* harmless pets.

The moral is: if the prediction derived from a theory is something that would *not be particularly unexpected anyway*, even on rival theories, then the fact that the prediction *is* true does not strongly confirm the theory. For strong confirmation, the prediction must be surprising in this sense: if the theory were not true, then what is predicted would not be particularly expected.

Putting these various points together, we can sum up by saying that, in order for a theory to be strongly confirmed, that theory has to stick its neck out with respect to the evidence. It has to be bold, to risk being proved wrong. If a theory either fails to make any predictions, or if it makes only vague and woolly predictions, or else if it predicts things that are not particularly unexpected anyway—if, in short, it takes no significant risks with the evidence—then not only is it not strongly confirmed, *it can't be.*

Let's now consider whether Young Earth Creationism and the theory of evolution are, or might be, strongly confirmed by empirical evidence.

STRONG CONFIRMATION BY THE FOSSIL RECORD?

We have seen that Young Earth Creationism can be endlessly adjusted so that it continues to "fit" whatever happens to be dug up. Does that mean that it is strongly *confirmed* by the fossil record?

No. Because Young Earth Creationists *don't predict very much at all about what fossils, if any, will be dug up*. If we find no fossils, they will say, "Hey, this fits my theory—there hasn't been enough time for fossils to form." If we find, as we do, fossils of only simple marine creatures in the lower layers and larger mammals in only the topmost layers, then Young Earth Creationists will say, "Hey, this fits my theory—this is explained by the differential rates at which corpses decompose and sink" or "This is explained by the fact that different ecological zones were submerged at different times." But suppose species had been found fairly randomly through the layers? Then Young Earth Creationists would say, "Hey, this fits my theory!—The flood drowned these creatures more or less simultaneously." Young Earth Creationists fail to make any bold predictions regarding the fossil record. They take no real risks with the fossil evidence. But then their theory can't be strongly confirmed by the fossil evidence.

What about the theory of evolution? Can that be strongly confirmed? Yes. The theory is a theory of common descent. It says that contemporary species evolved from common ancestors in a tree-like manner, with contemporary species at the tips of the branches and the most common ancestor at the base of the trunk. If the theory is true, the sedimentary layers should reveal fossils arranged in a very specific order, consistent with such a tree-like structure.

In its fully developed form, the theory of evolution also says that birds and mammals developed fairly late in the history of life, after the Devonian period. So the theory predicts that *not even one fossil of a bird or mammal will ever show up in the lower pre-Devonian deposits (which constitute over half the his-*

tory of multicellular organisms). As one scientist puts it: "Even *one* incontrovertible find of any pre-Devonian mammal [or] bird . . . would shatter the theory of common descent."[10]

These are both clear and precise predictions. They are also surprising predictions; for example, say the theory of evolution not true, and the flood theory were true instead. There would be no particular reason not to expect to find, among the countless thousands of fossils dug up each year, at least *one or two* avian or mammalian fossils in the pre-Devonian layers (Young Earth Creationists would not be remotely surprised if they did). Nor would there be any reason to expect fossils to line up in precisely the way predicted by the theory of common descent. Indeed, that the fossils should happen to line up precisely that way would be a gob-smacking coincidence if the theory weren't true.

So, in predicting that no such fossils will be found, the theory of evolution takes a very significant risk—which is why the fact that no such fossil has ever shown up very strongly confirms the theory of evolution. (And of course, this is just *one* example of how the theory of evolution is strongly confirmed. There are numerous others.)[11]

FALSIFICATION

Let's now turn from the notion of confirmation to that of falsification. What of the Young Earth Creationists' claim that their theory is not *falsified* by the fossil record? I am going to suggest that, not only is Young Earth Creationism not falsified by the fossil record—given the kind of immunizing strategies employed by its proponents—it *cannot* be falsified by the fossil record or indeed by anything else. It is, in effect, an unfalsifiable theory.

So far as the notion of falsification is concerned, a pivotal figure is the philosopher Karl Popper. Popper developed a philosophical theory called *falsificationism*, which describes how science progresses. Few philosophers now embrace falsificationism, and I certainly won't be relying on that theory here. Nevertheless, Popper did make a number of points relevant to our discussion.

We have already seen how scientific theories can be falsified—we can derive from them observational predictions that can then be checked. If the prediction turns out to be false, then the theory is falsified. However, Popper notes that various strategies can be employed by defenders of a theory to deal with an apparent falsification—to *protect* or *immunize* it against falsification. It is on such immunizing strategies that I am going to focus here. Let's begin with some examples.

Blame an Auxiliary Hypothesis

Here's one obvious way of protecting a theory from falsification. We have already seen that, in order to derive a prediction from a theory, it's often necessary to employ *auxiliary hypothesis*. We saw that Newton's theory of universal gravitation predicts a smooth, elliptical orbit for Uranus only if no other planet is exerting a gravitational effect on it. When Uranus turned out not to have a smooth, elliptical orbit—it wobbles slightly in and out of its predicted orbit—defenders of Newton's theory insisted that, rather than falsifying Newton's theory, this observation revealed only that there was another as-yet-unknown object in the vicinity of Uranus tugging it out of its elliptical orbit. In other words, the falsification was *deflected away from the core theory and onto an auxiliary hypothesis*. Scientists calculated where this mystery object would have to be in order to exert such a pull, looked for it, and discovered a new planet: Neptune.

Here's another example. When Galileo constructed his telescope, looked at the moon, and observed mountains and valleys, it seemed that Aristotle's theory that every heavenly body is perfectly spherical had been falsified. Instead of accepting this, some defenders of Aristotle's view suggested that there must be an invisible substance covering the surface of the moon, filling up its valleys right to the tops of the mountains, so that the moon is, after all, perfectly spherical. The falsification was in this case deflected away from Aristotle's theory and on to the auxiliary hypothesis that any material making up the surface of the moon must be visible.

Other strategies for defending a theory include exploiting vagueness and ambiguity in the theory or the predictions derived from it—to reinterpret them so that what is observed turns out to "fit" after all. This is, as already noted, a favorite trick of psychics and soothsayers.

Ad Hoc Maneuvers

Popper realized that even mainstream scientists can and do employ such strategies in order to defend their theories. He did not think this was *always* a bad thing. In particular, Popper thought that defending Newton's theory of universal gravitation by postulating a mystery planet was entirely acceptable, because it led to *new tests*—scientists could actually look to see if there was planet in the place predicted.

What Popper considered *particularly* suspect were attempts to defend a theory by means of modifications that introduced *no new tests*. So, for example, the postulation of an invisible substance on the surface of moon in order to salvage the Aristotelian theory that all heavenly bodies are perfectly spherical led to no new tests—there was nothing scientists could do at the time to check whether any such substance was there. Popper calls such untestable hypotheses introduced to immunize a theory against falsification "ad hoc."

Popper noted that the more such strategies are employed to protect a theory from falsification, the less falsifiable it becomes, until eventually we end up with a theory that is not falsifiable at all. In Popper's view, an unfalsifiable theory is not scientific. Theories that claim to be scientific but fail to meet the test of falsifiability are mere pseudoscience.

TWO KINDS OF IMMUNITY TO FALSIFICATION

My suggestion is that Young Earth Creationism, as promoted and defended by today's adherents, is also an unfalsifiable theory. But, before we look again at Young Earth Creationism, it's worth taking a short detour to look at two quite different ways in which theories can achieve unfalsifiability. We'll see, interestingly, that there are at least two versions of Young Earth Creationism, and they achieve unfalsifiability in a different way.

Popper himself distinguishes two ways in which a theory might be rendered unfalsifiable. Let's focus for a moment on Popper's own examples. He considered both Marx's theory of history and the psychoanalytic theories of Freud and Adler unfalsifiable, but for different reasons.

The problem with Freud's and Adler's psychoanalytic theories, thought Popper, is that, whatever human behavior is observed, it can always be interpreted to "fit" either theory. Popper, who knew Adler, remarks:

> As for Adler, I was much impressed by a personal experience. Once, in 1919, I reported to him a case which to me did not seem particularly Adlerian, but which he found no difficulty in analyzing in terms of his theory of inferiority feelings, although he had not even seen the child.

Popper believed the same was true of Freud's theories. They both appeared to fit the evidence and to thus be supported by the evidence, no matter what evidence might show up. Popper illustrated by considering two hypothetical situations—one in which a man pushes a child into water with the intention of drowning the child, and one in which a man sacrifices himself to save a child. Popper claims each of these two events can be explained with equal ease in Freudian and Adlerian terms:

According to Freud the first man suffered from repression (say, of some component of his Oedipus complex), while the second man had achieved sublimation. According to Adler the first man suffered from feelings of inferiority (producing perhaps the need to prove to himself that he dared to commit some crime), and so did the second man (whose need was to prove to himself that he dared to rescue the child).

Popper found he couldn't think of any human behavior that *wouldn't* fit either theory:

> It was precisely this fact—that they always fitted, that they were always confirmed—which in the eyes of their admirers constituted the strongest argument in favor of these theories. It began to dawn on me that this apparent strength was in fact their weakness.[12]

So Popper thought these two psychoanalytic theories were unfalsifiable, and for much the same reason. Popper also thought that Marx's theory of history was unfalsifiable, but for a different reason. According to Popper, unlike Freud's and Adler's theories, Marx's theory *started out* as a falsifiable theory. In fact, it made some rather risky predictions about how history would unfold. For example, it predicted the character of a coming social revolution (for example, it predicted the revolution would happen in an industrially advanced society such as Britain). However, this prediction turned out to be largely incorrect (there was a revolution, but it did not take place in the way Marx predicted—it actually happened in industrially backward Russia). Marx's theory was therefore falsified. Rather than accept this, Marx's followers employed an immunizing strategy, reinterpreting theory and evidence so that the theory continued to fit the evidence after all:

> Instead of accepting the refutations the followers of Marx reinterpreted both the theory and the evidence in order to make them agree. In this way they rescued the theory from refutation; but they did so at the price of adopting a device which made it irrefutable.[13]

Dave's Immunizing Strategy

Let's now return to Dave's theory that dogs are spies from the planet Venus. Mary and Pete tried to falsify Dave's theory, but each time they tried, Pete came up with yet another explanation for why his theory is, after all, consistent with the evidence. While some of Dave's moves are rather ad hoc in nature, others are not. His suggestion that the dogs' transmitters are located in their brains does in fact lead to a *new test*—we could look inside dogs' brains to check whether there are any transmitters. However, when no transmitters show up, Dave just makes another adjustment—he says the transmitters must be made of organic material indistinguishable from brain stuff. So while not every immunizing move Dave makes is ad hoc, his *overall strategy* renders his theory unfalsifiable. So, yes, today's Young Earth Creationists can say, "Our theory has not been falsified!" But that's only because, given their immunizing strategies, it *cannot* be."

Clearly, Dave's theory suffers from the same problem that Popper found with Marxism. Dave's theory *starts off* as potentially falsifiable. However, once it *is* falsified, Dave develops an immunizing strategy that makes it unfalsifiable. Every time his theory runs into trouble with the evidence, Dave just makes another modification to deal with it: to make it *fit* the evidence after all.

As should now be clear, the version of Young Earth Creationism outlined above is also unfalsifiable, and for much the same reason. The theory that the earth was created just as described in Genesis *starts out* as a falsifiable theory. Indeed, it is straightforwardly falsified by a mountain of evidence. In response to the evidence, proponents of Young Earth Creationism, like Dave, then devise ever more ingenious moves to account for it. Once they have embarked on this strategy, their theory *becomes* unfalsifiable. It's *the strategy developed to defend the core theory, rather than anything about the theory itself, that makes it unfalsifiable.* So, yes, today's Young Earth Creationists can say, "Our theory has not been falsified!" But that's only because, given their immunizing strategies, it *cannot* be.

So, yes, perhaps Young Earth Creationists can correctly say "Our theory has not been falsified!" But if so, that is only because, given their immunizing strategy, it *cannot* now be falsified.

Gosse's Omphalos Hypothesis

There is an interesting contrast to be drawn here with a rather different version of Young Earth Creationism developed by Philip Henry Gosse. In 1857, Gosse published a book titled *Omphalos: An Attempt to Untie the Geological Knot*. Gosse tried to explain how the discoveries then being made in geology—such as the fossil record—that were beginning to seriously challenge the view that the earth was just a few thousand years old, were in fact entirely compatible with Young Earth Creationism *Omphalos* means "navel," or "belly button." Some Christians wondered whether Adam had one. One the one hand, it seems he wouldn't, because he had no mother to whom he was attached by an umbilical cord. On the other hand, it would be seem odd if Adam didn't have one, as it's an otherwise universal feature of human beings.

Gosse thought Adam had a belly button, despite the fact that a belly button might seem to suggest Adam had a mother. Gosse took a similar view about the trees in the garden of Eden, which he thought would have tree rings that might seem to suggest greater age. Gosse then extended this line of thought to the earth itself. The sedimentary layers strewn with fossils were created just a few thousand years ago. Like Adam's navel, they were put there not to deceive or to test our religious faith (as some have suggested) but because such creations will inevitably bear the hallmarks of a nonexistent past. "It may be objected," Gosse wrote,

> that to assume the world to have been created with fossil skeletons in its crust—skeletons of animals that never really existed—is to charge the Creator with forming objects whose sole purpose was to deceive us. The reply is obvious. Were the concentric timber-rings of a created tree formed merely to

deceive? Were the growth lines of a created shell intended to deceive? Was the navel of the created Man intended to deceive him into the persuasion that he had a parent?[14]

Gosse concluded that the evidence provided by geology and other sciences failed to settle the age of the earth: *whether or not the biblical account was true, the earth would look just as it does.*

A striking feature of Gosse's version of Young Earth Creationism is that, unlike the contemporary version we have been examining, Gosse's version is immune to refutation by geological and other natural sciences *right from the start*. It is, in this respect, much like Bertrand Russell's famous hypothesis that the entire universe, with us in it, was created just five minutes ago, but with the appearance of a much longer past (including, of course, our own false memories of that nonexistent past). Both versions of creationism achieve *consistency* with the evidence. But they achieve it in different ways. Gosse's version does so by virtue of its *content*. The currently dominant version of Young Earth Creationism, by contrast, achieves unfalsifiability through the use of *immunizing strategies*.

To sum up: (1) Young Earth Creationism, unlike the theory of evolution and the theory that the universe is billions of years old, is not confirmed by the fossil record (or by anything else, for that matter); (2) Young Earth Creationism, as it is currently promoted and defended, is not only *not* falsified, it *cannot be* falsified (which is not a virtue in a theory, but a vice). Consequently, whether or not we want to call Young Earth Creationism "science" (and Popper would not), it's not *good* science.

BIASES AND PRESUPPOSITIONS

Let's now nail the myth that lies at the heart of the modern Young Earth Creationist movement. Young Earth Creationists will often cheerily admit that they endlessly adjust and develop their core theory that the biblical account of creation is literally correct to make it "fit" the evidence. But they typically deny that this entails that their account is not at least as well confirmed as the standard scientific account. Why? Because they think that *those who believe in the theory of evolution and a billions-of-years-old universe are doing the same thing.*

As a minister of a creationist organization explains, both the Bible-literalists and the evolutionists are doing no more than responding to the biases or presuppositions with which they start:

> There were a lot of influences in Darwin's background which would lead him almost inevitably to the point he reached. His father was clearly an atheist. And certainly there was a background of disbelief in the Bible. And certainly there was a belief about millions of years that existed before him. He started his theories from that point. Now I have a clear bias. The Bible. And I admit that. But most scientists do not want to admit these kinds of biases that they have themselves.[15]

Young Earth Creationists accuse the contemporary scientific orthodoxy of having its own bias—toward evolution in particular. Orthodox scientists are doing no more than taking whatever evidence shows up and making it fit *their* prior commitments. So they are, in this respect, really behaving no differently than Young Earth Creationists.

Young Earth Creationist Ken Ham concurs:

> Increasing numbers of scientists are realizing that when you take the Bible as your basis and build your models of science and history upon it, all the evidence from the living animals and plants, the fossils, and the cultures fits. This confirms that the Bible really is the Word of God and can be trusted totally.[16]

According to Ham, Young Earth Creationists and evolutionists do the same thing: they take the evidence and then look for ways to make it *fit* the axioms of the framework theory to which they have *already* committed themselves: "Evolutionists have their own framework . . . into which they try to fit the data."[17]

It should now be clear why *Ham is misrepresenting what real scientists do.* Science is not essentially about achieving fit between theory and data. As we have seen, any theory, no matter how nuts, can achieve that kind of fit, including Dave's ludicrous theory that dogs are Venusian spies. What a scientific theory requires if it is to be credible is not merely *consistency with* the evidence but *confirmation by* the evidence—the stronger the confirmation, the better. That is why real scientists prefer *bold* predictions. They take risks with the evidence wherever they can.

As a result of taking such risks, scientific theories can be, and often are, falsified. Even theories toward which scientists are initially very strongly biased can be, and historically have been, shown to be wrong. Sometimes the theoretical framework with which scientists begin is shown to be mistaken, resulting in a major scientific revolution.

However, because real scientists are prepared to take such risks, their theories can be, and sometimes are, strongly confirmed. Today's Young Earth Creationists avoid such risks. Like Dave, they have adopted an immunizing strategy such that, no matter what's discovered, it's never going to be allowed to falsify their framework theory. One way or another, the evidence will be shown to "fit." But then, because Young Earth Creationists take no such risks, their theory can never be strongly confirmed.

That Young Earth Creationists take no risks with the evidence is nicely illustrated by the following quote from proponent Bodie Hodge's "Why Don't We Find Human and Dinosaur Fossils Together?":

> If human and dinosaur bones are ever found in the same layers, it would be a fascinating find. . . . Those who hold a biblical view of history wouldn't be surprised. . . . Evolutionists, on the other hand . . . would have a real challenge. In the old-earth

view, man isn't supposed to be the same age as dinosaurs. . . .
As biblical creationists, we don't require that human and
dinosaur fossils be found in the same layers. Whether they are
found or not, does not affect the biblical view of history.[18]

Hodge makes no risky predictions regarding the fossil record.
Whatever shows up will be consistent with *his* theory. Dinosaurs
and humans discovered in different layers—fine. Dinosaurs and
humans in the same layers—no problem. Hodge is quite explicit
that neither discovery would constitute a "surprise."

What Hodge fails to realize is that *it is, precisely, the Bible-
literalist's lack of commitment about how human, dinosaur, and
other fossils should be found that gives the theory of evolution a
huge advantage over their own.* The bottom line is this: because
the theory of evolution takes a significant risk with that evidence,
it can be confirmed by it; because Young Earth Creationism
doesn't, it can't. Young Earth Creationism is no more "confirmed" than is the Dave's theory that dogs are spies from the
planet Venus.

THE BLUNDERBUSS

The strategy of making your theory "fit" the evidence and then
claiming it is not, after all, falsified (and is perhaps even confirmed) is often accompanied by another rhetorical strategy that
I call *The Blunderbuss* (a blunderbuss is a sort of early form of
shotgun that flares out widely at the muzzle). The strategy is this:
at the same time as you are employing *"But It Fits!"* to render
your own theory consistent with the evidence, you fire off endless
salvos of "problems" at your opponent's theory. Your salvos will
comprise (1) a few real but largely *irrelevant* problems, and (2)
various *invented* problems.

Almost every theory, no matter how well confirmed, faces
puzzles and problem cases. This is certainly true of the theory

that life on this planet is a product of natural mechanisms. There remain unanswered questions. Currently, orthodox science is not able to explain how life initially emerged on this planet. Genetic and evolutionary theory can explain how living organisms evolve over time, but it cannot yet fully explain how life initially appeared. Not surprisingly, then, Young Earth Creationists bring up these kinds of questions at every available opportunity. The truth, of course, is this: that life has evolved over many millions of years by mechanisms including natural selection is nevertheless overwhelmingly confirmed by the evidence. This genuine and intriguing puzzle for orthodox science does nothing to throw that fact into doubt. Nor does it lend the creationist theory that the entire universe and everything in it was created six thousand years ago any credibility whatsoever. So this "problem" is, in truth, *irrelevant* to the debate between Young Earth Creationism and orthodox science. The impression that Young Earth Creationists try to create by firing off such "problems"— that their own theory has something going for it, scientifically speaking—is entirely misleading.

That was an example of a genuine puzzle that orthodox science cannot currently solve. However, the vast majority of "problems" with which Young Earth Creationists pack their blunderbuss aren't genuine problems at all. More often than not, they are *invented*.

A nice example is *polystrate fossils*, such as vertically fossilized tree trunks. Young Earth Creationists will often wow audiences with dramatic images of fossilized trees that can be seen extended upward through many sedimentary layers. "How can our opponents explain *this*?" the Young Earth Creationists ask. "According to evolutionists, these sedimentary layers were produced over *millions of years*, far too long for this tree to have remained without rotting away! Clearly, this tree was buried by these layers of sediment very quickly. But that only makes sense with our flood theory!" One Young Earth Creationist concludes:

Such phenomena clearly violate the idea of a gradually accumulated geologic column since, generally speaking, an evolutionary overview of that column suggests that each stratum (layer) was laid down over thousands (or even millions!) of years.[19]

Except, of course, the "evolutionary overview" suggests no such thing. It allows that trees will sometimes be buried very quickly by a series of sedimentary layers, for example, if located near a riverbank, a volcanic eruption, or area of rapid subsidence. This so-called problem for the "evolutionary overview"—which is also supposed to confirm Young Earth Creationism—is pure bunkum.

Sometimes the so-called problems for the theory of evolution are quite literally fabricated. Attend a Young Earth Creationist event, and you may well be presented with photographs of dinosaur and human footprints in the same sedimentary layer. The tracks are right there in a rock bed at Paluxy River—"proof" that humans and dinosaurs walked the earth at the same time! What those peddling these photographs don't usually mention is that the granddaughter of George Adams, the man who originally discovered the prints, admits her grandfather carved the human prints by hand to make money.

Young Earth Creationists have amassed a vast arsenal of such irrelevant or invented problems to fire off at their opponents in debate. It usually takes time and patience to deal properly with even just one example. Often it also takes specialist knowledge, knowledge that scientists working in another field may not possess. So it's often fairly easy for Young Earth Creationists to get their rivals bogged down, seemingly stymied by the "problems" they raise. "Explain *this*! And *this*! And *this*!" they say, and watch with mounting satisfaction as looks of confusion and desperation begin to creep across their opponents' faces.

As a result, Young Earth Creationists are able to generate the illusion that not only does their theory "fit" the evidence, their opponents face all sorts of devastating objections. The audience to such a debate may depart, misled into thinking that, whether or not Young Earth Creationism is true, there at least remains a live, ongoing scientific debate.

YOUNG EARTH CREATIONISM IN SCHOOLS

Young Earth Creationism has been, and continues to be, taught in schools. Often this is done covertly (I know of two British schools in which Young Earth Creationism has been taught by a science teacher without the knowledge or permission of the school or other members of staff—and one was one of Britain's leading independent schools). Obviously I object to Young Earth Creationism being taught in schools as a rival to orthodox scientific theories. People often object to the teaching of Young Earth Creationism on the grounds that children should not be taught ludicrous, obvious falsehoods, but that's not my main objection. My central criticism is this: teaching children that Young Earth Creationism is scientifically respectable involves teaching children to *think like Dave*. It involves getting them to think in ways that, under other circumstances, might justifiably lead us to suspect the thinker is suffering from some sort of mental illness. By allowing Young Earth Creationism into the classroom, we run not only the risk that children will end up believing ridiculous falsehoods, which is bad enough, but, worse still, that they'll end up supposing that the kind of warped and convoluted mental gymnastics in which both Dave and Young Earth Creationists engage is actually *cogent scientific thinking*. We may end up corrupting not just *what* they think but, more important, *how* they think.

THE VISION THING

So effective can *"But It Fits!"* be in generating the illusion that a theory is overwhelmingly confirmed by the evidence that its defenders may come to think its truth is *just obvious for anyone with eyes to see*. This may in turn lead them to suspect that those who can't see its manifest truth must be suffering from something like a perceptual defect. We might call reaching this advanced stage achieving *The Vision Thing*.

Popper noted something like this effect in some followers of Marx, Freud, and Adler. He says:

> I found that those of my friends who were admirers of Marx, Freud, and Adler, were impressed by a number of points common to these theories, and especially by their apparent *explanatory power*. These theories appear to be able to explain practically everything that happened within the fields to which they referred. The study of any of them seemed to have the effect of an intellectual conversion or revelation, open your eyes to a new truth hidden from those not yet initiated. Once your eyes were thus opened you saw confirmed instances everywhere: the world was full of *verifications* of the theory. Whatever happened always confirmed it. Thus its truth appeared manifest; and unbelievers were clearly people who did not want to see the manifest truth; who refuse to see it, either because it was against their class interest, or because of their repressions which were still "un-analyzed" and crying aloud for treatment.[20]

Young Earth Creationist Ken Ham similarly puts down the inability of his opponents to "see" the manifest truth of creation to their arrogant and egotistical ways:

> Why can't the humanists, the evolutionists, see that all the evidence supports exactly what the Bible says? It is because they do not want to see it. It is not because the evidence is not there. They refuse to allow the evidence to be correctly interpreted in the light of biblical teaching.[21]

Evolutionists deliberately choose not to see what's right there in front of their noses. Clearly, Ken Ham has achieved The Vision Thing.

Young Earth Creationism, as defended and promoted by people like Ken Ham, is a very impressive Intellectual Black Hole. Indeed, Ham is one of the great contemporary masters of the *"But It Fits!"* strategy. However, *"But It Fits!"* is by no means restricted to Young Earth Creationism and fruitcakes like Dave. It crops up in all sorts of places. See the conclusion for more examples.

Chapter 3

Going Nuclear

Suppose Mike is involved in a debate about the truth of his own particular New Age belief system. Things are not going well for him. Mike's arguments are being picked apart, and, worse still, his opponents have come up with several devastating objections that he can't deal with. How might Mike get himself out of this bind?

One possibility is to adopt strategy I call *Going Nuclear*. *Going Nuclear* is an attempt to unleash an argument that lays waste to every position, bringing them all down to the same level of "reasonableness." Mike might try to force a draw by detonating a philosophical argument that achieves what during the Cold War was called "mutually assured destruction," in which both sides in the conflict are annihilated.

There are two main variants of *Going Nuclear*: skeptical and relativist. I'll begin with some skeptical versions.

SKEPTICAL VERSIONS OF GOING NUCLEAR

Skepticism about Reason

In philosophy, the term *skeptic* usually refers to someone who *denies we have knowledge in a given area* (outside of philosophy, the term is more commonly used to refer to someone unwilling to accept claims of the miraculous and extraordinary that don't withstand close critical and scientific scrutiny). Here is a classic example of a skeptical philosophical argument:

> *Whenever we argue about the truth or falsity of a belief, we apply our powers of reason. But why suppose that reason is itself a reliable route to the truth? We might attempt to justify our use of reason, of course. But any justification of reason that we offer will itself rely on reason. Relying on reason to justify our reliance on reason is a bit like taking a secondhand car salesman's word for it that he is trustworthy—it's an entirely circular justification, and so no justification at all! So it turns out that our reliance on reason is entirely unjustified. It's a leap of faith!*

From the claim that our reliance on reason is unjustified, it is seemingly then but a short step to the conclusion that no belief is justified:

> *But if reliance on reason cannot be justified, then, because every rational justification relies on reason, so no belief can be justified. But if no belief is justified, then, ultimately, everything is a faith position! But then your belief is no more reasonable than mine. Get out of that!*

Whether this is actually a good argument for the conclusion that no belief is justified is not a question I'll address here. The point is, at first sight, it does *look* pretty persuasive. It's not easy to spot precisely where the argument goes wrong, if, indeed, it goes wrong at all. This means that if Mike's belief system is

[handwritten margin note: this assertion actually relies on reason + logic]

taking a beating, rationally speaking, Mike can adopt the last-ditch tactic of employing this skeptical argument. Mike can then admit that while *his* belief might not be justified, *his opponent's beliefs can't be justified either*. The skeptical argument offers Mike a wonderful get-out-of-jail-free card. It allows him to walk away with his head held high, saying, "So you see? In the last analysis, our beliefs are *equally* (ir)rational! They're *both* 'faith positions!'"

You can see why I call this strategy *Going Nuclear*. Once Mike plays the skeptical card, all his opponent's hard work in constructing arguments against Mike's position counts for nothing. Kaboom! At one stroke, Mike demolishes them all. He lays waste to every rational argument, bringing every belief down to the same level.

In order for Mike's opponents to deal with his *Going Nuclear*, they will now have to refute his philosophical argument. That is a difficult, perhaps impossible, thing to do. They are certainly going to struggle. As a result, any audience to their debate will be struck not only by Mike's sophistication in employing such a devastating philosophical objection, but also by his opponent's mounting frustration as they wrestle with the thorny philosophical conundrum Mike has set them. It's quite likely Mike will be perceived to be the intellectual victor in this exchange. At the very least, he won't be thought to have lost.

This version of *Going Nuclear* can be employed in defense of a wide variety of beliefs. Believe in the curative powers of crystals or that there's a family of fairies living at the bottom of your garden? If you find yourself on the losing side of the argument, you can always employ *Going Nuclear* as a last-ditch, face-saving strategy.

So what, exactly, is wrong with this version of *Going Nuclear*? After all, it might be that the skeptical argument Mike has employed really is a good argument. Perhaps every belief system really is as rational as every other. So, if Mike finds himself argued into a corner, why shouldn't he employ such a skeptical argument?

Because it's almost certainly an intellectually dishonest ruse. Those who press the nuclear button rarely do so in good faith. Bear in mind that, in such discussions, playing the skeptical card really is the nuclear option. By *Going Nuclear*, Mike avoids defeat, but *only by utterly annihilating the rationality of every belief*. All positions, no matter how sensible or nuts, come out as equally (ir)rational.

If Mike is to be consistent, he must now accept that that the earth is flat, that the earth is round, that milk makes people fly, that it doesn't, that astrology is true, that it isn't—that all these beliefs are equally (un)reasonable. Now of course, Mike almost certainly doesn't believe any of this. The fact is, he does think reason is a fairly reliable tool for establishing what is true and what isn't. We all rely on reason in our day-to-day lives—Mike included. In fact, Mike constantly trusts his life to reason whenever, for example, he trusts that the brakes on his car will work, that a bridge will support his weight, that a medicine will save his life, and so on.

Indeed, those who employ this version of *Going Nuclear* are usually quite content to rely on reason to make their case just so long as they are not losing the argument. It's only when the tide of rationality turns against them that they reach for the nuclear button. And of course, once their opponent has left the room, they'll start using reason again to try to prop up their belief. That's downright hypocritical.

So this version of *Going Nuclear* is, in truth, almost always a ploy. Those who use it don't usually believe what they're saying about reason. They say it only to raise enough dust and confusion to make quick their escape.

A Religious Example

The skeptical version of *Going Nuclear* outlined above crops up quite often in debates about the truth of religion. For example, when responding to rational arguments raised against his belief, one Orthodox Jew writes: "The belief in reason seems no less a dogma than any other."[1]

Perhaps belief in reason is, ultimately, a dogma. However, *if* this person relies on reason in every other aspect of his life, and indeed appeals to reason whenever it appears to *support* his particular religious outlook, then he is guilty of hypocrisy. Playing the skeptical card is merely a ruse he selectively employs in order to avoid having to admit that what he believes is, by the standards that he accepts and employs in every other aspect of his life, unlikely to be true.

Skepticism about the External World

There are several variants of the skeptical version of *Going Nuclear*. Sometimes a different skeptical argument is employed. Here's another example.

Suppose a Theist finds herself on the losing side of a debate with atheists about the existence of God. Her own arguments for the existence of God have been shown to be weak, and she is struggling to deal with the evidential problem of evil (see Appendix B to my introduction) raised by her opponents. As a last-ditch strategy she may try this: she may admit that her own belief involves a leap of faith, but then add that her atheist opponents make a similar leap of faith when it comes to *trusting their senses.*

Atheists, after all, believe they inhabit a physical world filled with mountains, oceans, trees, houses, and people. But they believe this only because that is the kind of world their senses of sight, hearing, taste, touch, smell, and so on seem to reveal. How can they know their senses are a reliable guide to the truth? How can they know that their experiences are produced by a real world, rather than, say, a supercomputer generating a sophisticated virtual reality, as in the film *The Matrix*? After all, everything would seem exactly the same, either way. So, it seems atheists cannot justify their belief in such an external world. But if atheists cannot justify their belief in such an external world, then they don't know that such a world exists. Their belief that there is such a world must involve a huge leap of faith.

Having set up this skeptical argument, our Theist may then add that she happens to enjoy not only *sensory experiences* but also a *God experience*. God, she supposes, reveals himself to her. But then, precisely because she trusts her God experience—she supposes that it is not a delusion she then doesn't have to place any *additional* faith in the reliability of her other senses. Why? Because the kind of God she seems to experience is no deceiver. She can be sure that, if there is such a God, then he will have provided her with senses that are fairly trustworthy. So, for such a Theist, trusting her senses does not require any *further* leap of faith.

In which case, our Theist may conclude that, for someone who has such religious experiences, belief in God need be no more a faith position than the atheist's belief in the external world. The two beliefs are actually intellectually on par. It's *leaps of faith all round.*

Notice, incidentally, that our Theist may make the same suggestion about the atheist's use of logic and reason. She may say that atheists just *assume* that their use of logic is reliable—they cannot ultimately justify it (for the reason we saw above). But, because our Theist places her faith in her God experience, she *doesn't* have to make a further leap of faith so far as her use of logic is concerned, because her God would not allow her to be deceived about the reliability of logic.

Criticism

Perhaps it's true that atheism is a faith position, because any belief about how things stand outside our own minds is ultimately a faith position (although this is certainly controversial— some philosophers would say we are justified in supposing there is a physical world of mountains, oceans, trees, houses, and so on because that hypothesis provides the best available explanation of what we experience, a better explanation than the Matrix-type hypothesis that it's all an elaborate computer-generated illusion). However, even if any belief about the external world involves a leap of faith, it does *not* follow that it's as reasonable for Theists to place their trust in their God experience as it is for atheists to trust their senses.

First of all, note that, while we have no obvious grounds for supposing our ordinary senses are highly *un*trustworthy, *there are very obvious grounds for supposing that such religious experiences are, as a rule, untrustworthy* (see *"I Just Know!"* for details). The content of the religious experiences people report appears to be very largely a product of their culture and sometimes also the mind-altering practices they tend to engage in, rather than any sort of divine reality.

Secondly, and still more significantly, even if our Theist's assumption that she is experiencing God leads her to trust her other senses, her other senses then appear to furnish her with ample evidence that there is no such benevolent God. There is, for example, the evidential problem of evil—surely an all-powerful, all-good God would not have created a world of the sort her senses reveal: a world containing so much appalling suffering. So, unlike the assumption that our other senses are reliable, *her Theistic assumption ends up undermining itself.*

In short, this version of *Going Nuclear* doesn't work. The Theist's assumption that her God experience is reliable appears, on closer examination, to be far less reasonable than the atheist's assumption that our other senses are reliable. Perhaps it's leaps of faith all round, but some leaps are, it turns out, much bigger than others.

Beyond Going Nuclear

There is an interesting twist on *Going Nuclear* that is popular in certain religious circles—a twist that involves combining *Going Nuclear* with *"I Just Know!"* (see chapter 5). It runs as follows.

God, some Theists maintain, has provided them *direct and*

certain knowledge of his existence. So, they suppose, they don't have to *assume* God exists. They *just know* he does (see *"I Just Know!"*). Armed with this certain knowledge that God exists, such Theists can now go on to justify their reliance on logic and their senses. For the good God they just know exists would not allow them to be deceived by logic and by their senses. But the atheist, such Theists suppose, has no such justification. So the atheist remains mired in skepticism.

Such a Theist might be tempted to respond to her atheist critics by saying, "Ah, you are *attempting to use logic against me*, but of course, unlike me, *you are not entitled to—are you, are you?*" In fact, this is one of the main argumentative strategies of one well-known commenter on various religious and atheist blogs who, in response to any rational criticism of his particular extreme, Bible-literalist brand of Theism, typically ignores it, saying something like this: "I submit, that your worldview cannot justify the universal, abstract, invariant, laws of logic, which YOU presuppose in all of YOUR arguments, whereas mine can, and does."[2]

Notice that, although this particular Theist is playing the skeptical card, he is not, strictly speaking, *Going Nuclear*. *Going Nuclear* involves bringing all positions down to the *same* level of rationality. The claim made here is that *only* the atheist ends up mired in skepticism. Our Theist plays the skeptical card in order to undermine the arguments of his atheist critics. However, our Theist (he supposes) achieves a literally miraculous escape from skepticism himself. With one bound he is free—saved by the grace of God, whom, he supposes, provides him infallible knowledge of God's existence, knowledge that our Theist can then use to justify his own reliance on logic.

This way of dealing with criticisms of Theism also fails. Whether or not our Theist is right to claim the atheist is mired in skepticism, he's still obliged to deal with the atheist's arguments and objections. Suppose an atheist appears to have provided what looks like a cogent argument that our Theist's God does not exist, or good evidence that this Theist is deluded in supposing that he "just knows" his God exists. For our Theist to just ignore such arguments and say, "But you are using the principles of logic, which you can't justify, whereas I can!" is pure evasion. Whether atheists can ultimately justify the principles of logic is entirely beside the point. If the atheist's argument is cogent according to the principles of logic, then our Theist's beliefs are, by his *own* lights, refuted. So the onus is still on the Theist to show that what he has been presented with *isn't* a cogent argument. And of course, if the Theist can't do that, then he's dumped back in the skeptical swamp himself.

RELATIVIST VERSIONS OF *GOING NUCLEAR*

We have looked at two skeptical versions, one based on skepticism regarding reason, the other based on skepticism about the external world. However, there are also nonskeptical versions of *Going Nuclear*. Typically the nonskeptical versions are based on the thought that truth is *relative*.

Relativism about Truth

Relativism is the philosophical view that what is true is relative to believers. There's no objective Truth with a capital "T" out there to be discovered. Rather, truth is a construction—*our* construction. There's your truth, my truth, his truth, her truth. There is, in short, not one Truth, but *many truths*.

In its simplest form, this sort of relativism says that what is true is what the *individual* believes to be true. Suppose I believe we are visited by angels. Then, says such a relativist, for me it *is* true we are visited by angels. If you believe we are not visited by angels, then for you it's true that we're not. There's no fact of the matter as to which of us is actually correct.

Another form of relativism about truth makes truth relative not to individuals, but to *communities*. Most scientifically minded Westerners believe that stars and planets have no astrological influence on our lives. But in other cultures it's supposed that the stars and planets do have such an influence, and that astrologers can use star charts to accurately predict the future. According to this kind of relativist, that the stars and planets have such an influence is false for such Westerners but true for those other communities. Truth is a *social* construct. Scientific truth is just one truth among many, all of which are equally "valid."

Appeals to relativism about truth are popular in certain circles and might provide Mike with another get-out-of-jail-free card. If Mike finds he is losing the argument about the ability of astral plane therapy to cure disease, he might say: "Well, that astral plane therapy cures disease may not be true for you, but it's *true for me*!"

The implication is that what's true about astral plane therapy is a matter of what certain individuals or communities happen to believe about astral plane therapy. Mike's opponents not only have to figure out what Mike means by this cryptic remark, they're now faced with the job of refuting the relativist theory of truth to which Mike has, in effect, signed up. These are complicated tasks that will require time and patience to achieve. In the meantime, Mike's out the door, leaving his opponent bogged down in the philosophical mire he has created.

Notice that this is also a version of *Going Nuclear*, because, like the skeptical version, it *brings every belief down to the same level, rationally speaking*. Every belief is ultimately as "true" as every other.

The Absurdity of Relativism

It's worth making a detour at this point to explain just why this kind of relativism is absurd. One reason relativism can seem attractive is that there a few beliefs for which it might actually be true. Consider wichitee grubs, for example—the large larvae eaten live by some aboriginal Australians. Some aboriginals consider the grubs a delicacy. Most Westerners, on the other hand, find them revolting (when Jordan, the British glamour model, was challenged to eat several large squirming grubs on a reality TV program, she said the experience was "worse than childbirth").

So what's the truth about wichitee grubs? Are they delicious or are they not? The truth, perhaps, is that there is no Truth-with-a-capital-"T" about their deliciousness. For those who enjoy the taste of wichitee grubs, it's true that they're delicious. For those they don't, it's false. That's because the property of being delicious is ultimately rooted not objectively in the grubs themselves but rather in our subjective reaction to them.

So, yes, a small band of truths may be relative, but not all (for then, as Plato pointed out, the truth that all truths are relative would itself are relative, which entails that, if I believe it's false that all truths are relative, then I'm right).

One or two people might genuinely believe that individuals create their own reality—that reality is whatever the individual takes it to be. Perhaps actress Shirley MacLaine is an example. She writes: "I have learned one deep and meaningful lesson: LIFE, LIVES and REALITY are only what we each perceive them to be. Life doesn't happen to us. We make it happen."[3]

Such relativist views of reality often crop up in New Age circles. Another variant says that reality is not what we *perceive* or *believe* it to be but what we *want* it to be. One psychic, concerned about a disagreement between herself and a fellow psychic (who had told her she was about to receive a new "evolved" soul), consulted her spirit guides, who informed her they were *both* right:

I was told that there is no absolute truth. I was told that "truth" is a very personal, subjective thing. Something that is "true" = a perception or a belief that serves us personally.

My guides then explained this, using the law of attraction to illustrate it. They said:

"You know that your beliefs create your reality and that you can create any reality you want by changing your beliefs. If you focus your attention on something and hold it as a belief, whether you like it or not, you will begin to see evidence of it being true, all around you. Therefore, you must only believe things which feel good to you. Truth is that which feels good to you; that which serves you."

So, according to my guides:

Truth = something you have focused on, something you decided you want to experience = it shows up in your reality.

Untruth = something you reject, something you don't want to experience = it doesn't show up in your reality.[4]

This is an extraordinary quotation (particularly from a website called Psychic but Sane). Initially, it's suggested that *belief* creates reality. You should believe only what you want to be true, as whatever you believe (even if it's something you don't want) will become real. But as the quotation progresses, the author seems to switch from the view that reality is what you *believe* it to be to what we might call the *Disney theory of truth*—the truth is what you *want* it to be. In order to make something come true, you need only wish (on a star, perhaps) for it. If your wish doesn't come true, that's your own fault: you obviously didn't wish hard enough. The Disney theory of truth entails that if you get struck down with a horrible disease, then at some level you must have *wanted* to get ill.

Clearly, the MacLaine-type view that reality is whatever we perceive or believe it to be can't be correct. I cannot make it true that I can fly just by supposing that I can. Suppose I jump off this tall building, convinced I'll soar skyward by flapping my arms. Even if, as I jump, it seems to me I'm flying, the sad fact is I'll still end up a crumpled heap on the pavement below. Even if I jump off holding hands with my community, every member of which is convinced we'll fly, we'll still all plummet to our deaths. To suppose otherwise is, surely, to take the "power of positive thinking" too far.

Before Copernicus, was it true that the sun really went around the earth, because that's how it looked to people? Had Neil Armstrong and enough others believed the moon was made of cheese, might the *Eagle* have landed on a sea of Camembert? No. When it comes to whether we can fly by flapping our arms, whether the sun goes around the earth, or whether the moon is made of cheese, how things appear, and how things really are, can, and do, come apart.

The Selective Appeal to Relativism

The view that all truth is relative is supposedly widespread. According to academic Allan Bloom, "There is one thing a professor can be absolutely certain of: almost every student entering university believes, or says he believes, that truth is relative."[5]

Actually, I doubt almost every student really believes this. What I don't doubt is that many students have learned that relativism offers them a useful get-out-of-jail-free card when they find themselves cornered in an argument. They have learned that by saying, "Hmm, well, that may be true for you, but *it's not true for me*," they can raise enough intellectual dust to make quick their escape.

This is precisely what Mike does above, of course. Like the majority of people who play the relativist card when cornered, Mike doesn't *really* suppose the truth is whatever we believe it to be. If pressed, it would almost certainly turn out that Mike doesn't *really* accept the absurd view that if he really believes he can fly, then he can. Nor will Mike play the relativist card while the argument seems to be going his way. Mike's relativism is merely a convenient guise that he selectively adopts whenever he's on the losing end of an argument.

The relativist version of *Going Nuclear* is not popular with mainstream religious traditionalists who think that there is but One Truth and that their particular religion has privileged access to it. When such religious traditionalists *Go Nuclear*, they usually opt for the skeptical version. Relativist versions of *Going Nuclear* are more popular with New Age–type belief systems.

The "What Is Truth?" Smokescreen

To finish, I'll mention a related argumentative strategy. Rather than playing the relativist card, you might, if cornered, simply ask *what truth is*. Truth is a philosophically thorny notion, and it is by no means clear how to define it. So, if Mike finds that his New Age belief system is taking a pasting, intellectually speaking, he could try saying this to his critics:

> *Ah, you claim these things are true. You think you can show they are true. But let me ask you a more fundamental question—what is truth?*

Mike's opponents will no doubt be disoriented by this sudden change of direction in the conversation and will be baffled by the thorny philosophical question they have been set, giving Mike enough time to head out the door.

This very tactic seems to have been employed by Pontius Pilate, who served as judge at Jesus's trial. When he interrogated Jesus prior to the crucifixion, Jesus proclaimed, "Everyone on the side of truth listens to me." (John 18:37). Pilate replied, "What is truth?" and left. As philosopher Francis Bacon put it in his essay "On Truth":

> "What is truth?" said jesting Pilate; and would not stay for an answer.[6]

This kind of use of the question "What is truth?" is the intellectual equivalent of throwing dust in your opponent's face to make quick your escape. When arguments are going our way, we are generally quite happy to say that we have good grounds for supposing that what we believe is true. Only when things start going badly for us does it suddenly occur to us to ask, "Yes, but *what is* truth?!"

This is not, strictly speaking, a version of *Going Nuclear*, as it's not actually claimed that all beliefs are equally reasonable or equally true. However, it's related to *Going Nuclear*, in that it involves the selective use of a philosophical puzzle in order to generate enough confusion to make quick your escape.

Chapter 4

Moving the Semantic Goalposts

T he expression "moving the goalposts" refers to a certain disreputable strategy in an argument. Suppose I claim Fred has never been to Brazil. It's pointed out to me that Fred went to Brazil on his honeymoon. My claim has been shown to be false, but rather than admit this, I just switch claims: "Well, he's never been to Brazil on *business*." I have just moved the goalposts. The analogy is from football: it looks like someone's going to score a goal, but suddenly, at the last minute, the goalposts are moved and the ball misses the target.

Most of us will have come across this strategy. I focus here on a certain kind of example. It involves shifting one's *meaning*. I call it *Moving the Semantic Goalposts*.

Moving the Semantic Goalposts has been developed into something like an art form in certain theological circles, where it is capable of producing an interesting variety of Intellectual Black Hole. But it's a specialist gambit: comparatively few religious people engage in this sort of tactic, certainly not in the systematic fashion described here. Many would rightly condemn it.

Let's start with an example I call *effing the ineffable*.

EFFING THE INEFFABLE

This strategy is sometimes employed to deal with the evidential problem of evil. As we saw in the introduction (appendix B), traditional Theism faces an obvious objection: enormous amounts of seemingly pointless suffering look like very powerful evidence against the existence of a maximally powerful, knowledgeable, and good deity.

In response, some say, "Ah, yes. You may have succeeded in showing that there's no 'God,' if *that's* how you define him. But that's not what *sophisticated* theists such as myself mean by 'God.'" They then add, "What we're talking about is, in truth, *ineffable and beyond our comprehension.* So you have not refuted *my* sort of theism."

Here's an actual example made on a blog by a Christian minister in response to the evidential problem of evil:

> It is a central claim of the tradition that God is ultimately mysterious and not finally knowable. We cannot attain to a position of oversight with respect to God, we are always in an inferior position—that's part of what the word "God" means—something which is above and beyond our comprehension. Any analysis which seeks to render God's attributes definable is not engaging with a Christian analysis.[1]

Fair enough. If what this minister means by "God" is something indefinable, something beyond the grasp of our conceptual and linguistic apparatus, then obviously any criticism of his theism based on the assumption that the "God" he believes in is, say, maximally powerful, knowledgeable, and good must miss its mark. If all that's being claimed is that there's a transcendent something-or-other—an indescribable cosmic thingamajig—well, yes, that's certainly a hard claim to refute. I concede that it isn't vulnerable to the evidential problem of evil.

However, those who play the ineffability card to deal with the problem of evil typically don't stop there. Even while insisting on the ineffability of what they call "God," they nevertheless continue to eff the ineffable. They almost always go on to say all sorts of positive things about this being, such as that he is good, that he is something we ought to worship, and so on.

So, for example, our Christian blogger, in response to the suggestion that enormous amounts of pointless suffering are excellent evidence that there's no good God, adds:

> What's at stake is what is meant or understood by "God" in that sentence. I'm not persuaded that we can put much flesh on the bones of "good" when that term is ascribed to God; the God I worship is beyond good and evil, he doesn't fit within those categories. Though I'd still want to call him "good."

When it's pointed out that a good God would not, presumably, engage in the indiscriminate torture of children or unleash hundreds of millions of years of pain and suffering on animals for no good reason, God's goodness turns out to be of an ineffable variety. However, it subsequently turns out we can put *some* "flesh on the bones of 'good'" when applied to God, because it's then supposed that "good" is, say, a rather more appropriate way of describing God than, say, "indifferent," "callous," or "evil." Indeed, our blogger speaks of the "God I worship." But this raises the question: why is it that our grasp of the meaning of "good" as applied to God won't allow us to say that the horrendous suffering of children is evidence there's no such God, yet is sufficient to allow us to say that God nevertheless merits our boundless adoration, gratitude, and praise?

Let me be clear about what I am and am not criticizing here. Is God ineffable and beyond our comprehension? Let's acknowledge the possibility that the answer "In one way yes and in another no" might be correct. I'm neither rejecting that suggestion nor criticizing anyone for making it. What I'm objecting to is the *unjustified and partisan* use of this suggestion to immunize

Theism against powerful counterarguments, while at the same time allowing a degree of effability whenever, say, there appears to be something positive to be said in its favor.

SEESAW MEANINGS

Effing the ineffable involves an example of what I call a *seesaw meaning*. It relies on seesawing between two meanings of an expression. Suppose I ask someone to go to the bank. They say there are no such financial institutions nearby. I say I meant the riverbank. They say there's no point: you can't take money out of a river. This annoying individual is seesawing between two meanings of the word *bank*. When it suits them to use a word to mean one thing, they tilt the seesaw in one direction. When it suits them to use a word to mean the other thing, they tilt it back the other way. Effing the ineffable involves seesawing between effable and ineffable meanings of the word *God*.

DEFENDING THE EVIL GOD HYPOTHESIS

The mischievous character of effing the ineffable is nicely brought out by noting how the exact same seesaw strategy can be used to immunize other sorts of god hypotheses against similar criticisms.

Take the evil god hypothesis outlined in my introduction. Suppose the universe is the creation of a maximally powerful and evil being. As I pointed out, this claim faces an objection mirroring the evidential problem of evil—the evidential problem of good. Surely there's far too much good stuff—too much love, laughter, and ice cream—for the universe to be the creation of such an evil being?

But now imagine another earth-like planet where theists believe not in a good god but in this evil god. Call this planet Eth. The Ethians are struck by the problem of good, and some of them reject belief in an evil god on that basis. But other Ethians remain committed to their deity. And some of them attempt to deal with the problem of good by means of the same sort of semantic sleight of hand outlined above. When critics raise the problem of good, these Ethians say:

> *Ah, I see you are guilty of a crude misunderstanding. True, evil god creates love, laughter, and ice cream, and so on, but you must remember that "evil," as applied to God, means something other than it means when applied to us Ethians. Indeed, God's "evilness" is of an ineffable, incomprehensible sort.*

If these Ethians nevertheless continue to express horror at the boundless cruelty and malice of their deity, perhaps even using him to explain all the bad stuff that exists ("Look at all this terrible suffering—clearly this is evidence that evil god exists!") most of us would see through *their* linguistic ruse straightaway.

KAREN ARMSTRONG'S *THE CASE FOR GOD*

In *The Case for God*, Karen Armstrong, former Roman Catholic nun and bestselling author of several books about religion, defends her variety of religious belief against the attacks of the "new Atheists" such as Richard Dawkins and Christopher Hitchens, whom she condemns as theologically illiterate.[2]

Armstrong also addresses the evidential problem of evil. In response to the question "How do we account for the great evil we see in a world supposedly created and governed by a benevolent deity?" Armstrong maintains that this question *betrays a misunderstanding of what "God" means*. "God" says Armstrong, "is merely a symbol of indescribable transcendence," which points "beyond itself to an ineffable reality."[3] Armstrong insists that "all faith systems have been at pains to show that the ultimate cannot be adequately expressed in any theoretical system, however august, because it lies beyond the reach of words and concepts."[4] Of course, by insisting "God" is nothing more than a symbol of indescribable transcendence, Armstrong begs the question of whether there is any indescribable transcendence for "God" to label. Perhaps there isn't.

Still, Armstrong does at least succeed in rendering her brand of theism immune to the evidential problem of evil. If God can't be described, then he can't be described as, say, all-powerful, all-knowing, and all-good. Armstrong seems to concede that the problem of evil would indeed constitute an excellent argument against the existence of a God of *that* sort. But that's not the sort of God, she claims, that the vast majority of religious people down through the centuries have believed in.

So far, so good. Armstrong has dealt with the problem of evil. However, reading through Armstrong's book, it becomes apparent her God is not quite so mysterious and ineffable after all. Indeed, Armstrong says that "God" is a symbol of "*absolute* goodness, beauty, order, peace, truthfulness, justice."[5] Not only does Armstrong appear here to be effing the ineffable, it seems she also thinks she *knows* things about this indescribable transcendence of which "God" is the name. She *knows* not only that it is the sort of thing to which moral concepts apply, but also that the correct concept to apply is absolute goodness rather than, say, absolute indifference or absolute evil. How is she able to know this?

Because it turns out that what "God" symbolizes isn't something *entirely* incomprehensible and ineffable. "God," says Armstrong, refers to a "sacred reality" of which she supposes some of us, after lengthy immersion in the right sort of religious practices, can at least catch "momentary glimpses."[6]

Armstrong's book is in large measure an exercise in such dodging and weaving. When objections such as the evidential problem of evil are raised, Armstrong pulls the protective cloak of ineffability around her God, rendering him invulnerable. But then, when it suits her, she lets the cloak slip a bit, so that certain dedicated religious folk can take a peek and provide us with at least some hints about the nature of this "sacred reality" that she supposes is out there—a reality that, it turns out, can be described as absolute goodness, beauty, order, peace, truthfulness, justice, and so on after all. This is another example of seesawing between effable and ineffable meanings.

Of course, if Armstrong could *justify* her view that the use of "God" is such as to allow her to say God is absolute goodness, beauty, order, and so on, but not such as to allow critics to run the evidential problem of evil, then my suggestion that Armstrong is just seesawing back and forth between meanings to suit herself would be unfair. But I can find no such justification in Armstrong's book, nor even any attempt to provide one.

THE APOPHATIC THEOLOGIAN

Some theists hold the "apophatic" view that we cannot say what God *is*, only what he *is not*. Apophaticism is associated particularly with Christian philosopher Thomas Aquinas and Jewish philosopher Maimonides, who said, "No attributes of God can be inferred—He is Infinite and we can only say what He is not."

The immunizing potential of apophaticism is obvious. If you never say what God is, then you can never be contradicted or proved wrong. Refuse, for example, to say that God is maximally powerful, knowledgeable, and good, and the evidential problem of evil is no longer a problem.

Professor Denys Turner of the University of Cambridge is a theologian who embraces a version of apophaticism. According to Turner, "God" stands for something radically other—something beyond our understanding. "God" is not the name of a further "thing" that exists in addition to chairs, tables, planets, and the universe. To describe God, we would need to categorize him, but, argues Turner, he is beyond categorization—he is not an instance of any kind, not even a unique instance, for "there cannot be a kind of thing such that logically there can be only one of them."[7]

It might seem, then, that Turner's version of theism offers the atheist nothing to deny. The atheist says, "There's no such thing as God," to which Turner replies: "Yes, *I agree*, there's no such *thing*!"

Still, Turner thinks there remains *something* affirmed by theists that atheists can deny, and this is that "the world is created out of nothing."[8] "God," suggests Turner, is the name of whatever is the answer to the question "Why is there anything at all?"[9] Turner sums up what he thinks any decent sort of atheist has to do:

> It is no use supposing that you disagree with me if you say, "There is no such thing as God." For I got there well before you. What I say is merely: the world is created out of nothing, that's how to understand God. Deny that, and you are indeed some sort of decent atheist. But note what the issue is between us: it is about the legitimacy of a certain very odd kind of intellectual curiosity, about the right to ask a certain kind of question.[10]

Note Turner's concluding remark that *the* issue between the atheist and a theist like himself is whether a deep curiosity about such questions as "Why is there something rather than nothing?" is even legitimate. In fact, Turner then goes on to characterize the atheist as a person who isn't engaged by such questions, as a stodgy, unimaginative lump who remains steadfastly unamazed by the fact that there is anything at all. But if *that's* what an atheist is, then I'm not an atheist, and neither are most philosophers (which will come as a surprise to many of them). Personally, I'm fascinated by the question "Why is there anything at all?" and have been for as long as I can remember. Does that mean I am really a theist?

No. For a start, I acknowledge the *possibility* that there is no answer to that question, because no answer is required. Perhaps, as is sometimes the case with philosophical questions, there's something wrong with the question (perhaps asking, "Why is there something rather than nothing?" is a bit like asking, "What's north of the North Pole?").

[handwritten margin note: I'd say the atheist is the exact opposite.]

But in any case, even if the question is proper (and I acknowledge it might be), and indeed, even if it does have an answer, does it follow that the answer is what Turner calls "God"? Because Turner simply defines "God" as whatever is the answer to the question, it follows that his answer must be yes. But notice how very thin a notion of God Turner is working with. To say God might exist is to say no more than that *there might be an answer*—an answer about which, Turner adds, nothing positive can be said.

The truth, of course, is that most apophaticists aren't just suggesting we take the question of why there is anything at all seriously. Nor are they simply saying there's an answer to the question. Even while professing ignorance about the transcendent whatsit (I'm trying to avoid the word *thing*) they suppose is the answer, they usually have a great deal to say about it, even if it's all heavily qualified and couched in the language of analogy, metaphor, and so on. Indeed, most apophaticists appear to think this transcendent whatsit is worthy of our worship and gratitude, which raises the question of how, if "God" is a label for some unknowable, incomprehensible reality, they can be in a position to know that worship and gratitude are appropriate attitudes for us to have toward it. In fact, if Turner is right and the world is created, doesn't the appalling amount of suffering the world contains give us excellent grounds for adding two more characteristics to the list of those apophaticists say their God *is not*—their God *is not* worthy of either our worship or our gratitude?

THE UNEXPLAINED ANALOGY

Another example of *Moving the Semantic Goalposts* is the *unexplained analogy*. In my introduction (appendix B), I outlined an objection to a certain sort of argument for theism—the argument that the universe appears, for example, to be fine-tuned, and that an intelligent designer god provides the best available explanation for its fine-tuned character. If god is supposed to be a nontemporal agent—a sort a cosmic superintelligence that creates time and space—then we run up against the objection that talk of such a nontemporal agent appears to make scarcely more sense than, say, talk of a nonspatial mountain.

To recap: for something to be a mountain requires that it have parts spatially arranged in a particular way. It must have a summit and sides, for example, which requires that one part be *higher than* another. Strip away this spatial framework, and talk of there being a mountain no longer makes sense.

Similarly, to talk of an agent is to talk about a being that has beliefs and desires on the basis of which it more or less rationally acts. However, the concepts of belief and desire are concepts of psychological states having temporal duration. But if desires are states with temporal duration, how could this agent possess the desire to create the universe? And, we might add, how did this agent perform the act of creation if there was not yet any time in which actions might be performed?

In order to deal with this sort of difficulty, we might, as some theists do, insist that theistic talk of an "intelligent designer" should not be understood *literally*. We are positing not literally an intelligent agent but something merely *analogous to* such an agent.

But does this shift from literal to analogical talk succeed in salvaging the explanation of fine-tuning? Compare a similar case. Suppose I try to explain some natural phenomenon by appealing to the existence of a nonspatial mountain. Critics point out that talk of nonspatial mountains is nonsensical. I roll my eyes and insist they are guilty of a crude misunderstanding. I am not talking about a *literal* mountain, oh, no, but something merely *analogous to* a mountain. Does this save my explanation?

Not yet. Suppose my analogy is this: that the guilt of a nation concerning some terrible deed weighs down like a huge mountain on the collective psyche of its citizens. This is an interesting analogy that might be developed in various ways. Notice that it *does* actually avoid the conceptual problem that plagues the literal version of the claim. Guilt, it would appear, really isn't the kind of thing that occupies space in the way a literal mountain does. There's no conceptual problem with talk of a nonspatial mountain of *guilt*.

But remember—I'm supposed to be explaining some natural phenomenon by means of my analogy. Suppose the phenomenon is a major earthquake. People wonder why the earthquake occurred. I maintain the earthquake is a result of the vast weight of this something-analogous-to-a-mountain pressing down and causing a seismic shift.

Now that my analogy is spelled out, it's clear my explanation is hopeless. Collective guilt can't cause earthquakes. The weight of a real mountain might perhaps cause an earthquake, but not my something-merely-analogous-to-a-mountain. That which is merely analogous to a mountain doesn't possess the same set of causal and explanatory powers that a real mountain possesses.

You can now see why those who try to explain features of the universe by appealing to something merely *analogous* to an intelligent agent have some explaining to do. The onus is surely on them to explain:

1) what the intended analogy is,
2) how the analogy avoids the charge of nonsense leveled at the literally understood version of the claim, and
3) how this something-merely-analogous-to-an-intelligent-designer is nevertheless supposed to retain the relevant explanatory powers that a real intelligent designer would possess.

At least my explanation of the earthquake by appealing to a nonspatial mountain answered questions (1) and (2). However, I failed to explain how my something-analogous-to-a-mountain could cause or explain an earthquake.

Often, theists don't even bother to explain (1) and (2). When asked how we are supposed to make sense of such a nontemporal agent, they just say, "Oh, dear—you're guilty of a crude misunderstanding. You see, talk of an intelligent designer is not meant to be understood *literally*. It's merely an analogy." As if insisting that it's an analogy is, *by itself*, sufficient to deal with the problem raised! It is not.

Unless these theists can provide satisfactory answers to these questions, the problem with their explanation remains. Their introduction of an unexplained analogy brings the debate about intelligent design not—as its proponents seem to imagine—up to a level of great sophistication and profundity but down to the level of evasion and obfuscation. In truth, they're engaging in little more than a bit of sanctimonious hand waving.

None of this is to say that the use of analogy might not provide us with a useful tool in thinking about god. My objection is not to the use of analogy per se but to the shift from a literal to an unexplained analogical meaning as an immunizing strategy to deal with objections: "Ah, you've misunderstood. You see—it's merely an analogy. So—*problem solved*!"

APPEALS TO USE

One of the most intriguing methods of immunizing religious claims against possible refutation is to insist they're *not really claims after all*. If no claim is made, well, then, there's no claim there for the theist to be mistaken about or indeed for the atheist to refute.

If you choose to immunize your religious beliefs against rational criticism by this strategy, appealing to the philosophy of Ludwig Wittgenstein is useful, as Wittgenstein stressed the variety of ways in which language is used. Yes, language is used to make claims, but it's used in many other ways too. Wittgenstein warns us against being seduced by superficial similarities between sentences into overlooking these deeper differences in use.

So if, for example, your claim that God exists is met with some devastating-looking objections, you might try this:

Ah, I see you are guilty of a crude misunderstanding. You have understood me to be making some sort of claim that you might refute. But of course, as Wittgenstein explained, and as sophisticated religious people like myself know, "God exists" is not used to make a claim at all. The sentences "God exists" and "I believe God exists" might look similar to sentences such as "Electrons exist" and "I believe Mount Everest exists," but pay close attention and you will see that their use is very different.

But if religious language is used not to make claims but in some other way, *how* is it used? And, crucially, why does this difference in use entail that what is said is then immune to refutation?

Let's look briefly at three suggestions: that "I believe in God" is used (1) to express an attitude, (2) to make a promise, and (3) to express our trust.

Expressing an Attitude

Expressivist theories crop up in several areas of philosophy. Take moral discourse, for example. We say that things are morally good or bad, right or wrong, and so on. Of course the sentence "Killing is wrong" looks very much like it is used to make a claim—a claim that, we suppose, is true (the killing of innocent humans, at least). However, if those words are used to make a claim, and if claims are made true by facts—for example, if my claim "The pen is on the table" is made true by the fact that the pen is lying there on that table—then we face the philosophical puzzle of finding the peculiar fact that makes "Killing is wrong" true. Where is it? And how do we find out about it? Readers who have some knowledge of moral philosophy will know these are not easy questions to answer.

Philosopher A. J. Ayer developed an ingenious solution to this puzzle.[11] He maintained that although "Killing is wrong" might *look* like it's used to make a claim, it is actually used very differently—to express an attitude. Consider:

Hoorah for the Red Sox!
Boo to killing!

Neither of these sentences is used to make any sort of claim. They are used, rather, to express how we feel about something.

On Ayer's view, moral talk is also expressive. "Killing is wrong" is used, in effect, to say, "Boo to killing!" We use the sentence to express an attitude of disapproval toward killing. But if "Killing is wrong" is used expressively, then what is said is also neither true nor false. But then no mysterious moral fact is required to *make* it true. Puzzle solved! Ayer's theory of how moral language is used is called *emotivism* or, for obvious reasons, the *boo-hoorah theory.*

You have probably already guessed how an expressivist account of how "God exists" is used might be used to immunize what is said against any sort of refutation. True, the sentence "God exists" looks superficially similar to, say, "electrons exist," which is used to make a scientific claim. And when it comes to such scientific claims, it makes sense to ask what the evidence is for supposing it is true. The claim that electrons exist could also turn out to be false. But what if, despite the superficial similarity between the two sentences, "God exists" is used differently? What if it is used not to make a claim but to *express an attitude*?

What sort of attitude? Perhaps an attitude of awe and reverence toward the universe. Perhaps to say, "God exists" is, in effect, to say, "Oh, wow!" in amazement that the universe exists at all. If that's how "God exists" is used, then, because no claim is made, the theist cannot be making any kind of error, and *the atheist is left with nothing to refute.*

So, if having said, "God exists," the theist is faced with an objection, they might try to sidestep that criticism by saying, "Oh, dear, you appear to have misunderstood. You have supposed I was making some sort of *claim* that you might *refute*. No, no, no, I was . . . expressing an attitude of awe and wonder."

Again, notice how very thin a variety of Theism this is. Actually, given that atheists are also awed by the mystery of why there is anything at all, it seems it would also be appropriate for them to say, "God exists!" While this sort of Theism might succeed in immunizing itself against any sort of rational refutation, it does so at the price of making itself indistinguishable from the attitude of a great many atheists.

Making a Promise

Sometimes language is used not to make a claim about the world but to perform an action. Such "performatives" include, for example:

> I name this ship *Titanic*.
> I promise to clean the car.
> I bet you ten dollars.
> I apologize.

Let's focus on promises. When I say, "I promise to tell the truth, the whole truth, and nothing but the truth," in a court of law, I don't *make a claim* about the world, a claim that might turn out to be true or false. Rather, I make it true that I have promised by saying those words.

Now suppose we ask a Theist, "Do you believe in God?" They reply, "I do." This might look, superficially, much like this exchange: "Do you believe in electrons?" "I do."

But what if "I do" in the former case is understood not as expressing agreement with a certain theory or opinion, as in the electrons example, but rather as *making a promise*. Compare: "Do you take this woman to be your lawfully wedded wife?" "I do." Here, "I do" is used to make not a claim but a promise. But if that's also how "I do" is meant in response to "Do you believe in God?" then, similarly, no claim is made. Rather, a promise is given.

According to theologian Nicholas Lash, this is exactly how Theists such as himself respond to the question "Do you believe in God?"

If someone is asked: "Do you believe in God?" and replies "I do," they may be saying one of two quite different things, because the English expression "I believe in God" is systematically ambiguous. On the one hand, it may be the expression of an opinion; the opinion that God exists. On the other hand, as used in the Creed, in a public act of worship, it promises that life, and love, and all one's actions are henceforth set steadfastly on the mystery of God, and hence that we are thereby pledged to work towards that comprehensive healing of the world by which all things are brought into their peace and harmony in God. "Nicholas Lash, do you take Janet Chalmers to be your lawful wedded wife?" "I do." "Janet Chalmers, do you believe in God, the Father almighty, Creator of heaven and earth?" "I do." The grammar of these two declarations is the same.[12]

So there are, Lash says, two kinds of Theists. Those whom, in response to the question "Do you believe in God?" use "I do" to express agreement with an opinion, and those who use "I do" to express a promise. There are, correspondingly, two kinds of atheism: the atheism that rejects the opinion that God exists, and the atheism that involves a refusal to enter into any such promise.[13]

According to Lash, atheists like Richard Dawkins are attacking a crude, unsophisticated form of theism on which belief in God amounts to belief in the truth of a certain opinion. Lash says, "The atheism which is the contradictory of the opinion that God exists is both widespread and intellectually uninteresting."[14]

But then Lash actually *agrees* with Dawkins that *the opinion that God exists should be rejected*. Lash's kind of "belief in God," by contrast—which he maintains is the kind of belief shared by the Jewish, Christian, and Muslim traditions, *properly* understood—*offers no opinion for the atheist to contradict*. If these Theists make no claim, then their variety of "belief in God" can neither be contradicted nor shown to be false. In which case, *the arguments of critics like Dawkins must entirely miss their mark.*

Is Lash's brand of Theism really immune to the arguments of

critics like Dawkins? It's not clear to me that it is. Let's suppose, for the sake of argument, that Lash is correct and "I believe in God" is used not to state an opinion but to issue a promise. Does it follow that Lash holds no Theistic opinion into which Dawkins might sink his teeth?

While it may be that no claim is made in the issuing of a promise, such a claim may nevertheless be *presupposed*. Notice that when we issue a promise, we issue it to *someone*—to something like a person. You can't make a promise to a brick or a daffodil. If you tried, you would be guilty of anthropomorphizing—of mistakenly supposing that the brick or daffodil is something like a person. So if "I believe in God" really is used to make a promise, that raises the question: *to whom is this promise made?*

Presumably, Lash is not merely making a promise either to himself or to, say, other Christians (if he were, then they, or he, could choose to cancel it whenever they liked). If Lash is making a promise, it seems he is making a promise *to God*. But then, on Lash's view, even if "I believe in God" is not used to assert that one believes there is a God who is something like a person, it does seem that Lash nevertheless *presupposes* there's some such person-like being to whom such a promise might be made. In which case, Lash is committed to an opinion that might be refuted. In fact, it's precisely the opinion that there exists such a transcendent person to whom such a promise might be made that Dawkins is attacking.

An Expression of Trust

Some Theists maintain that "I believe in God" is used not to agree that a certain claim—God exists—is true but rather as an expression of *trust*. I believe in God in the same way as I believe in my wife or my bank manager. I believe they can be trusted. I believe they are dependable. When I say, "I believe in my wife," I don't mean that I suppose she exists but that I have faith in her.

According to these Theists, atheists who think they can show that religious belief is irrational by showing that the claim "God exists" is false are missing their target. Again, "God exists" is not used to make a claim.

Does this move succeed in immunizing theism against rational criticism? Again, I don't see how. Often, when we place our trust in someone, it's a reasonable thing to do. It's reasonable if we have good grounds to suppose the person in whom we are placing our trust exists and is likely to be reliable. It's not so reasonable if we have good grounds to suppose the person in whom we are placing our trust is, say, a convicted fraudster or entirely mythical.

Suppose I say, "I believe in fairies," meaning by this not that I believe in the truth of the opinion that fairies exists but that I place my faith, my trust, in fairies to keep the bottom of the garden tidy, say. If it's pointed out to me that there's excellent evidence that there are no fairies at the bottom of the garden, it won't do for me to say, "Ah, but *I never claimed there were*, did I?" Even if I made no such *claim*, the fact is that my placing my trust in fairies is highly unreasonable given the overwhelming evidence there's no such thing.

Similarly, even if someone who says "I believe in God" is not agreeing to the truth of a *claim*—the claim that God exists—but rather communicating their trust or faith in God, we might still have excellent grounds for supposing that this trust or faith is misplaced, if, for example, we have excellent evidence that there's no such transcendent, compassionate being that will ultimately right all wrongs, and so on. Which, arguably, we do (that, at least, is what the evidential problem of evil suggests). So, it's not clear that the suggestion that "I believe in God" is used to express faith or trust even works as an immunizing tactic.

NOW YOU SEE IT, NOW YOU DON'T

We have just looked at three strategies promising to immunize religious beliefs against refutation—strategies that turn on the suggestion that *religious language is not used to make claims, but in some other way.* We have seen that it's by no means obvious that the last two suggestions even work as immunizing strategies. However, let's suppose for the sake of argument that they do work. There remains a further problem with these strategies—the main problem with which I'm concerned here. The problem is that those employing these strategies *often appear to apply them in an inconsistent and partisan way.*

Take, for example, Nicholas Lash's suggestion that "I believe in God" is used to make a promise rather than offer an opinion. Even if this is true, Lash does also nevertheless seem to offer various opinions on the subject of God. Books full. For example, in the same article, Lash says God is both "the mystery we confess to be Creator of the world"[15] and that upon which we are absolutely dependent. So it does *seem*, at first sight, that Lash is of the opinion that there's a creator upon which we depend. God, Lash says, "freely, and forgivingly, communicates Himself."[16] Our creator, Lash adds, also issues invitations to us[17] and it is that upon which we should have our hearts set. In short, Lash regularly uses language that looks remarkably like literal talk about the sort of cosmic superperson that Dawkins denies exists.

Now an atheist will no doubt say, at this point, "But I *disagree* with these opinions offered by Lash. I *disagree* that the world has a creator that is something like a person—a person on whom we should have our hearts set." To this, Lash says, in effect, "Oh, dear. You're guilty of a crude misunderstanding. You take me to be offering *opinions* with which you might *disagree.*"

So is Lash offering us opinions, or isn't he? He seems to say plenty about God, but then, when it looks like what he said might be subjected to damaging critical scrutiny, it turns out he never said anything after all. Lash is undoubtedly a sincere and intelligent man who is genuinely aiming for rigor and, as far as it is achievable, clarity. But if Lash is doing something else with language other than giving opinions, why, then, doesn't he just clearly and unambiguously *do that other thing*? If you're not in

[handwritten margin note: Selective use of this immunizing strat, only when his ideas are criticized.]

the business of giving opinions, why choose to express yourself in such a quintessentially opinion-stating, and thus highly misleading, manner? It looks suspiciously as if Lash is just seesawing back and forth between opinion stating and non–opinion stating use of language to suit himself: opinions are given but then whipped away whenever anyone takes aim. If Lash is not doing that—if he *really isn't* offering any opinions—well, then, let's just take him at his word. Let's accept that Lash really means what he says when he says he has no opinions to offer, and move on.

THE META–GOALPOST-SHIFTING STRATEGY

I have presented several examples of goalpost-shifting strategies. To finish, let's look at one more example—perhaps the most effective of all. As a Theist presented with objections to your belief, you may employ not only the various strategies outlined above, you can also *shift the goalposts concerning which goalpost-shifting strategy you're using.* Say things suggestive of one strategy, but then say things suggestive of others too. Then, if you find yourself running into difficulty with one strategy, just switch to another, and, if necessary, to another. Later, when everyone's lost track of where the conversation started, you can switch back to the first one again. Mix in some references to clever and difficult thinkers (Wittgenstein is particularly useful here), pursue the Meta–Goalpost-Shifting Strategy with an air of calm intellectual and spiritual superiority, and many will be duped into thinking that, rather than a master of the dark arts of semantic sleight-of-hand, you are a deep and profound thinker. Indeed, you may succeed in fooling not only others but yourself too.

As I mentioned at the start of this chapter, *Moving the Semantic Goalposts* tends to be employed by small minorities within the academic wings of some mainstream religious traditions: intelligentsia who fancy they have a more sophisticated grasp of what religion is all about than rather more naive believers, whom they consider just as confused as atheists. When combined, in particular, with *Playing the Mystery Card*, *Pseudo-profundity*, and *"I Just Know!"* *Moving the Semantic Goalposts* is capable of producing an impressive Intellectual Black Hole.

Chapter 5

"I Just Know!"

When someone's claim is challenged, and they find themselves struggling to come up with a rational reply, they will often resort to saying, "Look, I *just know*!"

How reasonable is this response? It depends. Sometimes, by "I just know," people mean you should just take their word for it, perhaps because time is short and the evidence supporting their belief is too complex to present in a convenient sound-bite.

Suppose, for example, I'm asked how I know Tom can be trusted to pay back the five dollars you just loaned him. I could spend five minutes rehearsing several bits of evidence that would, together, show my claim was reasonable but that would take time and effort. So, instead I say, "Look, I *just know*, okay!" To which I might add, "Take my word for it!" And, if you know me to be a pretty good judge of character, you'll probably be justified in doing so.

Another situation in which it might be appropriate for me to say, "I just know" is to flag up that, rather than coming to a belief on the basis of evidence, I can, say, just *see*, clearly and directly, that such-and-such is the case.

Suppose I'm looking out the window and see our good friend Frank. You're convinced Frank is away on vacation, so you ask me if I'm sure. I might say, "Look, I *just know* it's Frank." What I'm trying to convey is that I can *see, very clearly*, that it *really is* Frank. I'm not just hazarding a guess that it's Frank on the basis of some passing resemblance (the shape of the back of his head, say). Again, knowing me to be a reliable witness, you would probably be justified in taking my word for it.

So saying "I just know" isn't always an inappropriate response to requests for supporting evidence. But then suppose I am asked how I know that God exists or whether crystals really can cure people. Why can't it be appropriate and reasonable for me to also say, "Look, I *just know*!" in such situations?

Maybe, just as I might directly experience Frank walking down the path to my front door, so I might *directly experience God*. I might just see, as it were, *very clearly*, that *God really does exist*. And if it's reasonable for you to take my word about Frank, then why isn't it reasonable for you to take my word about God?

Or, if I have a wealth of evidence that crystals really do have miraculous healing properties, but it would take considerable effort to organize that evidence into a cogent argument—effort I can't reasonably be expected to make under the circumstances—why isn't it appropriate for me to say, "Look, I *just know* crystals have these powers"? And if it's reasonable for you to take my word for it about Tom's trustworthiness, why isn't it reasonable for you to take my word about the healing power of crystals?

We can now begin to see why saying, "I *just know*!" offers those who believe conspiracy theories, wacky religious claims, psychic powers, and so on a potential get-out-of-jail-free card. Suppose you find your belief in such things running up against a stiff challenge. Say, "Look, I *just know*, okay," and you may succeed in putting your critics on the back foot. Make them feel that the onus is now very much on them to demonstrate that you *don't* "just know." Then make quick your escape, head held high, continuing to maintain the superior wisdom that they have failed to show that you don't know.

In this chapter we will be taking a closer look at this sort of appeal to "*I Just Know!*" to befuddle critics and shut down debate.

WHEN SAYING "I JUST KNOW" WON'T DO

While "Look, I *just know*" is *sometimes* an appropriate thing to say in response to a challenge to your belief, often, it isn't. First of all, while there are circumstances in which it might be unreasonable to expect someone to set out the evidence supporting their claim, there are other circumstances in which this excuse won't wash. If someone is writing a book on a subject, a book in which they have ample time and space available to properly set out their evidence, it obviously won't do for them to say, "Look, I *just know*."

The same is true of important political debates. Politicians are rightly expected to set out their case for raising taxes or invading another country clearly and in detail. Short of the decision being based on, say, top-secret information regarding national security, there's no legitimate excuse for not doing so.

"I just know" is an expression that also crops up at the race-track. Suppose Jane puts her money on a horse and says, "I *just know* it's going to win." She says this even though the evidence—the betting odds and so on—strongly suggest that the horse won't win. Even if Jane's horse does happen to win, we'll usually be inclined to think that not only did Jane not "just know," it wasn't reasonable for her to suppose she did.

DECIDING "WITH YOUR GUT"

We all go with our gut, intuition, or instinct on occasion. Some-times it's unavoidable. Suppose I don't know whether I should employ someone. The evidence concerning their reliability is somewhat mixed. I've received some very positive reports, but also some negative ones. I need to make a snap decision. Under such circumstances, I may just have to go with my gut. It's that or toss a coin.

It's been suggested that our gut feelings can be insightful. Police officers often have to make rapid decisions about, say, who is most likely to be armed in a rapidly unfolding and dangerous situation. There's no time to assess the evidence properly. Officers often just have to go with their instincts. But their instincts are, it's claimed, surprisingly accurate. They make fairly reliable judgments, despite not engaging in any conscious deliberation or evidence weighing at all.[1]

So there's not necessarily anything wrong with going with your gut *in certain situations*. However, none of this is to say that it's sensible to go with your gut feeling when you don't need to because, say, there's ample and decisive evidence available. We are also ill advised to place much confidence in the instincts of someone whose particular gut has a poor track record, or on topics on which we know that gut feeling has generally proven unreliable.

Bush's Gut

Notoriously, during George W. Bush's presidency, Bush's gut became the oracle of the state. Bush was distrustful of book learning and those with established expertise in a given area. When he made the decision to invade Iraq, and was subsequently confronted by a skeptical audience, Bush said that ultimately, he just *knew in his gut* that invading was the right thing to do. As writer Rich Procter noted prior to the invasion:

> Now we're preparing to invade a country in the middle of the most volatile "powder-keg" region on earth. We're going to toss out our history of using military force only when pro-

voked. We're going to launch a "pre-emptive" invasion that violates two hundred-plus years of American history and culture. We're on the verge of becoming a fundamentally different kind of nation—an aggressive, "go-it-alone" rogue state—based on Bush's gut.[2]

The invasion went ahead. A few months later, Senator Joe Biden told Bush of his growing worries about the aftermath. In response, Bush again appealed to the reliability of his "instincts," as author Ron Suskind here reports:

> "I was in the Oval Office a few months after we swept into Baghdad," [Biden] began, "and I was telling the president of my many concerns—concerns about growing problems winning the peace, the explosive mix of Shiite and Sunni, the disbanding of the Iraqi Army and problems securing the oil fields." Bush, Biden recalled, just looked at him, unflappably sure that the United States was on the right course and that all was well. "'Mr. President,' I finally said, 'How can you be so sure when you know you don't know the facts?'" Biden said that Bush stood up and put his hand on the senator's shoulder. "My instincts," he said. "My instincts." . . . The Delaware senator was, in fact, hearing what Bush's top deputies—from cabinet members like Paul O'Neill, Christine Todd Whitman and Colin Powell to generals fighting in Iraq—have been told for years when they requested explanations for many of the president's decisions, policies that often seemed to collide with accepted facts. The president would say that he relied on his "gut" or his "instinct" to guide the ship of state.[3]

How did Bush suppose his gut was able to steer the ship of state? He supposed it was functioning as a *sort of God-sensing faculty*. Bush believed that by means of his gut he could sense what God wanted of him. But how reasonable was it for Bush, or anyone else, to trust what his gut was telling him?

WHAT IS KNOWLEDGE?

Interestingly, a theory of knowledge developed over the last half century or so would seem to have the consequence that it is at least in principle *possible* (notice I don't say *likely*) that some psychics, religious gurus, and so on might "just know" things by means of some sort of psychic or divinely given sense. They might "just know" these things even if they don't have any *evidence* to support what they believe. In which case, might Bush perhaps "just know" what God wants of him by means of his gut? Let's make a short detour of a few pages into contemporary theory of knowledge to look more closely at these ideas.

What is knowledge? Under what circumstances can someone be correctly described as knowing that such-and-such? The classic definition of knowledge comes from the ancient Greek philosopher Plato, who thought that, in order to know that such-and-such, three conditions must be satisfied:

First, the person in question must *believe* that such-and-such. In order to know that, say, the Battle of Hastings was in 1066, or that there is a pen on my desk, I must believe it.

Second, the belief must be *true*. I can't know what isn't true. If there's no pen on my desk, then I cannot know that there is (although, of course, I might still *believe* it).

Third, I need to be *justified* in believing that such-and-such. In order to know that the Battle of Hastings was in 1066, or that there's a pen on my desk, I need to be *justified* in believing these things.

Up until the mid-twentieth century, this account of knowledge was widely accepted.

The third condition needs a little explanation. Justification can take various forms. Perhaps the most obvious way in which you might be justified in believing something is if you have good *evidence* that what you believe is true. Incidentally, those who sign up to this definition of knowledge don't normally mean that your justification must *guarantee* the truth of your belief. They typically allow that you can be justified in believing something even if you're mistaken. For example, surely you're justified in supposing that John is an expert on chemistry after he has shown you around a chemistry laboratory and you have seen various credentials hanging on his study wall, even though it still remains *possible* (if unlikely) that John is a con man and you are the victim of some elaborate, *Mission: Impossible*–type fraud.

EVIDENTIALISM

Let's now quickly turn to a well-known claim about evidence made by the philosopher W. K. Clifford. Clifford claimed that "it is wrong, always and everywhere, to believe anything on insufficient evidence."[4] This quotation is often used to condemn those who believe in such things as the Loch Ness monster, angels, fairies, and even God. People who believe despite not possessing good evidence that their belief is true are being downright irresponsible, thought Clifford. Such beliefs, it is suggested, are not well supported by the evidence. So it is *wrong* for people to believe them.

The idea that it is, at the very least, *unwise* to accept claims for which we possess little or no supporting evidence is certainly widespread. Richard Dawkins, for example, writes:

> Next time somebody tells you something that sounds important, think to yourself: "Is this the kind of thing that people probably know because of evidence? Or is it the kind of thing that people only believe because of tradition, authority or revelation?" And next time somebody tells you that something is true, why not say to them: "What kind of evidence is there for that?" And if they can't give you a good answer, I hope you'll think very carefully before you believe a word they say.[5]

Let's call the view that we ought not to accept any belief not well supported by evidence *evidentialism*. Is evidentialism true?

Problem w/ evidentialism

Probably not. Evidentialism faces some obvious difficulties. Perhaps the most glaring is this: suppose I believe some claim A because I suppose I have supporting evidence B. But now ought I to believe *that evidence B obtains*? If evidentialism is true, it seems I ought to believe B obtains only if I possess, in turn, evidence for that—C, say. But then I should believe that C obtains only if there is, in turn, evidence for *that*, and so on ad infinitum. Evidentialism seems to entail that, *before I adopt any belief, I must first acquire evidence to support an infinite number of beliefs*—which, as a finite being, I can't do. In short, Clifford's injunction that I ought not to believe anything on the basis of insufficient evidence appears to have the disastrous consequence that I *ought not to believe anything at all*!

A PROBLEM FOR PLATO'S THEORY

Let's now return for a moment to Plato's theory that knowledge is justified true belief. It is widely supposed that Plato's theory runs into a similar problem. The theory says that, in order to know that such-and-such, my belief must be justified. But if my justification is supplied by another belief of mine, then, presumably, I am only justified in believing the first belief if I am justified in believing the second. But then the second belief will require a third belief to justify it, and so on ad infinitum. So, in order to justify even one belief, I will have to justify an infinite number. Being a finite being, I cannot justify an infinite series of beliefs. It seems, then, that I cannot justify any belief and thus *cannot know anything at all*!

How do we escape from this conclusion? The theory of knowledge known as *reliabilism* provides one solution.

RELIABILISM

Here is a simple reliabilist theory of knowledge. In order for person a to know that P,

1) P must be true,
2) a must believe that P, and
3) a's belief that P must be brought about by the fact that P via a reliable mechanism.

You will notice that the first two conditions are the same as for Plato's definition of knowledge. But the third is different and requires a little explanation.

What's meant by a "reliable mechanism"? A reliable mechanism is a mechanism that tends to produce true beliefs. My sense of sight is a fairly reliable belief-producing mechanism. It allows my beliefs to fairly reliably track how things are in my environment.

Suppose, for example, someone puts an orange on the table in front of me. Light bounces off the orange into my eyes, which in turn causes certain cells to fire in my retina, which causes a pattern of electrical impulses to pass down my optic nerves into my brain, eventually bringing about my belief that there's an orange before me. Remove the orange, and that will in turn cause me, by means of the same mechanism, to believe the orange has gone.

The same goes for my other senses—they are fairly reliable belief-producing mechanisms. Blindfold me and put me in a crowded street, and my ears and nose will, in response to the sound of car horns and the odor of hot dogs, cause me to believe I am in a crowded street. Move me to a fragrant garden filled with singing birds, and those same senses will cause me to believe I am in such a garden. My senses of sight, touch, smell, hearing, and taste cause me to hold beliefs that tend to accurately reflect how things actually are around me.

I don't say our senses are 100 percent reliable, of course.

Sometimes we get things wrong. They are occasionally prone to illusion. But they are *fairly* reliable.

Let's now apply our reliabilist definition of knowledge. Suppose someone puts an orange on the table in front of me. I look at the orange and so come to believe there's an orange there. Do I *know* there's an orange on the table?

According to our reliabilist, I do. The simple reliabilist theory says that if (1) it's *true* that there's an orange there, (2) I *believe* there's an orange there, and (3) my belief is produced via a reliable mechanism—for example, sight—by the presence of an orange there, then I *know* there's an orange there.

Now here is an interesting twist to this theory—a twist that will prove relevant to our discussion of psychic powers and George Bush's gut. Notice that, according to reliabilism, in order to know there's an orange on the table, I need not *infer* there's an orange there. I need not arrive at my belief on the basis of good grounds or evidence. *No evidence is required.* All that's required is that I hold the belief and that it be produced in the right sort of way—by a reliable mechanism.

Also notice that if, by saying that a belief is "justified," we mean we have good grounds for believing it, then reliabilism says that *we can know without justification.* In which case, the regress problem with Plato's theory that knowledge is justified true belief is also sidestepped by reliabilism.

RELIABILISM AND PSYCHIC POWERS

Many contemporary philosophers accept some form of reliabilism (although they have developed it in various ways). You can now see why reliabilism might also appeal to, say, a psychic who believes she "just knows" things about the dead.

Suppose a psychic (notice that by "psychic" I mean someone who is supposed to have psychic powers, whether or not they actually do)—call her Mary—finds herself believing that her dead

Aunt Sarah is currently in the room with her. Also suppose, for the sake of argument, that Mary really does have some sort of reliable psychic sense that dead Aunt Sarah really is in the room with Mary, and that Mary's psychic sense is what is causing Mary to believe Aunt Sarah is present. Then, says our reliabilist theory, *Mary knows that Aunt Sarah is in the room with her.*

Notice that Mary doesn't *infer* that Aunt Sarah is present on the basis of *evidence*. Mary just finds herself stuck with that belief that Aunt Sarah is present, caused as it is by her reliable psychic sense. Yet, says our reliabilist, despite the fact that Mary doesn't possess any evidence that Aunt Sarah is present, Mary knows Aunt Sarah is there. In fact, were Mary to claim that she "just knows" that Mary is in the room with her right now, *she'd be right*!

Of course, that they do "just know" such things despite not having any publicly available evidence is a claim psychics make on a daily basis. So, while few psychics will have heard of reliabilism, reliabilism nevertheless opens up at least the *possibility* that these psychics are actually correct—they *do* know, despite not possessing any evidence.

"But hang on," you may object. "Even if reliabilism is correct and Mary does know her dead aunt is in the room with her, that is not something she *ought* to believe. The fact is, Mary is being downright irresponsible in just accepting at face value this belief that happens to have popped into her head. Clifford is still correct—she *shouldn't* believe it. It's still *unwise* for her to believe it."

In her own defense, Mary might appeal to a further principle. Surely, Mary may insist, *if something seems very clearly and obviously to be the case, then, other things being equal, it's reasonable to believe it's true.* It's reasonable to take appearance at face value. For example, if it seems clear and obvious to me that there's on orange on the table before me, then surely it's reasonable for me to believe there's an orange there.

This principle does seem intuitively plausible. And it entails that, if it seems just clearly and obviously true to Mary that her dead aunt is in the room with her, then, other things being equal, it *is* reasonable for Mary to hold that belief, whether or not she can provide any publicly available evidence.

RELIABILISM AND RELIGIOUS EXPERIENCE

Let's now return to George Bush's gut. Bush believes he can directly know, by means of his gut, what God wants him to do.

Many people believe that they "just know" directly, rather than on the basis of evidence, that God exists and that, say, the Bible is true. Ask them *why* they believe, and they may give reasons and justifications of one sort or another. But typically, even if such grounds are provided, not much weight is placed on them. Many Theists say that they don't believe on the basis of evidence. Rather, they "just know" God exists. They believe they directly experience God, perhaps in something like the way I just directly experience that orange on the table in front of me. To them, it seems perfectly clear and obvious that God exists.

Reliabilism seems to open up the possibility that some people might, indeed, "just know" that God exists. Suppose God has provided us with a sort of *sensus divinitatis*—a reliable, God-sensing faculty (in Bush's case, that would be his gut). On the reliabilist view, it seems that a *sensus divinitatis* could provide such knowledge.

Moreover, a religious person might add, just as, if it seems clearly and obviously true to me that there's an orange on the table, then it is reasonable for me to suppose there's an orange there, so *if it seems clearly and obviously true to someone that God exists, then it's reasonable for them to believe God exists.* There's certainly nothing wrong, or irresponsible, about them taking their experience at face value.

This view about religious experience has been developed by several contemporary Christian philosophers, chief among whom is Alvin Plantinga. Plantinga's version is detailed, but the gist is essentially this, that something like reliabilism is essentially correct, that God has indeed given every one of us a God-sensing faculty or *sensus divinitatis*, and that consequently, some of us can know, directly and without evidence, that God exists. Indeed, that God exists is an entirely *reasonable* thing for such people to believe, if that's very much how things clearly and obviously seem to them even after careful reflection.[6]

Plantinga adds that, if there is a God, he probably would want us to know of his existence directly by means of such a reliable God-sensing faculty. So, if there is a God, then some of us probably do know by such means that God exists.

You may be wondering: "But if we all have a *sensus divinitatis*, as Plantinga supposes, why don't we all enjoy such clear and unambiguous God experiences?" Because, Plantinga explains, in many cases our *sensus divinitatis* has been damaged by sin:

> Were it not for sin and its effects, God's presence and glory would be as obvious and uncontroversial to us all as the presence of other minds, physical objects and the past. Like any cognitive process, however, the *sensus divinitatis* can malfunction; as a result of sin, it has been damaged.[7]

The reason I don't have such God experiences, then, is because my *sensus divinitatis* has been damaged by sin. Obviously, it doesn't follow that if I don't happen to have such experiences, then others aren't, by means of them, able to know that God exists.[8]

ASSESSING PSYCHIC AND RELIGIOUS CLAIMS TO "JUST KNOW"

We have seen how the reliabilist theory of knowledge appears to open up the possibility that some people might "just know" that their dead relative is in the room with them, or "just know" that God exists. We have also seen that evidentialism has been challenged, and that, according to Plantinga and others, it can be entirely reasonable for people to take their religious experiences at face value. If it seems just as clearly and obviously true to them that God exists, then it can be entirely reasonable for them to believe God exists, whether or not they possess any evidence. Psychics might say much the same thing about their psychic experiences. Let's now begin to assess these various claims.

Let me say at the outset that I find reliabilism plausible. I suspect that some version of reliabilism may well be correct. Let me also be clear that I do not rule out in principle the possibility that some people might be equipped with reliable psychic powers, or a *sensus divinitatis*, or whatever.

I also agree that evidentialism is probably false, and that, generally speaking, it is indeed reasonable for us to take appearances at face value. If it seems just as clearly and obviously the case that there's an orange on the table in front of me, well, then, other things being equal, it's reasonable for me to believe there's an orange on the table in front of me.

However, I remain entirely unconvinced that anyone who claims to "just know" that the dead walk among us or that God exists knows any such thing. Not only do I think the rest of us have good grounds for doubting their experience; I don't believe it's reasonable for them to take their own experience at face value either. I'll explain this by means of what I call *the case of the mad, fruit-fixated brain scientist*.

The Case of the Mad, Fruit-Fixated Brain Scientist

Suppose Jane is shown what appears, quite clearly and obviously, to be an orange on the table in front of her. Surely then, it is, other things being equal, reasonable for Jane to believe there's an orange there.

But now suppose the orange is presented to Jane in a rather unusual situation. Jane is one of several visitors to the laboratory of a mad brain scientist with a weird fruit fixation. She, like the other visitors, is wearing an electronic helmet that can influence what happens in her brain. From his central computer terminal, the mad brain scientist can, by means of these helmets, control what people are experiencing. He can create vivid and convincing hallucinations.

The scientist demonstrates by causing one of the visitors to hallucinate an apple. There's much hilarity as the victim tries to grab for the fruit that's not there. The visitors are then invited to wander around the lab where, the scientist tells them, they may experience several other kinds of virtual fruit. Jane then comes across what appears to be an orange on a table. Now, as a matter of fact, it is a real orange—one that fell out of someone's packed lunch bag. Jane's faculty of sight is functioning normally and reliably. This is no hallucination.

Now ask yourself two questions: (1) does Jane *know* there's an orange on the table? And (2) is it *reasonable* for Jane to suppose there's an orange on the table?

Intuitively, it seems Jane *doesn't* know there's an orange present. After all, for all Jane knows, it could be one of the many hallucinatory fruit she knows about. But what would a reliabilist say? Well, sight is generally a reliable belief-producing mechanism, and sight is what's producing her belief. So some reliabilists may say that, yes, Jane does know. On the other hand, very many reliabilists say that, while in a standard environment sight is reliable, *it isn't reliable in other kinds of environment*, for example, the kind of environment in which we will often as not be deceived by visual hallucinations. But then it follows that, because Jane is in just such an environment, she doesn't know.

Now let's turn to question (2), which is the pivotal question: is it reasonable for Jane to believe there's an orange before her? Surely not. Given Jane knows that she is in an environment (the mad brain scientist's laboratory) in which people regularly have compelling fruit hallucinations (indistinguishable from real fruit experiences), Jane should remain rather skeptical about her own fruit experience. For all she can tell, she's probably having a mad-scientist-induced fruit hallucination.

I draw two morals for religious experience:

First of all, even if reliabilism is true, and even if some of us do have God experiences produced by a *sensus divinitatis*, it remains debatable whether such people *know* that God exists. If human beings are highly prone to delusional religious experiences that they nevertheless find entirely convincing, then, even if, as a matter of fact, I happen to be having a wholly accurate religious experience revealing that, say, the Judeo-Christian God exists, it's by no means clear I can be said to *know* that the Judeo-Christian God exists, anymore than Jane, coming upon a real orange in the brain scientist's lab, can be said to *know* that there's an orange on the table in front of her.

Second, and more important, even if it's true, because of my religious experience, that I *do* know that the Judeo-Christian God exists, surely it still isn't reasonable for me to take my experience at face value. For I find myself in a situation much like Jane finds herself in the brain scientist's lab. Even though it looks to Jane clearly and obviously to be true that there's an orange on the table in front of her, Jane should, surely, remain pretty skeptical about whether there's actually an orange there, given that, for all she knows, she might very easily be having one of the many delusional fruit experiences currently being generated in the lab. Jane would be foolish to take appearance at face value. Similarly, if I have good evidence that many religious experiences are delusional—even the most compelling examples—then surely I should be equally skeptical about my own religious experiences, no matter how compelling they might be. It would be foolish for me to take my experiences at face value.

A similar moral might be drawn about psychic experiences. If most—including even the most compelling examples—are delusional, then it's debatable whether the psychic can be said to *know*. However, even if the psychic can be said to know, if they're aware that many such experiences are delusional, then it surely isn't reasonable for such a person to take their experience at face value. They would be foolish to do so.

THE DUBIOUS NATURE OF RELIGIOUS EXPERIENCE

The above argument presupposes that there is good evidence that most psychic and religious experiences are delusional—even the most compelling examples. Which of course there is. Let's focus on religious experience. We know that:

(1) *Religious experiences tend to be culturally specific.* Christians experience the guiding hand of Jesus, while Muslims experience Allah. Just like experiences of alien abduction (reports of alien abduction pretty much stop at certain national borders), the character of religious experiences often changes at national borders. In Catholic countries, the Virgin Mary is often seen, but not over the border in a predominantly Muslim country. This strongly suggests that to a significant degree, religious experiences are shaped by our cultural expectations—by the power of suggestion (see *Piling Up the Anecdotes*). And once we know that a large part of what is experienced is a result of the power of suggestion, we immediately have grounds for being somewhat suspicious about what remains.

(2) *Religious experiences often contradict each other.* George W. Bush's gut told him God wanted war with Iraq. However, the religious antenna of other believers—including other Christians—told them God wanted peace. Some religious people claim to know by virtue of a revelatory experience that Christ is divine and was resurrected. Muslims, relying instead on the religious revelations of the Prophet Muhammad, deny this. Religious experience reveals that some gods are cruel and vengeful—some even requiring the blood of children (the Mayan and Aztec gods, for example), while others are loving and kind. The religious experiences of some Buddhists reveal there's no personal God, whereas those of many Christians, Jews, and Muslims reveal that there is but one personal God. Other religions have a pantheon of gods. Take a step back and look at the sweep of human history, and you find an extraordinary range of such experiences. Religious revelation has produced a vast hodge-podge of contradictory claims, many of which

must, therefore, be false. Even those who believe they have had things directly revealed to them by God must acknowledge that a great many equally convinced people are deluded about what has supposedly been revealed to them.

There are similar reasons for supposing the bulk of psychic experiences are also delusional. What is revealed to psychics is often wrong, often contradicted by what other psychics claim, and so on.

For these reasons, then, it's not reasonable for me to take my psychic or religious experience at face value—not even if it's very vivid and convincing. It *might* be genuinely revelatory. But, under the circumstances, it would be rather foolish of me to assume that it is. Those who, like George W. Bush, place a simple trusting faith in their gut, or wherever else they think their *sensus divinitatis* is located, are being irresponsible and foolish.

Notice that it would be *particularly* foolhardy for, say, someone who believes in a maximally powerful, knowledgeable, and good God, but who is confronted with the evidential problem of evil, to sweep the problem to one side, saying, "But look, I *just know* in my heart [or gut, or wherever] that my God exists!" While it might remain a theoretical possibility that they do "just know," it's certainly not *reasonable* for them to maintain this—not if they have been presented with both good evidence that many such experiences are delusional and powerful empirical evidence that what they believe is false. To insist one "just knows" under these circumstances is very unreasonable indeed.

THE COMMON CORE OF RELIGIOUS EXPERIENCE—
"INEFFABLE TRANSCENDENCE"?

Some will say that it is unfair to lump all religious experiences together. There is a certain kind of experience—the sort enjoyed by the mystics of many different religions down through the centuries—that is essentially the same. What is this experiential common denominator? According to Karen Armstrong, it is an experience of "indescribable transcendence." As we saw in "*Moving the Semantic Goalposts*," Armstrong's view is that "God" is merely a symbol for this transcendence. Once we strip away the cultural artifacts peculiar to the different mainstream religions, we find they all have this common, experiential core.

According to Armstrong, such experiences of indescribable transcendence typically don't *just happen*. Usually, they emerge only after subjects have committed themselves over an extended period of time to a particular sort of lifestyle—a *religious* lifestyle. Religion, on Armstrong's way of thinking, is not a body of *doctrine* (how could it be, if that toward which religion is oriented is ineffable?) but an *activity*: the kind of activity that produces experiences of this sort. Religion, says Armstrong, is "a practical discipline, and its insights are not derived from abstract speculation but from spiritual exercises and a dedicated lifestyle."[9] By engaging in certain religious practices and forms of life, maintains Armstrong, people can come to live "on a higher, divine or godlike plane and thus wake up their true selves."[10]

SOME NOTEWORTHY FEATURES OF RELIGIOUS PRACTICE

Suppose, then, that having immersed themselves in such a lifestyle, someone claims to "just know" that there is indeed such an ineffable transcendence? Is it reasonable for us, or for them, to suppose they've achieved awareness of Armstrong's "sacred reality"?[11]

I don't believe so. As Armstrong acknowledges, religious practice takes many forms involving a variety of activities. An interesting feature of many of these activities is that we know they can induce interesting—sometimes rather beneficial—psychological states, even outside of a religious setting. Let's look at some examples:

Meditation and prayer. Consider meditation. It has proven effects on both our psychology and physiology. It can reduce stress, lower blood pressure, and induce feelings of calm and contentment. Even atheists meditate to gain these benefits. Prayer can be a form of meditation, of course. Sometimes prayer and other devotional activities are accompanied by repetitive swaying or rocking motions known to induce a sense of well-being—the so-called jogger's high (though this is not, as is widely believed, a result of releasing endorphins).

Isolation. Isolation can have a powerful psychological effect on people. It can render them more easily psychologically manipulated (which is why isolation is a favorite tool of interrogators) and can produce hallucinations and other altered states of consciousness. Many religions encourage periods of isolation for spiritual purposes—several days in the wilderness, say.

Fasting. Fasting, too, is known to produce some peculiar psychological states, including hallucinations, even outside of a religious setting.

Collective singing/chanting. Coming together in a large group to chant or sing can also be a very intoxicating experience, as anyone who has gone to a football game can testify.

Architecture. If you have ever entered a large cave by torchlight, you will know that such a setting can induce a powerful emotional experience. The darkness, echoing sounds, and glimpses of magnificent structures make one fearful and yet excited at the same time and lead us to start talking in whispers. The echoing grandeur of many places of worship has a similar psychological effect.

Giving. Helping others in a face-to-face situation can be an immensely powerful psychological experience—often a deeply gratifying and positive experience, whether or not you happen to do it in a religious setting.

Ritual. Engaging in ritualistic activity often has a calming and beneficial effect, whether or not performed within a religious setting. For example, sportsmen and sportswomen often engage in rituals before competing and can become very disturbed if for some reason the ritual cannot be performed because, for example, their lucky shirt has been lost.

Religious practice typically involves at least some of, and usually many of, these activities—activities we know can have a powerful psychological effect even outside any religious setting. If people collectively engage in such activities with intensity of purpose over a long period of time, this might very well have a marked psychological effect. It might well produce some interesting, and quite possibly beneficial, psychological states.

If we then mix into this heady and intoxicating brew the suggestion that what people are experiencing or becoming psychologically attuned to as a result of long-term engagement in such a regime is some sort of ineffable transcendence, then, given the power of suggestion (see chapter 7 on *Piling Up the Anecdotes*), many will probably become quite convinced that this is what's going on.

The experiences and insights that, as a result of the regime, then coalesce under the label "God" will no doubt be complex and difficult to articulate. There probably is a sense in which someone who has never been through such a regime will not fully appreciate what the experience is actually like for the subject "from the inside," as it were. Those who have had such an experience will no doubt struggle to communicate to its character in the same way that someone who has been through, say, a war or childbirth may struggle. They may well have to resort to poetry or music or other art forms in order to convey the unique intensity of their experience.

Armstrong says:

It is clear that the meditation, yoga and rituals that work aesthetically on a congregation have, when practised assiduously over a lifetime, a marked effect on the personality—an effect that is another form of natural theology. There is no "born again" conversion, but a slow, incremental and imperceptible transformation. . . . The effect of these practices cannot give us concrete information about God; it is certainly not a scientific "proof." But something indefinable happens to people who involve themselves in these disciplines with commitment and talent. The "something" remains opaque, however, to those who do not undergo these disciplines.[12]

While it may indeed be difficult for those of us who have not been through such a process to appreciate exactly what it's like to be in the kind of psychological state it can produce, surely we have pretty good grounds for doubting that what is experienced is some sort of transcendent reality. Given what we know about human psychology, it's likely that people put through such an intense regime over an extended period of time will think they have become attuned to such a reality anyway, whether or not any such reality exists, and whether or not they have obtained any sort of genuine insight into it.

I don't wish to deny there is value in engaging in meditation, yoga, and so on. It may well be that those who engage in such practices gain some valuable insights into themselves and the human condition as a result. Certainly, there may be some positive psychological effects, such as a lasting sense of peace and contentment, from determinedly engaging in such activities over a long period of time, effects that will undoubtedly by magnified by the accompanying thought that what they are becoming attuned to is "God."

But the claim that they have thereby become attuned to some sort of "sacred reality" is dubious, to say the least. Surely, given our understanding of human psychology, by far the best explanation of what people experience after having engaged in religious practice with dedication over long periods of time is not that they have become attuned to some sort of ineffable transcendence, but that they have succeeded in altering their own psychology by fairly well-understood mechanisms common to both the religious and nonreligious spheres, and that they have then mistakenly interpreted this alteration as their becoming attuned to such a reality.[13]

CONCLUSION

As we have seen, "*I Just Know!*" isn't *always* an unreasonable thing to say. But sometimes it is. Indeed, sometimes it's a foolish thing to say.

Consider these two examples: "Sometimes I see images and I just know something terrible has happened to them" (psychic Margaret Solis quoted in "The Scots Psychic Helping Hollywood Stars—and Hunting Down Murder Victims," *Daily Record*, September 14, 2010), and "How do I know when God is talking to me? I just know" (Internet comment).[14]

Suppose these individuals claiming to "just know" can't provide any sort of publicly available evidence or rational argument to back up what they claim they know. We have seen that, if reliabilism is true, then the fact that they don't have any such evidence or argument does not rule out the *possibility* that they "just know." However, given what we, and presumably they, know about the unreliability of such psychic and religious experiences generally, surely it's not reasonable for either us, or them, to take such seemingly revelatory experiences at face value. It's not reasonable for them to insist they "just know."

Chapter 6

Pseudoprofundity

Some marketing, religious, and lifestyle gurus have genuinely profound insights to offer. Others spout little more than pseudoprofundity. *Pseudoprofundity* is the art of sounding profound while talking nonsense. Unlike the art of actually being profound, the art of sounding profound is not particularly difficult to master. As we'll see, there are certain basic recipes that can produce fairly convincing results—good enough to convince others, and perhaps even yourself, that you have gained some sort of profound insight into the human condition.

If you want to achieve the status of a guru, it helps to have some natural charisma and presentational skills. Sincerity and empathy, or at least the ability to fake them, can be useful. Props also help. Try wearing a loincloth, a fez, or, in a business setting, a particularly brash waistcoat. But even without the aid of such natural talents or paraphernalia, anyone can produce deep- and meaningful-sounding pronouncements if they are prepared to follow a few simple recipes.

STATE THE OBVIOUS

To begin with, try pointing out the *blindingly obvious*. Only do it i-n-c-r-e-d-i-b-l-y s-l-o-w-l-y and with an air of superior wisdom. The technique works best if your pronouncements focus on one of life's big themes, such as love, money, and death. So, for example:

> We were all children once.
> Money can't buy you love.
> Death is unavoidable.

State the obvious in a sufficiently earnest way, perhaps following up with a pregnant pause, and you may find others begin to nod in agreement, perhaps murmuring, "Yes, how very true that is."

CONTRADICT YOURSELF

A second technique is to select words with opposite or incompatible meanings and cryptically combine them in what appears to be a straightforward *contradiction*. Here are a few examples:

> Sanity is just another kind of madness.
> Life is often a form of death.
> The ordinary is extraordinary.

Such sentences are interpretable in all sorts of ways and can easily appear profound. In George Orwell's novel *Nineteen Eighty-Four*, two of the three slogans of the Party have this character:

> War is peace.
> Freedom is slavery.
> Ignorance is strength.

If you're an aspiring guru, why not produce your own contradictory remarks? The great beauty of such comments is that they make your audience do the work for you. Their meaning is not for you, the guru, to say—it's for your followers to figure out. Just sit back, adopt a sage-like expression, and let them do the intellectual labor.

The thought that contradiction is a mark of profundity sometimes crops up in a religious context. Nonbelievers will suppose contradictions within a religious doctrine reveal that it contains falsehoods. The faithful are likely to take the same contradictions as a mark of profundity. Contradictions have other advantages too. A series of simple, unambiguous claims is easy to refute; not so a series of such cryptic remarks. So, if you're planning to start your own religion and want to say things that will appear profound and also be invulnerable to criticism, try making a series of contradictory pronouncements. Assert, but then deny. For example, say that your particular god is—and yet, he is not. Your god is everything, and yet nothing. He is one, and yet he is many. He is good. But then again he isn't.

None of this is to say that such seemingly contradictory remarks can't convey something genuinely profound. They can certainly be thought provoking (I bet you can find even *some* sort of truth in all of Orwell's poisonous examples). But, given the formulaic way contradictions can be used to generate *Pseudoprofundity*, it's wise not to be too easily impressed.

DEEPITIES

Another recipe for generating *Pseudoprofundity*, identified by philosopher Daniel Dennett,[1] is the *deepity*. A deepity involves saying something with two meanings—one trivially true, the other profound sounding but false or nonsensical. Dennett illustrates this with the expression "Love is just a word."

On one reading, this sentence is about the *word* "love" (but notice that, if the sentence is about the word, then it really ought to appear in quotation marks). The word *love* is indeed just a word, as are the words *steel* and *concrete*. So, on this reading, the sentence is trivially true. On the other reading, the sentence is not about the word *love* but *love itself*—that which the word *love* refers to. Love is often defined as a feeling or emotion. Love may even, arguably, be an illusion. But the one thing it definitely isn't is a word. So on this second reading, "Love is just a word" is obviously false.

Deepities trade on the ambiguities between such readings. It's the ambiguity that generates the "Oh, wow!" response, that makes people gasp, "Golly, yes, actually love *is* just a word, isn't it?!" as if they have suddenly been struck by something terribly profound.

TRITE-NALOGIES

Here's a particularly effective way of generating *Pseudoprofundity*. First, take some fairly trite observation about the human condition, such as:

- life is often surprising
- people often feel there's something missing from their lives
- we should appreciate things while we can
- we should make the most of the opportunities we get.

Then, *wrap your chosen trite observation in an analogy*. I call the result a *trite-nalogy*. "Life is like a . . ." provides one popular template. Here are a few examples I quickly found on the Internet:

> My momma always said life was like a box of chocolates. You never know what you're gonna get. (Forrest Gump)

Life is like a taxi. The meter just keeps a-ticking whether you are getting somewhere or just standing still. (Lou Erickson)

Life is a grindstone. Whether it grinds us down or polishes us up depends on us. (Thomas L. Holdcroft)

Life is like a coin. You can spend it any way you wish, but you only spend it once. (Lillian Dickson)

The result can often be terribly deep sounding.

Sermons and homilies sometimes involve trite-nalogies. Alan Bennett produced a hilarious spoof in his sketch "The Sermon" (which Bennett delivered while wearing a dog collar):

Life, you know, is rather like opening a tin of sardines. We are all of us looking for the key. And I wonder how many of you here tonight have wasted years of your lives looking behind the kitchen dressers of this life for that key. I know I have. Others think they've found the key, don't they? They roll back the lid of the sardine tin of life. They reveal the sardines, the riches of life, therein, and they get them out, and they enjoy them. But, you know, there's always a little bit in the corner you can't get out. I wonder is there a little bit in the corner of your life? I know there is in mine!

Author Douglas Adams, no doubt irritated by such "Life is like a . . ." pseudoprofundities, produced his own surreal version:

Life . . . is like a grapefruit. It's orange and squishy, and has a few pips in it, and some folks have half a one for breakfast.

Parables, too, are sometimes trite-nalogies. Take this example:

The young man was at the end of his rope. Seeing no way out, he dropped to his knees in prayer. "Lord, I can't go on," he said. "I have too heavy a cross to bear." The Lord replied, "My son, if you can't bear its weight, just place your cross inside this room. Then open another door and pick any cross you wish." The man was filled with relief. "Thank you, Lord," he sighed, and did as he was told. As he looked around the room he saw many different crosses; some so large the tops were not visible. Then he spotted a tiny cross leaning against a far wall. "I'd like that one, Lord," he whispered. And the Lord replied, "My son, that's the cross you brought in."[2]

Take the important but obvious truth that we often overestimate our own woes and fail to realize how serious are the problems of others, draw an analogy with carrying heavy crosses, and *voilà*—you're profound! In this example, the *Pseudoprofundity* also serves to distract the listener's attention from more troubling questions, such as: Why does God insist on loading people with such horrendous burdens in the first place?

USE JARGON

Whether you're a business guru, lifestyle consultant, or mystic, introducing some jargon can further enhance the illusion of profundity. Here is a common trick. Make up some words that appear to have meanings similar to those of certain well-known terms but that differ in some never fully explained way. For example, don't talk about people being sad or happy; talk about them having "negative or positive attitudinal orientations."

Next, translate some truisms into your new vocabulary. Take the trite observation that happy people tend to make other people feel happier. That can be recast as "positive attitudinal orientations have high transferability."

It also helps to adopt the vocabulary of "forces," "energies," and "balances." The use of these words will suggest that you have discovered some deep power that can be harnessed and utilized by others. That will make it much easier to persuade them that they may seriously miss out if they don't sign up for one of your seminars.

So, if you're a marketing guru, try running seminars on "Harnessing Positive Attitudinal Energies within the Retail Environment." If some smart aleck is brave enough to put up his hand at one of your seminars and ask *exactly* what a "positive attitudinal energy" is, just define it using other bits of your jargon. That way, you'll never have to explain what any of your gibberish means. Yet the several truisms around which all your jargon has been wrapped will generate the illusion that you must really be on to *something*, even if your listeners cannot fully grasp what it is. So you'll leave them anxious to hear more.

Adding some scientific jargon or references can be particularly useful in lending your ramblings further fake authority and gravitas. Many purveyors of *Pseudoprofundity* have learned the insight expressed by the great nineteenth-century scientist James Clerk Maxwell that such "is the respect paid to science that the most absurd opinions may become current, provided they are expressed in language, the sound of which recalls some well-known scientific phrase."[3]

References to quantum mechanics are particularly popular among peddlers of pseudoscientific claptrap. Quantum mechanics is widely supposed to make weird claims, and hardly anyone understands it, so if you start spouting references to it in support of your own bizarre teachings, people will assume you must be very clever and probably won't realize that you are, in fact, just bullshitting. So perhaps, if you're feeling ambitious, put on another seminar titled "Positive Attitudinal Energies and Quantum Mechanics."

POSTMODERN PSEUDOPROFUNDITY

Sadly, some corners of academia are dominated by intellectuals whose writing amounts to little more than *Pseudoprofundity*. Strip away the academic jargon and pseudoscientific references from their impressive-sounding pronouncements, and you'll find there's precious little left.

Those thinkers often referred to as "postmodern" include more than their fair share of such jargon-fueled wafflers. So easy is it, in fact, to produce convincing-looking postmodern gobbledygook that a wag called Andrew Bulhak constructed a computer program that will write your own "postmodern" essay, complete with references. For the *Postmodern Essay Generator*, go to http://www.elsewhere.org/pomo/.

I just did and received an essay that begins:

> The primary theme of Cameron's model of neostructural Marxism is the common ground between society and culture. Sontag's analysis of Debordist situation states that society has objective value. However, Marx promotes the use of Marxist socialism to analyse class. Debordist situation holds that the goal of the observer is deconstruction. Therefore, the subject is interpolated into a neostructural Marxism that includes art as a paradox. Several materialisms concerning semanticist subdialectic theory may be found.

This may be nonsense, but it makes scarcely less sense than the real thing. Possibly more. Consider this example from the French intellectual Félix Guattari:

> We can clearly see that there is no bi-univocal correspondence between linear signifying links or archi-writing, depending on the author, and this multireferential, multi-dimensional machinic catalysis. The symmetry of scale, the transversality, the pathic non-discursive character of their expansion: all these dimensions remove us from the logic of the excluded middle and reinforce us in our dismissal of the ontological binarism we criticised previously. A machinic assemblage, through its diverse components, extracts its consistency by crossing ontological thresholds, non-linear thresholds of irreversibility, ontological and phylogenetic thresholds, creative thresholds of heterogenesis and autopoiesis.[4]

In 1997, Alan Sokal, a professor of physics at New York University (eminently qualified to comment on the use of scientific terminology), annoyed with the way in which some postmodern writers were borrowing terms and theories from physics and applying them in a nonsensical way, published, along with his colleague Jean Bricmont, the book *Intellectual Impostures*. *Impostures* carefully and often hilariously exposes the scientific jargon–fueled nonsense of various intellectuals writing in this vein. About the longer passage from which the Guattari quotation is taken, Sokal and Bricmont say that it is the "most brilliant mélange of scientific, pseudo-scientific and philosophical jargon that we have ever encountered; only a genius could have written it."[5]

Intellectual Impostures followed the "Sokal Hoax" in 1996. Sokal submitted to the fashionable US postmodern journal *Social Text* an essay packed full of pretentious-sounding, pseudoscientific claptrap. The editors of *Social Text*, unable to distinguish claptrap from profundity, published it. After all, Sokal's "Transgressing the Boundaries: Towards a Transformative Hermeneutics of Quantum Gravity" seemed to make as much sense as other papers they published. The publication of "Transgressing the Boundaries" became an "Emperor's New Clothes" moment for the style of philosophy published by the journal. *Social Text* became a laughingstock.

About Jean Baudrillard's work, which is full of references to chaos theory, quantum mechanics, non-Euclidean geometries, and so on, Sokal and Bricmont write:

> In summary, one finds in Baudrillard's works a profusion of scientific terms, used with total disregard for their meaning and, above all, in a context where they are manifestly irrelevant. Whether or not one interprets them as metaphors, it is hard to see what role they could play, except to give an appearance of profundity to trite observations about sociology or history. Moreover, the scientific terminology is mixed up with a non-scientific vocabulary that is employed with equal sloppiness.

> When all is said and done, one wonders what would be left of Baudrillard's thought if the verbal veneer covering it were stripped away.[6]

I include this quotation from Sokal and Bricmont because it nicely summarizes what might be said about *Pseudoprofundity* more generally—*Pseudoprofundity* consists of a thin mixture of the trite, the nonsensical, and/or the obviously false, whipped up into an impressive-looking linguistic soufflé. Prick it with a fork, let out the hot air, and you'll find there's little left. Certainly nothing worth eating.

In defense of Guattari, Baudrillard, and others, some might say that Sokal and Bricmont have misunderstood what these writers are trying to do. Such postmodern thinkers are themselves engaging in game playing and spoofery. So the joke is really on Sokal and Bricmont. This won't wash. As Richard Dawkins points out in his review of *Intellectual Imposteurs*, if Sokal and Bricmont's targets

> are only joking around, why do they react with such shrieks of dismay when somebody plays a joke at their expense. The genesis of *Intellectual Impostures* was a brilliant hoax perpetrated by Alan Sokal, and the stunning success of his *coup* was not greeted with the chuckles of delight that one might have hoped for after such a feat of deconstructive game playing. Apparently, when you've become the establishment, it ceases to be funny when somebody punctures the established bag of wind.[7]

DEALING WITH PSEUDOPROFUNDITY

Hopefully, this brief sketch of some of the ways *Pseudoprofundity* can be generated will help you spot it more effectively. If you find yourself on the receiving end of such blather, how should you respond? How can we best reveal *Pseudoprofundity* for what it is?

Pseudoprofundity's greatest enemy is clarity. One of the most effective methods of disarming it is to translate what is said into plain English. Say, "Right, so you are saying . . ." and proceed to jot down in clear, unambiguous prose on back of an envelope precisely what they do mean. Such a translation will typically reveal that what was said is one of three things: (1) an obvious falsehood, (2) nonsense, or (3) a truism.

However, combating *Pseudoprofundity* is rarely quite as easy as that. Those who spout it are often aware, at some level, that clarity is likely to unmask them, and they will probably resist your attempts to rephrase what they mean in clear and unambiguous terms. They will almost certainly accuse you of a crude misunderstanding (see chapter on *"Moving the Semantic Goalposts"*). Of course, they still won't explain clearly what they *do* mean. They'll just keep giving you the runaround by changing the subject, erecting smokescreens, accusing you of further misunderstandings, and so on. For this reason, the unmasking of *Pseudoprofundity* typically requires both time and patience.

Mockery and satire can have a role to play, as Allan Bennett's "The Sermon" and the Postmodern Essay Generator illustrate. The Hans Christian Andersen story "The Emperor's New Clothes" ends with much hilarity when the small boy points out that the emperor is wearing no clothes at all. The public's laughter at the emperor parading around naked finally breaks the spell that the charlatan weavers had, in effect, cast over them all. Laughter can similarly help break the spell that *Pseudoprofundity* casts over us. A little satire may help us recognize that we have been taken in by someone spouting little more than truisms, falsehoods, or nonsense *dressed up as* profundity. That is why those who spout pseudoprofundity often strongly discourage satire and mockery—taking enormous, exaggerated offense at it.

There is an important caveat when it comes to the use of humor, however. Obviously, any belief—even a genuinely profound belief—can be mocked. I'm not suggesting mockery should *replace* clear, rigorous criticism of the sort I have attempted to provide here. No one should be encouraged to abandon a belief just because people laugh at it. But, because of its ability to help break the spell that pseudoprofundity casts over its victims, allowing us to entertain for a moment or two the thought that perhaps we have been somewhat gullible or foolish, a little mockery can form an appropriate part of a response. Mockery may be both useful and legitimate if we can show that it is deserved.

Chapter 7

Piling Up the Anecdotes

An anecdote involves the recounting of a short story or episode, supposedly true and often testimonial in nature. There's nothing wrong with anecdotes per se—they can usefully be used to spice up a dinner party conversation, provoke a discussion, or illustrate a point. I've told a few in my time. However, alarm bells should start ringing whenever anecdotes are supposed to provide significant *evidence* in support of a claim, particularly a supernatural claim. Here are a few examples:

> I know I'm psychic. For example, last week I was thinking about Aunt Sue, whom I hadn't talked to for ages, when the phone rang. And it was her.
>
> Prayer clearly works. I prayed for Mark, John, Karen, and Rita and they all got better.
>
> I have no doubt that ghosts are real. My mother saw one just last week. And she's a trustworthy woman not prone to making things up.

Anecdotal evidence is also a staple of snake-oil salesmen everywhere, who can usually produce a handful of supporting testimonials to the efficacy of their remedies:

John ate three of my patented magic beans, and his cancer dis-appeared. Here's his sworn testimony!

People are attracted to anecdotes. We especially love hearing tales of the extraordinary and supernatural. Many of us are easily swayed by anecdotal evidence for the existence of psychic powers, ghosts, or the efficacy of prayer or of some alternative medicine. Yet, as supporting evidence, such anecdotes are almost entirely worthless. Why? For a range of reasons. Here are a few examples.

AMAZING COINCIDENCE

First of all, note that amazing coincidences are inevitable. There are billions of people living on this planet, each experiencing thousands of events each day. Inevitably, some of them are going to experience some really remarkable coincidences.

Such coincidences will be thrown up by chance. The odds of flipping a coin and getting a run of ten heads by chance is very low if you flip the coin only ten times. But if billions of people do the same thing, it becomes very likely indeed that a run of ten heads will occur.

Such coincidences can easily generate the appearance of supernatural activity. For example, such coincidences can suggest that prayer can cure people of terminal diseases. Among people diagnosed with terminal cancer, a small percentage will sponta-neously get better. Such rare occurrences are just a natural fact about cancer. Huge numbers of people are diagnosed with ter-minal cancer each year. And a significant proportion of them are prayed for. It's likely, then, that a few of those diagnosed with ter-minal cancer and prayed for will recover. Is the existence of such people evidence that prayer works? Clearly not. These are people who would have gotten better anyway, prayed for or not. A handful of reports of such amazing recoveries is not good evi-dence of the efficacy of petitionary prayer.

What would be more impressive is if, say, after being prayed for, someone's amputated leg grew back. That's something that would really run contrary to everything we know about how our bodies function. If, in response to prayer, God really did heal people by supernatural means, and if his powers are unlimited, then he could just as easily grow someone a new leg as cure them of terminal cancer. However, well-documented cases of people growing legs back after being prayed for do not, so far as I am aware, exist. Interestingly, reports of "miraculous" medical recoveries tend to be largely restricted to the kinds of cases in which such spontaneous remission is known to occur.

What about the phone-ringing episode? Just the other day, I was booked to play at a wedding in some fairly remote countryside about fifty miles from where I live. When I arrived, my brother walked out of the building to meet me. He was as amazed to see me as I was to see him. The venue was miles away from where either of us lived. But, by sheer chance, we ended up at the same place at the same time. A month or two ago, my wife took a train journey to a station in the north of England. When she stepped onto the platform, her father was standing there. Again, both were amazed. Again, this was a coincidence. The fact is, coincidences happen. Every now and again, people will run into each other in unexpected locations. Every now and then, the phone will ring, and at the end of the line will be someone you were just thinking about.

Coincidence also accounts for at least some sightings of monsters. Consider the many thousands of people who look out over Loch Ness each year. All sorts of shapes are created in the water by floating logs, otters, wind patterns, the wakes of boats, and so on. Just by chance, a few will look a little monster-like. So, if a monster is what people are looking for, we should expect a few such reports of a monster, whether or not there's a monster in the loch.

Those finding hidden codes in ancient texts also tend to rely heavily on coincidence. In the book *The Bible Code*, journalist Michael Drosnin claims to have discovered within the Bible a code revealing events that happened thousands of years after the text was written, events such as the assassination of John F. Kennedy in Dallas. Drosnin also claims no mere human could have encoded these hidden messages, and that he has therefore discovered mathematical proof that "we are not alone."[1]

Has Drosnin really discovered such deliberately hidden predictive messages within the pages of the Bible? Critics note that Drosnin's method of revealing his messages looks suspiciously as if it would throw them up by chance. Drosnin denies this. He claimed in *Newsweek*, "When my critics find a message about the assassination of a prime minister encrypted in *Moby Dick*, I'll believe them."[2]

One critic then proceeded to do just that. Mathematician Brendan MacKay subsequently used Drosnin's method to find encrypted in *Moby Dick* "predictions" of the assassinations of Leon Trotsky, Indira Gandhi, Martin Luther King, René Moawad, and Robert F. Kennedy. In fact it turns out that by using Drosnin's method you can find such "messages" hidden in any large text. They're thrown up by chance among the vast number of letter sequences that Drosnin's method generates.

The important thing to remember about coincidences is this— what would be *really* odd is if they *didn't* happen. If no one ever unexpectedly ran into a friend or relative, or if we never received phone calls from people we just happened to be thinking about— well, that really would be pretty peculiar. The fact that amazing coincidences happen is, or should be, entirely unsurprising and requires no supernatural explanation.

THE POST HOC FALLACY

People often assume that because one thing happens after another, that one is the *cause* of the other. But there needn't be any causal link. To assume that because B followed A, A *caused* B is to commit the fallacy known as *post hoc ergo propter hoc* (which means "After this, therefore because of this"). Suppose my kettle boils immediately after a comet crashes into Mars. Did the comet cause my kettle to boil? No. That's just a coincidence.

Similarly, the fact that someone diagnosed with terminal cancer recovers after prayer does not establish that prayer caused the recovery. To suppose otherwise is also to commit the post hoc fallacy.

Recovery after diagnosis of terminal cancer might be an amazing one-off coincidence. But what if we spot a *pattern*? What if, *whenever* A happens, B always, or very often, follows? Would *that* establish that A causes B?

Suppose, for example, that there is a New Age medical treatment advertised like so:

> Ninety percent of those suffering from unexplained lower back pain who took magic beans as treatment reported a significant improvement after just a few weeks!

Wow, that sounds impressive—*90 percent*! Surely we have here evidence that magic beans really do effectively treat lower back pain, right?

No, we don't. Ninety percent of cases of unexplained lower back pain will have improved significantly after six weeks, even with *no treatment at all*. So the fact that 90 percent of those with unexplained lower back pain improve significantly after receiving magic beans, crystal healing, homeopathy, or a rubdown with pink blancmange is no evidence at all that any of these treatments have any sort of beneficial effect.

What we tend to overlook is the extent to which the supposed "effect" happens *anyway*, whether or not the alleged "cause" is present. One hundred percent of those people who drink water eventually die. That doesn't establish that drinking water is the cause of their death.

COUNTING THE HITS AND IGNORING THE MISSES

Francis Bacon, a pivotal figure in the development of the scientific method, once said, "The general root of superstition is that men observe when things hit, and not when they miss; and commit to memory the one, and forget and pass over the other." Anecdotes can appear to provide compelling evidence of psychic abilities and supernatural events, particularly when many are collected together in a book or article. Page upon page of anecdotes about the amazing insights of psychics can leave people thinking, "Well, there's got to be *something* to it, surely!" But how is this evidence accumulated? Typically, as Bacon notes, people *look for cases that seem to support the theory they believe in, and ignore those that don't.* This is called *confirmation bias.*

For example, someone who believes they are psychic will usually focus on the few "hits," for instance, those times when they received a phone call from someone they just thought about. They forget about the many "misses": all those times when they thought about someone but the person didn't immediately call. By collecting together several such "hits" and ignoring the innumerable "misses," it's not difficult to convince yourself that you have psychic powers, even if you don't.

Similarly, someone who believes in the efficacy of prayer will typically ignore all those cases in which people diagnosed with terminal cancer were prayed for and didn't recover—the overwhelming majority—and will focus exclusively on the handful of cases in which there was a full recovery. By ignoring the "misses"—all those occasions on which sick people were prayed for but they experienced no recovery, and collect together only on the "hits"—the small proportion of occasions the person recovered, we can, again, easily convince ourselves that we have amassed powerful evidence of the miraculous efficacy of prayer.

We can now see more clearly one of the main reasons why anecdotal evidence is such poor evidence. When we are simply presented with a large collection of anecdotes, we have no idea how *idiosyncratic* the cases are. If I casually take a sawn-off shotgun and pepper the side of a barn on which a small target is hanging, and a couple of shotgun pellets happen to fall inside the target, that's not evidence of my great marksmanship. Someone who initially looks only at the two holes in the target might be impressed, but once they take a step back and see all the misses, it becomes obvious that there's no evidence of marksmanship after all. The "hits" were highly atypical.

Not only do we tend to count the "hits" and forget about the "misses," we also tend, when recounting anecdotes, to focus on those features that make the story sound dramatic and downplay details that make it less so. There's often also an incentive to "sex up" anecdotes—sometimes even a financial incentive. Tabloid newspapers and TV production companies know that, as a rule, their audiences tend to be more interested in dramatic and extraordinary tales than in articles or programs that shed doubts on such stories. As a result, even while pretending to be "balanced," TV programs on the paranormal are often little more than puffs for self-styled psychics. Doubts, if voiced at all, tend to be in the background. As a result of all this anecdote generating and peddling by the media, many people have become convinced there is abundant evidence that ghosts exist, that some people really are blessed with psychic powers, that some people have been abducted by aliens, and so on.

THE POWER OF SUGGESTION AND OUR TENDENCY TO "SEE" WHAT IS NOT THERE

Human beings are remarkably prone to "see" things that are not, in truth, there. Take, for example, the *power of suggestion*, nicely illustrated by Kenneth Arnold's famous sighting of the very first flying saucer back in 1963. Arnold was flying his light plane near Mount Rainier in Washington when he saw a series of mysterious shapes in the distance. On landing, he reported these unidentified flying objects. The news media picked up the story of Arnold's flying saucers, and, soon after, many other people were reporting the saucer-shaped objects in the sky. They have been reporting them ever since. The saucer-shaped spacecraft has become a staple of science fiction. But here's the thing—*Arnold did not report seeing flying saucers*. What Arnold said he saw were boomerang-shaped craft that bobbed up and down, somewhat like a saucer would do if skimmed across a lake. The reporter misheard, the story of "flying saucers" entered the public sphere, and other people started reporting saucers too. Why? Assuming most of them were sincere, and assuming it's unlikely our alien visitors just happened to switch from using boomerang-shaped craft to saucer-shaped craft in 1963, it seems the saucer reports that followed were, and are, largely a product of the power of suggestion. People see something in the sky, and, because they expect it to be saucer shaped, that's how it looks to them. Expectation strongly shapes perception.

Rigorous investigation of reports of unidentified flying objects has thrown up numerous examples of how our eyes can deceive us. In the autumn of 1967 there was a rash of reports of a UFO appearing nightly over the construction site of a nuclear plant. Sanitation workers reported it, then a guard. The police showed up. An officer confirmed, "It was about half the size of the moon, and it just hung there over the plant. Must have been there nearly two hours." The strange object disappeared at sunrise. The next night the same thing happened. A county deputy sheriff described a "large lighted object." An auxiliary police officer described "five objects—they appeared to be burning. An aircraft passed by while I was watching. They seemed to be 20 times the size of the plane." A Wake County magistrate saw "a rectangular object, looked like it was on fire. . . . We figured it about the size of a football field. It was huge and very bright." There was also a report from air traffic control of an unidentified blip on the radar scope.

When newspaper reporters arrived to investigate the mysterious object, it appeared again at 5:00 a.m. The reporters attempted to chase it in a car. They discovered that no matter how fast they drove, they couldn't get any closer. Finally, they stopped to take pictures of the mysterious object. The photographer looked through his long telephoto lens and said, "Yep . . . that's the planet Venus alright."[3]

Once the planet had been mistaken for a large hovering object by one person, well, that's how everyone else saw it too, until, finally, someone finally looked at it through a magnifying lens and realized the truth. You might be surprised to discover that Venus is one of the biggest sources of UFO reports. Anyone who thinks that a group of honest, experienced, trained eye-witnesses—police officers, no less—can't be seriously and repeatedly misled by the power of suggestion should think again. Also notice how coincidence threw into the mix of this story an apparent "independent" confirmation—that spurious radar blip.

It's not just visual perception that's affected by the power of suggestion. An auditory example, widely available on the Internet, is provided by the song "Stairway to Heaven" by rock band Led Zeppelin, one passage of which, when played backward (easy to do on an old-style record player), is supposed to say:

Oh here's to my sweet Satan.
The one whose little path would make me sad,
    whose power is Satan.
He will give those with him 666.
There was a little tool shed where he made us suffer,
    sad Satan.

Actually, if people listen to the song backward without having seen the suggested lyrics (obviously, I've ruined this for you now), they can't make out much at all, except maybe one or two words, such as "Satan." Play the reversed passage to people with these words in front of them, on the other hand, and they find it almost impossible *not* to hear the words.

How did the myth of the hidden message in "Stairway to

Heaven" arise? Someone playing rock records backward—either messing around, or actually looking for hidden messages—came across what sounds like the dramatic and noteworthy word "Satan" (thrown up by chance) in "Stairway to Heaven," and they then constructed lyrics suggested to them by the surrounding noises. Having produced the satanic lyrics, the more they listened, the more obvious it seemed to them that the words were really there. The truth, of course, is that the satanic lyrics people "hear" are a product of the minds of listeners, not the mind of Led Zeppelin's lyricist, Robert Plant.

Even setting aside the power of suggestion, various other factors can shape perception, including our obvious perceptual sensitivity to faces. Look up at passing cumulus clouds or stare into the embers of a fire, and all sorts of things start to appear. By far the most common are faces. We are naturally attuned to them and can easily "find" a face in most randomly generated patterns.

In 1976, the space probe Viking Orbiter 1 was busy photographing the Cydonia region of Mars. On July 25 it took a picture of what appeared to many to be an enormous alien face carved onto the planet's surface. The Mars Face, as it has come to be known, caused much speculation. One author, Richard Haugland, suggested in his book *The Monuments of Mars: City on the Edge of Forever*, that the reptilian-looking face was a vast monument created by some ancient Martian civilization—the Martian equivalent of the Great Pyramid of Giza. However, other photographs of the same region reveal that the Mars Face is just a hill that doesn't look very face-like at all unless lit at a certain angle, when it happens by chance to take on a face-like appearance.

In fact, the Mars Face is a product of two factors: (1) Chance eventually threw up a rather face-like set of shadows among the hundreds of photographs of a planet's surface. This face-like image was then further enhanced by (2) our tendency to "see" faces in such patterns anyway. These same two factors account for the many reports of mysterious faces appearing in things. If you have five minutes to spare, a quick trawl through the Internet will reveal Mother Teresa's face in a bun, Jesus's face on the back of a bedroom door, and a demon's face appearing in a cloud of smoke emerging from the Twin Towers.

The placebo effect provides another example of the power of suggestion. During the Second World War, anesthetist Henry Beecher, faced with a lack of morphine at a military field hospital, tried a rather desperate ploy. He injected a wounded soldier with inert saline solution but told the soldier it was a powerful painkiller. Amazingly, the soldier relaxed and stopped exhibiting signs of significant pain or distress. When Beecher repeated the ploy on other soldiers, he got the same effect. We are remarkably prone to the power of suggestion when it comes to medical treatment. Tell people something will make them better—that it will relieve their pain, give their joints better mobility, reduce their acne, or whatever—and they'll believe, and report in all sincerity, that it does. The placebo effect, as it's known, can create the illusion that a treatment is medically effective when it is not. However, it can also contribute to the effectiveness of even bona fide medicines.

Beecher subsequently went on to publish a seminal paper, "The Powerful Placebo,"[4] in which he argued for the importance of conducting *double-blind, placebo-controlled clinical trials of treatments to establish their efficacy.* If we want to know whether, say, homeopathic remedies have any effect other than placebo, we need two large groups into which individuals have been randomly assigned, one group receiving the homeopathic drug, the other, the medically inert placebo. The trial should be double-blind: the subjects should not know who is receiving the genuine treatment and who is receiving the inert alternative. The experimenters should also be blind to this information, in order to counter the "experimenter effect" (it is well established that experimenters can inadvertently influence the outcome of such trials if they know who is and isn't receiving the genuine treatment). Unfortunately for homeopathy, such well-conducted trials have failed to provide any convincing evidence of the efficacy of homeopathic treatments for any particular ailment.

It is not just perception that can be led astray by the power of suggestion. Psychologist Jean Piaget once claimed his earliest memory was of nearly being kidnapped at the age of two while being walked in his pram by his nurse:

> I can still see, most clearly, the following scene, in which I believed until I was about fifteen. I was sitting in my pram, which my nurse was pushing in the Champs Elysées, when a man tried to kidnap me. I was held in by the strap fastened round me while my nurse bravely tried to stand between me and the thief. She received various scratches, and I can still see vaguely those on her face. Then a crowd gathered, a policeman with a short cloak and a white baton came up, and the man took to his heels. I can still see the whole scene, and can even place it near the tube station.

Later, when Piaget was about fifteen, his family received a letter in which the nurse admitted the story was false:

> She had made up the whole story, faking the scratches. I, therefore, must have heard, as a child, the account of this story, which my parents believed, and projected into the past in the form of a visual memory.[5]

Studies reveal that in somewhere between 18 and 37 percent of subjects, researchers can successfully "implant" false memories of events such as animal attacks, riding in a hot air balloon with one's family, and witnessing a demonic possession.[6]

OTHER MECHANISMS: CHINESE WHISPERS, DECEPTION AND FAKERY, AND SO ON

Another factor that further undermines the credibility of much anecdotal evidence is what I call the *Chinese whispers effect*. When amazing tales are transmitted from one person to another, the retellings often involve some subtle or not so subtle editing. Those details that are dramatic tend to be remembered and exaggerated. Those that undermine the credibility of the anecdote tend to be airbrushed out. Even if each reteller reshapes the original story only slightly, it takes just a handful of retellings for the story to change significantly. So we can place even less credence in stories that reach us fourth-, fifth-, or sixth-hand.

We should also remember that, when it comes to anecdotes about faith healing, spoon bending, mind reading, communication with the dead, and so on, many people have been revealed as deceptive. In 1983, Christian healer Peter Popoff, who regularly "cured" people of serious illnesses during his revival meetings, was exposed by magician James Randi. Popoff would wheel subjects onto the stage in wheelchairs—subjects who were then miraculously able to walk. It turned out that these people could already walk, and that Popoff had simply brought them on in wheelchairs. Popoff was also caught receiving information about audience members given to him by his wife via a radio earpiece.

The list of fakes and deceivers is long and includes the three Fox sisters, who helped generate huge mid-nineteenth-century interest in communication with the dead. The sisters conducted séances in New York in which the dead would communicate by making rapping noises. The Foxes performed in public theaters, and their work attracted many notable people. Two of the sisters were later to admit "perpetrating the fraud of Spiritualism upon a too-confiding public."[7] Though they later retracted their confessions, Margaret Fox had nevertheless demonstrated how she could produce the mysterious raps by cracking her toe joints at will.

Not all the claims made about the Fox sisters' séances were, however, a result of deception. In some cases, members of the public were to add dramatic details of their own. Margaret was to say:

A great many people when they hear the rapping imagine at once that the spirits are touching them. It is a very common delusion. Some very wealthy people came to see me some years ago when I lived in Forty-second Street and I did some rappings for them. I made the spirit rap on the chair and one of the ladies cried out: "I feel the spirit tapping me on the shoulder." Of course that was pure imagination.[8]

Another form of fakery by psychics and mediums is the use of hot and/or cold reading. Hot reading involves research in advance. A psychic may prepare for a reading by researching the client on the Internet. Some psychics will place stooges in the foyers of theaters in which they are performing to overhear the conversations of audience members, make notes, and pass information back to the psychic. Sometimes the person for whom a public reading is done will be known to the psychic or to someone close to the psychic, who may then pass on information. Sometimes stooges will join the audience, pretending to be ordinary members of the public.

Cold reading is more of an art form and involves creating the illusion that the psychic knows things about her subject. Psychic readings typically begin like so:

PSYCHIC: I am getting someone whose name begins with "G." George . . . [pause] . . . Or Gerald.
CUSTOMER: Gerald! My uncle's name was Gerald.
PSYCHIC: Yes, Gerald is here with me now. He is saying Hello!
CUSTOMER: That's amazing!
PSYCHIC: He being quite shy, quite coy.
CUSTOMER: [No reaction]
PSYCHIC: Which is odd, because he was such an outgoing chap, wasn't he?
CUSTOMER: Yes, that's right. He loved the social club.
PSYCHIC: Ah, yes, he was just saying he missed his friends there.
CUSTOMER. [Gets a little weepy] It's really him!
PSYCHIC: I'm sensing he had some back trouble.
CUSTOMER: Yes he did! A slipped disc.
PSYCHIC: That's right. He says that disc is all better now.

This customer may go away and tell her friends that the psychic knew she had a dead uncle named Gerald who was outgoing, missed his friends at the social club, and had a slipped disc. Her friends may well be amazed and think that perhaps there's *something* to this psychic business after all.

However, our psychic, in reality, knew nothing. Let's go through the reading again. The psychic tries a name. No reaction. Then another, and this time she gets a hit. But she does not say whether Gerald is living or dead (it could be a message concerning a living person called Gerald). It's the customer who supplies the information that she has a dead uncle of that name. The psychic then suggests Gerald is shy. No reaction, so the psychic switches to saying Gerald was outgoing and gets another hit. The customer supplies the information that Gerald attended a social club. The psychic then suggests Gerald had back trouble. "So-and-so had back trouble" is what is known as a *Barnum statement*. It sounds pretty specific, but it is actually true of most people. Almost everyone has back trouble at some point, so it's not surprising the psychic gets another hit. Other examples of Barnum statements are: "You had an accident when you were a child involving water" and "You have been worrying about money recently." Psychics will typically make lots of Barnum statements. But notice that even if Gerald's back was always problem free, the psychic can switch tactics and say, "No, sorry, I misheard—Gerald is saying *you* have had some back trouble." Even if that fails to score a hit, chances are the customer will quickly forget about it. As we have already noted, it's the hits we remember—the misses are soon forgotten.

By using a combination of hot and cold reading, professional magicians can fake everything that supposedly genuine psychics can apparently do—often fooling audiences into believing they are genuinely psychic before revealing the truth. In fact, it is striking how often the methods of many supposedly genuine psychics resemble those of honest cheats.

However, it would be a mistake to conclude that everyone

who believes they are psychic—and who presents himself or herself as a psychic—is a deceiver. Several years ago, a friend and I played a simple mind-reading trick on another friend of ours. It's a simple trick you can try yourself. One person holds up a playing card and then mentally "transmits" the color of the card to the other person, who has to guess the color. To the amazement of onlookers, the guesser keeps getting it right. It looks like they are "mind reading," but actually they are using a simple code: when the person holding the card says "OK," the card is black, and when they say "Right," it's red. It's a fairly obvious deception, and it's astonishing that people fall for it. But many do, especially if you set up the trick so that it seems to emerge as a bit of spontaneous larking about. Throw in a few misses to give the scenario credibility, and the trick works better still.

What was interesting on this occasion was that, after impressing our victim with our psychic powers, we decided to test her to see if she, too, could read the mind of the card holder. She found, to her astonishment, that she could. She got more and more excited about her amazing psychic ability, until we finally had to disappoint her by revealing the truth—that she was merely subliminally picking up on the OK/Right code.

Just like my friend, some psychics lacking any genuine psychic ability may nevertheless sincerely believe they are psychic. They may be picking up on all sorts of entirely natural signals and clues without realizing they are doing so.

We may also unwittingly provide psychics with information through our body language. Consider the strange case of Clever Hans, a horse that could apparently perform mathematical calculations—tapping out the answers with his hoof. In 1907, psychologist Oskar Pfungst conducted an investigation into the horse's alleged mathematical abilities and discovered that the horse was not doing math but picking up on the very subtle reactions of his human trainer. The trainer was, without realizing it, cueing the horse when to stop tapping. When the trainer did not know the answer, it turned out that the horse didn't either. The

Clever Hans effect, as it became known, illustrates how we can "leak" information without realizing it.

"TELL ME A STORY"

We have conducted a brief survey of some of the main ways anecdotal evidence for the existence of psychic powers, ghosts, alien abduction, monsters and so on can be generated. It indicates why such evidence is almost entirely worthless. You will remember in *"But It Fits!"* that we said evidence supports a hypothesis to the extent that *the evidence is to be expected if the hypothesis is true, but not particularly expected otherwise.* The evidence has to be, in a certain sense, "surprising."

The problem with anecdotal evidence for such extraordinary claims is that, knowing what we do about how such testimony tends to be generated, a great deal of it is to be expected *anyway*, whether or not the claims happen to be true. The existence of quantities of such anecdotal evidence is not, then, good evidence for the truth of such extraordinary claims.

Anecdotal evidence may be largely worthless as evidence, but it can be highly persuasive. Humans love a story, especially if it's shocking, weird, or emotionally arresting. We enjoy comedies, tragedies, stories of wrongs righted, of revenge, of ghosts, of aliens. One reason we find such stories appealing is that they tap into our tendency to feel empathy with others. We enjoy imaginatively putting ourselves in the subject's position, imagining how it must have felt to exact that bloody revenge, to see a ghost, or to be abducted by aliens. The more emotional impact the story has, the more memorable it is.

As a consequence, a juicy story can psychologically trump a dry statistic, even when the statistic is rather more informative. The result of a double-blind clinical study of the efficacy of prayer is a dull set of figures easily forgotten, whereas a handful of emotionally arresting anecdotes about prayers answered may resonate with us for a long time.

THE AMAZINGLY PERSUASIVE POWER
OF ACCUMULATED ANECDOTES

Pulling several anecdotes together can be particularly persuasive. A shower of anecdotes often explains why people become convinced that certain medical treatments are effective when they are not.

Bloodletting, popular from antiquity until the late nineteenth century, was used to treat almost every disease. In 1799, George Washington asked to be bled after he developed a throat infection. He died after large quantities of blood were removed. Benjamin Rush, a physician and one of signatories to the Declaration of Independence, was, like most of his contemporaries, entirely convinced that removing significant quantities of blood from patients helped cure many ailments. Rush, like other physicians, believed in the efficacy of bloodletting entirely on the basis of anecdotes about people being bled and then recovering. Here he cites two examples:

> I bled a young man James Cameron, in the autumn of 1794, four times between the 20th and 30th days of a chronic fever, in consequence of a pain in the side, accompanied by a tense pulse, which suddenly came on after the 20th day of his disease. His blood was sizy. His pain and tense pulse were subdued by the bleeding and he recovered. I bled the late Dr. Prowl twelve times, in a fever which continued thirty days, in the autumn of the year 1800. I wish these cases to be attended by young practitioners.[9]

It was not until Parisian doctor Pierre Louis conducted a controlled experiment in 1836—treating one group of patients with pneumonia with aggressive bloodletting, and another group with modest bloodletting—that the truth began to be revealed. The number of patients who died after aggressive bloodletting turned out to be greater.

Consider homeopathy. In their book *Trick or Treatment*, Simon Singh and Edzard Ernst (the latter is both a professor of medicine and a trained homeopathic practitioner) conclude of their assessment of the scientific evidence regarding homeopathy that "it would be fair to say that there is a mountain of evidence to suggest that homeopathic remedies do not work."[10] So why do people *think* they work? Because of numerous anecdotes about the efficacy of homeopathy. These anecdotes are, in reality, a result of people just getting better anyway, the placebo effect, and other factors such as conventional medicines also having an effect, subjects not wanting to disappoint those interviewing them, and so on.

Many people also believe in the power of intercessionary prayer to help people through medical crises. In 2006, the *American Heart Journal* published the results of a 2.4 million-dollar experiment involving 1,802 heart-bypass patients, conducted under the leadership of Herbert Benson, a cardiologist who had previously suggested that "the evidence for the efficacy of intercessionary prayer is mounting" (so he was hardly biased against the claim that prayer works). The results were clear-cut: prayer had no beneficial effect on the patients.[11] Another large-scale trial of patients undergoing angioplasty or cardiac catheterization also found prayer had no effect.[12] Unsurprisingly, such studies don't convince all those who believe in the power of prayer. After these studies, Bob Barth, spiritual director of a Missouri prayer ministry involved in the Benson prayer experiment, said, "A person of faith would say that this study is interesting, but we've been praying a long time and we've seen prayer work, we know it works, and the research on prayer and spirituality is just getting started."[13]

How did Bob Barth "know" prayer works? In the same way Benjamin Rush "knew" that bloodletting worked. On the basis of anecdotal evidence—that's to say, various cases in which the treatment was "seen to work."

CHRISTIAN SCIENCE

It's often said that "the plural of anecdote is not data." And yet a pile of anecdotes can be made to *look* very much like solid scientific data. Attempts have even been made to build a science on the basis of anecdotal evidence. I will finish this chapter with a brief look at just such an attempt—Christian Science.

As Caroline Fraser, a former Christian Scientist herself, explains in her book *God's Perfect Child* (on which much of this section is based), Christian Scientists believe that they have rediscovered Christianity by rediscovering the "*exact method and means* by which Jesus healed. Only Christian Scientists believe they can duplicate those healings systematically and repeatedly over a lifetime."[14]

According to Mary Baker Eddy, the founder of the Christian Science movement, matter does not exist and disease is a product of the mind. A Christian Science practitioner's training typically involves two weeks of religious instruction. Practitioners are not trained to diagnose illness, and in fact they do not even believe in the reality of illness. The treatment carried out by trained practitioners of Christian Science is primarily prayer.

How do Christian Scientists know they have discovered methods that work? Because of the "scientific" evidence they have amassed over the years—tens of thousands of published testimonies of cases in which the methods of Christian Science have been applied and people have subsequently recovered. The "science" in Christian Science is meant literally. The suggestion is that the thousands of testimonies or anecdotes that the movement has accumulated over the years constitutes solid, statistical evidence that Christian Science works.

By 1989, around fifty-three thousand testimonies had been published in Christian Science periodicals. Early on, the cured were allowed to write up their own cases. More recently, Christian Science publications have prefaced such testimonials by saying:

The statements made in testimonies and articles with regard to healing have been verified in writing by those who can vouch for the integrity of the testifier or know of the healing. Three such written verifications or vouchers are required before testimony can be published.[15]

While this might strike some as being very "scientific," the appearance of scientific rigor is misleading.

Notice, first of all, that the Christian Science movement *ignores all cases of failure*. It counts only its "hits" and ignores all its "misses." Extraordinarily, there are no records of those who died after having received treatment. In their "Empirical Analysis" conducted by Christian Scientists of over seven thousand treatments, the authors admitted that the study "does not provide comparative cure or mortality rates, nor does it consider cases in which healing prayer has not been effective."[16] This fact, all by itself, renders the evidence more or less worthless.

Worse still, many of the testimonials look very dubious indeed. In 1954, the academic R. W. England of the University of Pennsylvania published his analysis of a sample of five hundred letters published in the *Christian Science Journal* testifying to the power of Christian Science to heal. As Fraser notes, England found that the self-diagnoses of Christian Scientists were often unreliable:

The number of cancers, tumors, broken bones, and cases of pneumonia and acute appendicitis which were self-diagnosed by the writers seemed large. . . . It seems likely that most of the more dramatic cures are due simply to mistaken diagnoses. In scores of letters the writers describe how they broke their skulls, dislocated organs, awoke in the night with pneumonia, decided mysterious lumps were cancers, or found themselves in other ways serious victims of mortal mind. Their next move was to begin divine treatment, with or without a practitioner's aid. Elated and gratified when the skulls mended, their organs returned to place, their pneumonia and cancers vanished, they wrote letters of testimony to the Journal.[17]

Moreover, most letters concerned fairly trivial—sometimes psychosomatic—conditions that tend to get better anyway:

> Most conspicuous was an apparent ignorance of or indifference to the natural healing powers of the human body. Thus, a vast number of minor ailments, ranging from athlete's foot to the common cold, were treated and cured by the application of Divine Truth. Furthermore, there is, among the 500 communicants, considerable attention given to types of disorders so insignificant as to be of practically no consequence so far as one's daily life is concerned. Chapped hands, lone warts, a burned fingernail, hangnails, vague fleeting pains, a momentary dizziness were not infrequently the "healings" for which testimony was given.[18]

It should be fairly obvious by now why the "scientific evidence" for the efficacy of Christian Science is no such thing. It's just a vast collection of anecdotes—tens of thousands of them—anecdotes of a sort that we might well expect to be produced by the kind of mechanisms described in this chapter, whether or not Christian Science actually works.

If Christian Science really worked, then that fact could be established by a controlled experiment, as scientist Richard Feynman points out in his book *The Meaning of It All*:

> There is, in fact, an entire religion that's respectable, so called, that's called Christian Science, that's based on the idea of faith healing. If it were true, it could be established, not by the anecdotes of a few people but by careful checks.[19]

The Christian Science movement has no interest in conducting such careful checks. They just stick with their accumulation of anecdotes, which they *dress up as* "science."

Christian Science has cost lives. People can and have died as a result of their rejecting conventional medical services and plumping for the power of Christian Science instead. Hundreds, perhaps thousands, of children have received Christian Science treatment rather than conventional medicine. One of the most notorious cases is the 1979 incident involving twelve-year-old Michael Schram. As Michael started showing increasingly serious symptoms of gastric distress, his mother, a devout Christian Scientist, decided to rely on the services not of a doctor but of a Christian Science practitioner. As a result, Michael died unnecessarily from a ruptured appendix. We don't know how many children have died in this way, because Christian Science keeps no record of its failures.

Christian Science is undoubtedly an Intellectual Black Hole and a potentially dangerous one at that. While other mechanisms described in this book also play a role in providing Christian Science with a veneer of reasonableness, it is *Piling Up the Anecdotes* that does the bulk of the work.

Chapter 8

Pressing Your Buttons

O ne way in which we can shape the beliefs of others is by rational persuasion. Suppose, for example, that I want someone to believe Buckingham Palace is in London (which it is). I could provide them with a great deal of evidence to support that belief. Or I could also just take them to London so they can see with their own eyes that that's where Buckingham Palace is located.

But what if these methods aren't available? Suppose I have little or no evidence to support the belief I nevertheless want people to accept. Suppose I can't just show them that it's true. How else might I get them to believe?

I might try to dupe them, of course. I could produce fraudulent evidence and bogus arguments. But what if I suspect this won't be enough? What if I think my deceit is likely to be detected?

Another option is to dispense with even the pretense of rational persuasion and rely on the strategy I call *Pressing Your Buttons* instead. As I'll explain, *Pressing Your Buttons*, applied in a systematic and dedicated way, amounts to *brainwashing*. I'll set out exactly what I mean by *Pressing Your Buttons* toward the end of this chapter. In the meantime, in order to prepare the ground for that discussion, let's survey some of the many mechanisms that can influence what we believe.

BELIEF-SHAPING MECHANISMS

One very obvious way in which our beliefs are shaped is by social and psychological mechanisms such as peer pressure and a desire to conform. Finding ourselves believing something of which our community disapproves can be a deeply uncomfortable experience, an experience that may lead us unconsciously to tailor what we believe so that we remain in step with others. We're far more susceptible to such social pressures than we like to believe (as several famous psychological studies have shown).[1]

Belief can also be shaped through the use of reward and punishment. A grandmother may influence the beliefs of her grandson by giving him a sweet whenever he expresses the kind of beliefs of which she approves, and by ignoring or smacking him when he expresses the "wrong" sort of belief. Over time, this may change not just the kind of beliefs her grandson expresses, but also the kinds of beliefs he holds.

Perhaps certain beliefs might also be directly implanted in us. Some suppose God has implanted certain beliefs in at least some of us. Our evolutionary history may also produce certain beliefs, or at least certain predispositions to belief. For example, there's growing evidence that a disposition toward religious belief is part of our evolutionary heritage, bestowed on us by natural selection. But even if neither God nor evolution have implanted beliefs in us, perhaps one day we'll be able to implant beliefs using technology. Perhaps we'll be able to strap a brain-state-altering helmet onto an unwitting victim while they sleep, dial in the required belief, press the red button and Bing! our victim will wake up with the belief we've programmed them to hold. That would be a rather cruel trick. Some hypnotists claim a similar ability to, as it were, directly "inject" beliefs into people's minds.

Obviously, such causal mechanisms can operate on us *without our realizing what's going on*. I might *think* I condemn racism because I have good grounds for supposing racism is morally wrong, but the truth is I have merely caved into peer pressure and my desire not to be ostracized by my liberal family and friends. If a belief has been implanted in me by, say, natural selection, or by some brain-state-altering device then, again, I may not be aware that this is the reason why I believe. Suppose, for example, that some prankster programs me to believe I have been abducted by aliens using the belief-inducing helmet described above. I wake up one morning and find, as a result, that I now very strongly believe I was taken aboard a flying saucer during the night. I have no awareness of the real reason why I now hold that belief—of the mechanism that actually produced the belief in me. If asked how I know I was abducted, I'll probably say, "*I Just Know!*"

ISOLATION, CONTROL, UNCERTAINTY, REPETITION, EMOTION

I'm going to focus here on five important belief-shaping mechanisms that can play a major role in producing and sustaining an Intellectual Black Hole: *isolation, control, uncertainty, repetition,* and *emotion*.

Isolation is a useful belief-shaping tool. An isolated individual is more vulnerable to various forms of psychological manipulation. If you want someone to believe something that runs contrary to what their friends and family believe, it's a good idea to have them spend some time at a retreat or remote training camp where their attachment to other ideas can more easily be undermined. Cults often isolate their members in this way. Cult leader Jim Jones physically moved both himself and all his followers to the Guyanan jungle (where they all eventually committed suicide). Isolation is also recommended by some within more mainstream religions. In many countries, hermetically sealed-off religious schools are commonplace.[2]

A related mechanism is *control*. If you want people to accept your belief system, it's unwise to expose them to alternative systems of belief. Gain control over the kind of ideas to which they have access and to which they are exposed. Censor beliefs and ideas that threaten to undermine your own. This kind of control is often justified on the grounds that people will otherwise be corrupted or confused. Totalitarian regimes will often remove "unhealthy" books from their libraries if the books contradict the regime. All sorts of media are restricted on the grounds that they will only "mislead" people. Schools under strict religious regimes will sometimes justify preventing children from discovering or exploring other points of view on the grounds that they will only succeed in "muddling" or "corrupting" the children. Take a leaf out of the manuals of such regimes and restrict your followers' field of vision so that everything is interpreted through a single ideological lens—your own.

If you want people to abandon their beliefs and embrace your own, or if you want to be sure they won't reject your beliefs in favor of others, it also helps to raise as much doubt and *uncertainty* as possible about those rival beliefs. Uncertainty is a potent source of stress, so the more you associate alternative beliefs with uncertainty, the better. Ideally, offer a simple set of geometric, easily formulated and remembered certainties designed to give meaning to and cover every aspect of life. By constantly harping on the vagaries, uncertainties, and meaninglessness of life outside your belief system, the simple, concrete certainties you offer may begin to seem increasingly attractive to your audience.

Encourage *repetition*. Get people to recite what you want them to believe over and over again in a mantra-like way. Make the beliefs trip unthinkingly off their tongues. It doesn't matter whether your subjects accept what they are saying, or if they even fully understand it to begin with. There's still a fair chance that belief will eventually take hold. Mindless repetition works especially well when applied in situations in which your subjects feel powerful pressure to confirm. Lining pupils up in playgrounds for a daily, mantra-like recitation of your key tenets, for example, combines repetition with a situation in which any deviation by an individual will immediately result in a hundred pairs of eyes turned in their direction.

Emotion can also be harnessed to shape belief. Fear is particularly useful. In George Orwell's novel *Nineteen Eighty-Four*, the regime seeks control not just over people's behavior but, even more important, what they think and feel. When the hapless rebel Winston is finally captured, his "educators" make it clear that what ultimately concerns them are his *thoughts*:

> "And why do you imagine that we bring people to this place?"
> "To make them confess."
> "No, that is not the reason. Try again."
> "To punish them."
> "No!" exclaimed O'Brien. His voice had changed extraordinarily, and his face had suddenly become both stern and animated. "No! Not merely to extract your confession, not to punish you. Shall I tell you why we have brought you here? To cure you! To make you sane! Will you understand, Winston, that no one whom we bring to this place ever leaves our hands uncured? We are not interested in those stupid crimes that you have committed. The Party is not interested in the overt act: the thought is all we care about."[3]

It is of course fear—the terrifying contents of Room 101—that ultimately causes Winston to succumb. He ends up genuinely believing that if Big Brother says that two plus two equals five, then two plus two *does* equal five. Many real regimes have been prepared to employ similarly brutal methods to control what goes on in people's minds. But emotional manipulation can take much milder forms yet still be effective. For example, you might harness the emotional power of iconic music and imagery. Ensure people are regularly confronted by portraits of Our Leader accompanied by smiling children and sunbeams emanating from his head (those Baghdad murals of Saddam Hussein spring to mind). Ensure your opponents and critics are always portrayed accompanied by images of catastrophe and suffering, and perhaps even Hieronymus Bosch–like visions of hell. Make people emotionally dependent on your belief system. Ensure that what self-esteem and sense of meaning, purpose, and belonging they have is derived as far as possible from their belonging to your system of belief. Make sure they recognize that abandoning those beliefs will involve the loss of things about which they care deeply.

It goes without saying that these five mechanisms of thought control are popular with various totalitarian regimes. They are also a staple of many extreme religious cults.

Applied determinedly and systematically, these mechanisms can be highly effective in shaping belief and suppressing "unacceptable" lines of thought. They are particularly potent when applied to children and young adults, whose critical defenses are weak, and who have a sponge-like tendency to accept whatever they are told.

Note that traditional, mainstream religious education has sometimes also involved heavy reliance on many, sometimes all, of these five mechanisms. I was struck by a story a colleague once told me that, as a teenage pupil of a rather strict Catholic school in the 1960s, she once put up her hand in class to ask why contraception was wrong. She was immediately sent to the headmaster, who asked her why she was obsessed with sex. Interestingly, my colleague added that, even before she asked the question, she knew she shouldn't. While never explicitly saying so, her school and wider Catholic community had managed to convey to her that asking such a question was unacceptable. Her role was not to think and question but passively to accept. My colleague added that, even today, nearly half a century later, despite the fact that she no longer has any religious conviction, she still finds herself feeling guilty if she dares to question a Catholic belief. So effective was her religious upbringing in straitjacketing her thought that she still feels *instinctively* that to do so is to commit a thought crime.

Of course, religious education doesn't have to be like this. Often it isn't. An open, questioning attitude can be encouraged rather than suppressed. Still, it's clear that some mainstream religions have historically been very reliant upon such techniques so far as the transmission of the faith from one generation to the next is concerned. In some places, they still are.

BRAINWASHING

Applied in a consistent and systematic fashion, these five techniques add up to what many would call "brainwashing." Kathleen Taylor, a research scientist in physiology at the University of Oxford, upon whose work I am partly drawing here, has published a book on brainwashing. In an associated newspaper article, Taylor writes:

> One striking fact about brainwashing is its consistency. Whether the context is a prisoner of war camp, a cult's headquarters or a radical mosque, five core techniques keep cropping up: isolation, control, uncertainty, repetition and emotional manipulation.[4]

Taylor adds that within the discipline of psychology, *brainwashing* is an increasingly superfluous word. It can be a misleading term, associated as it is with *Manchurian Candidate*–type stories of seemingly ordinary members of the public transformed into presidential assassins on hearing a trigger phrase. As Taylor says, that kind of brainwashing is a myth. Case studies suggest there is

> no "magic" process called "brainwashing," though many (including the U.S. government) have spent time and money

looking for such a process. Rather the studies suggest that brainwashing . . . is best regarded as a collective noun for various, increasingly well-understood techniques of non-consensual mind-change.[5]

THE UNWITTING AND WELL-INTENTIONED BRAINWASHER

Often, those who use such techniques are despicable people with the evil aim of enslaving minds. Edward Hunter, the CIA operative who coined the phrase back in 1950, characterized brainwashing in emotive terms:

> The intent is to change a mind radically so that its owner becomes a living puppet—a human robot—without the atrocity being visible from the outside. The aim is to create a mechanism in flesh and blood, with new beliefs and new thought processes inserted into a captive body. What that amounts to is the search for a slave race that, unlike the slaves of olden times, can be trusted never to revolt, always to be amenable to orders, like an insect to its instincts.[6]

Perhaps this very often was the intent so far as the regimes of which Hunter had experience were concerned. However, the intent to produce mental slaves is not required for brainwashing. Sometimes those who apply these techniques genuinely believe themselves to be doing good. Their intention is not to enslave but to *free* their victims from evil and illusion (this is often true of religious brainwashers). Yet, despite the absence of any evil intent, heavy reliance on such techniques still adds up to brainwashing. Brainwashers can be good people with little or no awareness that brainwashing is, in reality, what they're engaged in.

THE CONSENTING VICTIM

In the second Taylor quotation above, Taylor says that brain-washing involves various techniques of *nonconsensual* mind change. That can't be quite right. Of course, prisoners of war don't usually consent to being brainwashed. But people can in principle consent. In one well-known thriller, the trained assassin at the heart of the film turns out to have agreed to be brainwashed. Surely the fact that he consented to have such techniques applied to him doesn't entail that he wasn't really brainwashed after all.

People do sometimes willingly submit themselves to brain-washing. They sign up to be brainwashed at a cult's training camp, say. Admittedly, they will not usually describe what they have signed up to as "brainwashing." As they see it, even while they are fully aware that the above techniques will be applied to them, they nevertheless suppose they are merely being "edu-cated"—being put through a process that will open up their minds and allow them to see the truth.

REASON VS. BRAINWASHING

So what *is* brainwashing, then, if it can even be consensual? What marks it out from other belief-shaping mechanisms if it can even be consensual? At this point, some readers might be wondering whether what I am calling "brainwashing" is really any different than any other educational method. Isn't the application of reason to persuade really just another form of thought control? Just another way of wielding power over the minds of others? So why shouldn't we favor brainwashing over reason? Particularly if no one is actually being coerced, threatened, or harmed?

In fact, there's at least one very obvious and important differ-ence between the use of reason to persuade and the use of these kinds of belief-shaping techniques. Reason is *truth sensitive*. It favors true beliefs over false beliefs. Try making a rational case for believing that New Jersey is populated with ant-people or that the earth's core is made of yogurt. Because these statements are false, you're not going to find it easy to believe them.

Reason functions, in effect, as a filter on false beliefs. It's not 100 percent reliable, of course—false beliefs can still get through. But it does tend to weed out false beliefs. There are innumerable beliefs out there that might end up lodging in your head, from the belief that Paris is the capital of France to the belief that the earth is ruled by alien lizard-people. Apply your filter of reason, and only those with a fair chance of being true will get through. Turn your filter off, and your head will soon fill up with nonsense.

And yet many belief systems do demand that we turn our filters off, at least when it comes to their own particular beliefs. In fact, those who turn their filters off—those whose minds have become entirely passive receptacles of the faith—are often held up by such belief systems as a shining example to others. Mindless, uncritical acceptance (or, as they would see it, a simple, trusting faith) is paraded as a badge of honor.

Reason is a double-edged sword. It does not favor the beliefs of the "educator" over those of the "pupil." It favors those beliefs that are true. This means that if you try to use reason to try to bring others around to your way of thinking, you run the risk that they may be able to demonstrate that it is actually you who's mistaken. That's a risk that some "educators" aren't prepared to take.

The contrast between the use of reason to persuade and the use of the kind of belief-shaping mechanisms outlined above is obvious. You can use emotional manipulation, peer pressure, censorship, and so on to induce beliefs that happen to be true. But they can just as effectively be used to induce the belief that Big Brother loves you, that there are fairies at the bottom of the garden, and that the earth's core is made of yogurt. Such techniques do indeed favor the beliefs of the "educator" over those of the "pupil," which is precisely why those "educators" who suspect they may end up losing the argument tend to favor them.

I call the application of such non-truth-sensitive belief-producing methods *Pressing Your Buttons*. Brainwashing involves the systematic and dedicated application of such button-pressing techniques.

A MATTER OF DEGREE

Of course, to some extent, we can't avoid pressing the buttons of others. Nor can we entirely avoid having our own buttons pressed. The fact is, our beliefs are often shaped by such non-truth-sensitive mechanisms. No doubt we flatter ourselves about just how "rational" we really are. And, like it or not, you will inevitably influence the beliefs of others by such means too.

For example, my own children's beliefs are undoubtedly shaped by the kind of peer group to which I introduce them, by their desire to want to please (or perhaps annoy) me, by the range of different beliefs to which I have given them access at home, and so on. But of course, that's not yet to say I'm guilty of brainwashing my children. The extent to which we shape the beliefs of others by pressing their buttons, rather than by relying on rational means, is a matter of degree. There's a sliding scale of reliance on non-truth-sensitive mechanisms, with brainwashing located at the far end of the scale. There's clearly a world of difference between, on the one hand, the parent who tries to give her child access to a wide range of religious and political points of views; who encourages her child to think, question, and value reason; and who allows her child to befriend children with different beliefs; and, on the other hand, the parent who deliberately isolates her child, who ensures her child has access only to ideas of which the parent approves, who demands formal recitation of certain beliefs, who allows her child to befriend children who share the same beliefs, and so on.

THE DEHUMANIZING EFFECT OF BUTTON PRESSING

We have seen that one key difference between relying on reason to influence the beliefs of others and relying on button pressing is that only the former is sensitive to truth. Button pressing can as easily be used to induce false or even downright ridiculous beliefs as it can be used to induce true beliefs.

There is also a second important difference worth noting. As philosopher Immanuel Kant observed, when you rely on reason to try to influence the beliefs of others, you respect their freedom to make (or fail to make) a rational decision. When you resort to pressing their buttons on the other hand, you are, in effect, stripping them of that freedom. Your subject might think they've made a free and rational decision, but the truth is they're your puppet—you're pulling their strings. By resorting to button pressing—peer pressure, emotional manipulation, repetition, and so on—you are, in effect, treating them as just one more bit of the causally manipulatable natural order—as mere *things*. The button-pressing approach is, in essence, a dehumanizing approach.

CONCLUSION

Clearly, a cult that employs full-blown brainwashing at a training camp is a matter of serious concern. If the beliefs it induces are pernicious—if, for example, followers are being lured into terrorism—then obviously we should alarmed. However, even if the beliefs induced happen to be benign, there's still cause for concern.

One reason we should be concerned is the *potential* hazard such mindless and uncritical followers pose. They may as well have cotton wool in their ears so far as the ideas and arguments of nonbelievers are concerned. They are immune to reason. Trapped inside an Intellectual Black Hole, they are now largely at the mercy of those who control the ideas at its core. The dangers this poses are obvious.

Such extreme examples of brainwashing are comparatively rare. Still, even if not engaged in full-blown brainwashing, if the promoters of a belief system come increasingly to rely on button pressing to shape the beliefs of others, that, too, is a cause for concern. The more we rely on button pressing, the less sensitive to reason and truth our beliefs become.

Conclusion

Intellectual Black Holes are belief systems able to suck people in and hold them intellectual prisoner. Their captivating character does not depend on the beliefs at their core being either reasonable or true. In this book, I have set out eight key mechanisms that contribute to the seductive nature of such belief systems. I'll now close by illustrating how these eight mechanisms can be combined in different ways to produce different kinds of Intellectual Black Hole.

The eight mechanisms are as follows:

1. *Playing the Mystery Card* involves immunizing your beliefs against refutation by making *unjustified appeals to mystery*. For example, deal with any scientific evidence against your paranormal beliefs by insisting, without justification, that what you believe is "beyond the ability of science to decide."

2. *"But It Fits!"* involves *coming up with ways of making evidence and theory "fit" after all.* As we have seen, any theory, no matter how absurd, can be made *consistent* with the evidence (even Dave's theory that dogs are Venusian spies).

3. *Going Nuclear* involves *exploding a skeptical or relativist*

philosophical argument that appears to bring all beliefs down to the same level, rationally speaking. You can thereby *force a draw* in any debate. Then, once the threat has receded, the skepticism/relativism may be conveniently forgotten.

4. *Moving the Semantic Goalposts* involves dodging possible refutations by *switching back and forth between meanings* (between effable and ineffable meanings, for example).

5. *"I Just Know!"* involves suggesting that the truth of your belief has somehow been revealed to you, by, for example, some sort of a psychic or god-sensing faculty (this suggestion is unreasonable if you are aware of grounds for supposing that at least a large proportion of these supposedly revelatory experiences are, in fact, delusional).

6. *Pseudoprofundity* is the *art of making the trite, false, or nonsensical appear both true and deep*. Various linguistic recipes are able to create the illusion that you have achieved some sort of profound insight into the human condition.

7. *Piling Up the Anecdotes*. Anecdotes are in most cases almost entirely worthless as evidence, particularly in support of supernatural claims. But they can be highly persuasive, especially when collected together.

8. *Pressing Your Buttons* involves reliance on certain kinds of non-truth-sensitive techniques for shaping belief, such those I termed *isolation, control, uncertainty, repetition,* and *emotional manipulation*. These techniques are a mainstay of the "educational" programs of many cults and totalitarian regimes. Applied in a consistent and systematic way, they amount to brainwashing.

The table on page 211 is based on my impression of how these various strategies tend to be applied to different areas of belief. I have checked boxes where I believe a significant number of people holding those kinds of beliefs tend to rely fairly heavily on those kinds of strategies in convincing themselves and others that what they believe is reasonable, or at the very least not unreasonable.

The table is meant only to be indicative. We can argue about the details. Perhaps you think certain boxes should be checked

	Playing the Mystery Card	"But It Fits!" and The Blunderbuss	Going Nuclear	Moving the Semantic Goalposts	"I Just Know!"	Pseudo-profundity	Piling Up the Anecdotes	Pressing Your Buttons
Homeopathy	X						X	
Conspiracy theories/alternative histories	X	X					X	
Alien abduction	X				X		X	
Self-Help blather		X				X	X	
Psychic powers and angelic visitation	X		X		X		X	
Prophecies of Nostradamus		X				X	X	
Political/economic theories		X					X	X
A certain sort of "sophisticated" theology	X		X	X	X	X		
My evangelical friend's beliefs	X		X		X		X	X

that I have left blank, or other boxes should be unchecked. I'm open to persuasion on that front. Many other beliefs might be added, of course.

Notice that the extent to which a belief system qualifies as an Intellectual Black Hole is not determined by the *number* of boxes checked. Young Earth Creationism is surely an Intellectual Black Hole, despite the fact that its proponents rely primarily on just one strategy, *"But It Fits!"* (combined with *The Blunderbuss*). The reason Young Earth Creationism qualifies as an Intellectual Black Hole is that, while it may check only one or two boxes, its proponents typically rely very heavily on those strategies to generate an impression of "reasonableness" and convince themselves that what they believe is true.

As I mentioned in the introduction, I'm not primarily concerned with judging the content of the belief systems in question here (though in many cases, it's clear what I think). Whether or not some people have psychic powers, whether or not 9/11 was the result of a government conspiracy, whether or not homeopathy works, and whether or not any particular religion is true is not the issue.

Nor am I claiming that there may not be perfectly good reasons for holding at least some of the beliefs we have examined. Argue, if you like, that homeopathy really does work, that a particular political belief is correct or that a particular religion is true. What I'm pointing out is the extent to which *many* (if not all) of those holding these kinds of belief tend to rely on these kinds of strategy in order to generate an impression of "reasonableness" and convince themselves that they're true. If you believe in the efficacy of homeopathy, and you do so because you have good, nonanecdotal evidence that it works, that's fine—I'm not suggesting that you're the victim of an Intellectual Black Hole. However, to the extent that you find yourself relying very heavily on one or more of these strategies in order to convince yourself and others that what you believe is both reasonable and true, you should be concerned.

THE EXAMPLES

Let's go through my nine examples.

Homeopathy

As we saw in *Piling Up the Anecdotes*, those who believe in the efficacy of homeopathy typically rely heavily on anecdotal evidence to create the impression that what they believe is reasonable. However, they also tend to *Play the Mystery Card*. That's because there's a puzzle about how homeopathy could possibly work, given that it involves diluting substances to such a degree that there's not even a molecule of the supposedly active ingredient left. In other words, what homeopaths are prescribing is, quite literally, just water (or a drop of water in a sugar pill). In which case, how can homeopathic remedies possibly have any genuinely medicinal effect? Homeopaths usually admit they don't know. "But still," they'll say, "homeopathy *works*, so there must be *some* mysterious mechanism in play." They remind us that there are, after all, "more things in heaven and earth."

In fact, were there some solid evidence that homeopathy worked, putting its effectiveness down to some as-yet-unknown mechanism would not be so very unreasonable. However, there appears to be no such evidence. While other devices may also come into play, it's primarily *Piling Up the Anecdotes* and *Playing the Mystery Card* that do most of the work in transforming homeopathy into what can be, for at least *some* of its practitioners, an Intellectual Black Hole.

Conspiracy Theories/Alternative Histories

If you want to create and promote your own conspiracy theory or alternative history, here's a simple recipe you might follow. First, identify some intriguing mystery to which you might provide the "solution." In fact it doesn't matter whether it's a genuine mystery (perhaps scientists solved it long ago). It is enough that many people find what you offer to explain intuitively baffling.

Second, produce your own explanation. The suggestion that mysterious unseen agents with extraordinary powers are involved is likely to go down well, given our natural tendency, noted in the introduction, to switch to such an agent-based explanation when other explanations aren't available.

For example, someone noting the striking way in which the twin towers of the World Trade Center collapsed (vertically, with puffs of smoke appearing below the collapsing structure, as in a demolition), might claim they were actually brought down by explosive charges set by a secret cabal of government conspirators. Or, like the alternative-science historian Erich von Däniken (author of *Chariots of the Gods?*),[1] explains the extraordinary architectural achievements of ancient civilizations, such as the Mayan temples or the Great Pyramid of Giza, by suggesting these ancient people were aided by advanced extraterrestrial visitors. Use your imagination. You shouldn't find it too difficult to bestow upon your mysterious agents whatever extraordinary powers they'll need to get the job done. It's particularly easy if they're advanced aliens or supernaturally gifted beings of some sort.

Of course, the criticisms will come. Many will be skeptical about the role of the mysterious agents you've invoked. Deal with such criticisms by using a combination of *"But It Fits!"* and *Playing the Mystery Card*. Suppose critics point out that alien civilizations based around other stars would be too far away to make regular trips back and forth to the earth to help ancient civilizations with their construction projects. The journey would take too long, even at the speed of light (the maximum speed limit of the universe). In response, say the aliens must have developed mysterious technology beyond our comprehension that somehow allows them to travel faster than light. Or suggest that they are really time travelers from the earth's future, and/or that they live inside the earth itself, perhaps coming and going through holes at the poles (if it's pointed out there are no such

use your imagination to make it fit.

holes, you might insist, as some have, that the photographic and *haha* other evidence has been removed by government conspirators).

You can also empty *The Blunderbuss* at your critics—firing off numerous genuine but irrelevant or invented "problems" for more orthodox theories to cope with. Let off enough salvos in quick succession, and your critics will soon start to struggle. There is all sorts of information and misinformation about the destruction of the World Trade Center that might provide you with ammunition—from (false) reports of some of the hijackers later being found alive to (false) reports that many Jewish people failed to show up for work at the WTC that day, to dubious footage of one of the airliners with mysterious "pods" attached. Trot out a long series of such "problems," saying: "Explain *this*, and *this*, and *this*!" and your critics will find themselves either hopelessly bogged down or else, if they refuse to deal with them, looking evasive.

You might further bolster your theory by trawling around for anecdotal and other "evidence" to support your theory. For example, von Däniken points out how the figures in some ancient carvings look a bit like they are wearing space helmets (of course, plow through enough ancient imagery, and you'll probably be able to "discover" all sorts of other "alien" paraphernalia), and that some ancient images such as the Nazca Lines in Peru can only be seen from the air and so were probably made for the benefit of passing aliens (never mind that there are other more prosaic explanations for these images, such as that they were designed to be seen by gods). Von Däniken also interprets some ancient texts as referring to alien astronauts, claiming, for example, that Ezekiel's revelation in the Old Testament is a detailed description of a landing spacecraft. Mixing in further tall tales about UFOs and alien abduction may help lend further credibility to your ancient astronaut theory. Dig around, and you should be able to amass a significant quantity of other supporting "evidence." The Internet is awash with it. If you are really stuck, you can, of course, just make some up.

Alien Abduction

really? *Source?* According to some surveys, up to 6 percent of US citizens believe they have been abducted by aliens. Victims are often taken while in bed. Many are supposedly subjected to peculiar medical examinations. Some abductions involve a sexual dimension.

There are reasons to be suspicious about such reports. Some sound very much like the phenomenon known as sleep paralysis, which people have been reporting for centuries (though the little creatures that they report vary from culture to culture). In "*I Just Know!*" we saw that religious experiences tend to be highly culturally specific and also contradictory. The same is true of alien abduction experiences. Just like religious experiences, abduction experiences tend to halt at certain culturally significant national borders. And what gets reported also seems to a very large extent to be shaped by the power of suggestion—the kind of "aliens" tending to reflect what people expect aliens to look like. The abduction reports also tend to contradict each other to some extent (though this can partly be put down to our being visited by lots of different kinds of aliens).

Consider, for example, the 1961 case of Betty and Barney Hill, the first widely reported abduction case. In 1964 the Hills were interviewed independently and while under hypnosis about their experience. Barney's unusual description of the aliens having "wraparound eyes" and speaking with their eyes using "thought transference" was remarkably similar to characteristics of the aliens shown on an episode of the TV show *Outer Limits* just twelve days prior to his interview (moreover, Barney never previously mentioned these peculiar details during the previous three years). In addition, despite being involved in the same encounter, Betty's description of the aliens differed from Barney's—her aliens had no hair or noses. These and various other features of their accounts strongly suggest that, while Betty's and Barney's reports were almost certainly sincere, they did not, in fact, have any sort of genuine extraterrestrial encounter.

Given that the evidence for alien abduction is so poor, why are so many people convinced that it is a real phenomenon? Typically, they are persuaded by two things: in some cases, by personal experience. They say, in effect: *"I just know* I was abducted."* However, given there are excellent reasons for supposing that, even while entirely convincing, very many of these experiences aren't genuine, surely someone who believes they've had such an experience themselves ought not to take their experience entirely at face value. Second, people are often also convinced by *Piling Up the Anecdotes*—by the combined testimony of various supposed abductees, such as that of the Hills. Objections to belief in alien abduction, such as that surely any alien civilization would be too far away to travel here on a regular basis, tend to be dealt with by *Playing the Mystery Card* (see above). So three mechanisms in particular—*"I Just Know!" Piling Up the Anecdotes*, and *Playing the Mystery Card*—combine to transform belief in alien abduction into something like an Intellectual Black Hole.

Self-Help Blather

Many books promise you THE SECRET—be it of success in dating, marketing, business, or life generally. The self-help industry is huge, its gurus filling auditoriums with people prepared to pay significant sums of money for their advice. There's often some value in what these self-styled experts say. However, as often as not, what the self-help "experts" are selling are little more than truisms padded with *Pseudoprofundity*. The impression that they possess THE SECRET is often bolstered by means of numerous testimonials from people who say that they followed the advice and now they are millionaires or happily married or whatever. That is to say, sellers of THE SECRET tend to rely heavily on *Piling Up the Anecdotes* to generate the impression that there's good evidence to back up their claims. Cases in which THE SECRET hasn't actually been successful are typically either ignored or explained away using *"But It Fits!"* (if Bert lost a fortune after applying the techniques described in "The Secret of Gambling Success," then that's because he didn't follow the instructions properly).

Other mechanisms may also come into play in selling THE SECRET, including *Pressing Your Buttons*. Those who have paid to hear about THE SECRET firsthand in an auditorium may find themselves on the receiving end of various forms of psychological manipulation. Indeed, such events often have a "cult" feel.

As a result of the combined effects of *Pseudoprofundity*, *Piling Up the Anecdotes*, *"But It Fits!"* and *Pressing Your Buttons*, it may seem to those walking out of an auditorium after a rousing performance from the seller of THE SECRET that their eyes have now been opened. They can now just "see" how things *really* are. Everything "fits"! They have achieved The Vision Thing. In reality, of course, they've just been sucked into an Intellectual Black Hole.

Psychic Powers and Angelic Visitation

Those who believe in the abilities of psychics, when asked why this is a reasonable thing for them to believe, typically rely heavily on *Piling Up the Anecdotes*. When asked for evidence, they'll say they were just thinking about so-and-so when the phone rang and it was them, that Psychic Sue told them all sorts of things she could not possibly have known if she wasn't psychic, and so on. When, in reply, it's pointed out that there's no solid, nonanecdotal evidence to support belief in any genuine psychic ability, defenders often *Play the Mystery Card*, saying "there are more things in heaven and earth." As we saw in *Going Nuclear*, those who believe in psychic powers sometimes also press the nuclear button when their beliefs are challenged, either playing a general skeptical card or embracing relativism about truth (they may say, "That psychic abilities exist may not be true for you, but it's *true for me*.").

Claims of angelic visitation are currently popular. All sorts of people insist they have been helped by an angelic presence. You can even receive lessons on how to summon your own angel. Again, these beliefs are usually propped up by a combination of *Piling Up the Anecdotes* and *"I Just Know!"* Books on angelic visitation are for the most part just large collections of anecdotes. Of course, *Playing the Mystery Card* and *Going Nuclear* can crop up too. Róisín Ingle concludes her interview with Lorna Byrne, author of *Angels in My Hair*, in the *Irish Times* by coming close to doing both:

> Spending time with [Lorna Byrne] is both challenging and inspirational. I say goodbye reluctantly and all the way home I keep thinking about that Hamlet quote, that there's "more things in heaven and earth, Horatio, than are dreamt of in your philosophy." Is Lorna Byrne telling the truth? Well, she's telling her truth. It may or may not be yours.[2]

Prophecies of Nostradamus

This sixteenth-century apothecary published collections of prophecies, which, many believe, accurately predict important world events, including the Great Fire of London, the rise of Hitler, the *Challenger* space shuttle disaster, and the destruction of the World Trade Center.

Here is one of Nostradamus's best-known "predictions":

> In the year of the new century and nine months, from the sky will come a great King of Terror. In the city of York there will be a great collapse; two twin brothers torn apart by chaos while the fortress falls; the great leader will succumb; third big war will begin when the big city is burning.

In fact, this is a hoax (exposed by magician and skeptic James Randi). The passage does not exist anywhere in the writings of Nostradamus. An actual passage from Nostradamus (note the similar first two lines) that does supposedly accurately predict the future is this:

> The year 1999 seven months from the sky will come the great King of Terror to resuscitate the great king of the Mongols. Before and after Mars reigns by good luck.

So what does this predict? As Robert T. Carroll at the online *Skeptic's Dictionary* points out:

> Nobody, not even the most fanatical of Nostradamus's disciples, had a clue what this passage might have meant before July 1999. However, after John F. Kennedy Jr., his wife Carolyn Bessette and her sister Lauren Bessette, were killed in a plane crash on July 18, 1999, the retroprophets shoehorned the event to the "prophecy." Here is just one example culled from the Internet: "Could the crash of John F. Kennedy Jr.'s airplane in July of 1999 fulfill the line 'from the sky will come the great King of Terror'? Could the human fear of death and bodily injury be the intended definition of 'the great King of Terror'? It might be possible." "It might be possible"—now *there* is a precise bit of terminology. Other disciples were generous enough to think that Nostradamus was referring to a solar eclipse that would occur on August 11, 1999. Others feared a NASA space probe would come crashing down on earth.[3]

Another famous Nostradamus prediction, supposedly about the rise of Hitler, actually turns out to be about Hister—the Latin name for the Danube River. By switching an "s" for "l," and flipping the letters, Nostradamus's contemporary interpreters were again able to demonstrate his amazing predictive powers.

What rarely happens, of course, is that someone is able to predict some major event *before it occurs*. Plenty of such predictions are made in the many books published about Nostradamus. Check a volume printed several years ago, and you'll find its predictions rarely come true. For example, one 1980 volume predicts war in 1999 between China and a Soviet-American alliance; another says prominently on its back cover "1992—George Bush re-elected."[4] Bush lost.

So how are people able to convince themselves that Nostradamus could accurately predict the future? Primarily, by means of *"But It Fits!"* Nostradamus's writing is so vague and woolly (see the example above), that it is not difficult to come up with a reading on which the passage turns out to have "come true." Whatever happens can, with a little ingenuity, be "predicted."

Piling Up the Anecdotes also plays a role. We should expect a few of the countless clear and concrete predictions made by commentators on Nostradamus's writings to come true by chance. One or two "hits" among the hundreds of misses is likely anyway, whether or not Nostradamus had any real predictive gift.

Pseudoprofundity also helps to contribute to the impression that Nostradamus should be taken seriously. The fact that he wrote in such a bombastic manner lends his writing an air of profundity and portentousness it doesn't deserve.

Political/Economic Theory

Have a particular political or economic theory you want to promote? Anecdotal evidence for your favored theory, whatever it happens to be, can almost certainly be found. Believe tax cuts for the rich help raise the income of the poor? Just dig up one or two cases where tax cuts for the rich were followed by the poor becoming richer and voilà! by the power of *Piling Up the Anecdotes* your case is "proved"! Believe tax cuts for the rich make the poor poorer? Again, no problem. You'll no doubt be able to find some cases that "prove" your theory. But what if you claim tax cuts for the rich make the poor richer, and someone points out cases where this did not happen? Just explain such counterexamples away using *"But It Fits!"*

None of this is to say that political or economic theories are never reasonable, of course. No doubt some are. But if you want your belief in such a theory to be genuinely reasonable, you had better not make it too reliant on anecdotal evidence and *"But It Fits!"*

Notice that an unscrupulous media mogul who wanted to promote a particular economic or political theory might fill his programs and publications with supporting anecdotes (the more emotive, the better) and have his pundits employ *"But It Fits!"* to deal with any apparent counterexamples. They could also use all sorts of button-pressing techniques to shape the belief of viewers and readers, employing emotional manipulation, censorship, uncertainty, and so on. Audiences on the receiving end of relentless programming of this sort might well end up achieving The Vision Thing: they'll suppose they can *just see* what's *really* going on, and that everyone is either a victim or perpetrator of some dark conspiracy to hide the truth.

The truth, of course, is that such passionately committed audiences will be among the least knowledgeable, not the most. They're also likely to be extremely hard to reach, rationally speaking. Such political and economic "true believers" have fallen victim to a particularly insidious, media-generated form of Intellectual Black Hole.

A Certain Sort of "Sophisticated" Theology

Plenty of religiously minded theologians are content to adopt an intellectually honest and rigorous approach when discussing religious matters. However, there is a minority of theists who, when presented with any sort of intellectual challenge to their faith, tend to rely heavily on *Playing the Mystery Card*, *Going Nuclear*, *"I Just Know!"* and above all, *Moving the Semantic Goalposts* to neutralize the threat. Criticize what they believe, and they'll accuse you of being arrogantly wedded to scientism and remind you "there are more things in heaven and earth." Persist, and they'll say, in a condescending tone, "Ah, I'm afraid you are guilty of a crude misunderstanding." Either that, or they'll *Go Nuclear*, insisting (probably without even bothering to explain why) that "atheism is a faith position too." Ask them what they *do* believe, and they'll spout *Pseudoprofundity*, reveling in the obscure, opaque, and contradictory. Ask for further clarification, and you'll be told that what they believe is ultimately ineffable, or that religious language is not used to make claims that might be refuted. And yet, come Sunday morning, there they are at the pulpit, saying a great deal of literal-sounding stuff about, say, God, Jesus, and the Resurrection, without providing their congregations the slightest clue that they (so they told *you*) don't believe a word of it, literally understood. What such Theists offer, in truth, is not intellectual sophistication but intellectual sleight of hand. Whether or not their particular religious beliefs are true (whatever their beliefs are, exactly—who can be sure?), they have succeeded in transforming them into an Intellectual Black Hole.

My Evangelical Friend's Beliefs

A friend of mine (not a particularly close one, but I do count her as a friend) believes in the inerrancy of the Bible. She believes it is all absolutely and literally true. Every last word. My friend is, of course, a Young Earth Creationist. Not surprisingly, when I question her about Young Earth Creationism, she relies heavily on *"But It Fits!"* to defend her position. She has also acquired a great deal of ammunition for *The Blunderbuss*—firing off all sorts of irrelevant or invented "problems" for me to deal with. Setting her Young Earth Creationism to one side, my friend's religious convictions are defended more generally by *Playing the Mystery Card*—she constantly reminds me there are "more things in heaven and earth." She says I should show a little humility (ironic, given she is the one claiming certainty). She also appeals regularly to her own religious experience. If I raise objections to some aspect of her belief, she often responds by saying she *just knows* in her heart that the Bible is all literally true and that Jesus is her savior (and she insists I would know this too if I wasn't blinded by sin). Sometimes my friend also points to the miraculous healings she has received as conclusive proof that what she believes is true. She claims she was unable to have children, but then received a miracle pregnancy. She also insists that she used to have a minor physical disability that was instantly cured at a religious event. This is, of course, all anecdotal evidence. I strongly suspect, given what my friend says about her conversion (she was dramatically "born again") that she was, and continues to be, subject to quite a bit of *Pressing Your Buttons*, though I can't be sure.

*   *   *

That completes my nine examples. Of course, they are just examples. My hope is that this "spotter's guide" to Intellectual Black Holes will help readers to both spot other examples when they come across them.

We have a duty to our children to ensure that they have at least some immunity to the kind of intellectual snake oil identified in this book. When some smiling, wide-eyed true believer presses a leaflet into our son's or daughter's hand as they walk down the street, how confident can we be that they won't end up suckered into some ridiculous, financially exploitative, and possibly even downright sinister belief system by people employing the kinds of techniques outlined here?

If we want to immunize the next generation against such bullshit, let's at least make sure they understand the warning signs.

The Tapescrew Letters

Letters from a Senior to a Junior Guru

(Inspired by C. S. Lewis's *The Screwtape Letters*.)

PREFACE

I have no intention of explaining how the correspondence that I now offer to the public fell into my hands. One or two details have been changed to save reputations, but the letters are substantially unrevised and intact.

Bear in mind that the author—an eminent guru within some minor, recently invented cult—is a charlatan, as are her colleagues. She cannot be trusted to tell the truth, not even to her nephew. Her views about mainstream religion—and Christianity in particular—are clearly cynical and no doubt unreliable. I leave you to judge what is true and what is not.

The letters contain few clues as to the specific teaching of the cult. There is a limited amount of jargon. "Glub" seems to be the name of some sort of deity or god, "Boogle," the name of some particularly evil and terrifying being, and "doob," a term that members of this cult use to refer to outsiders. Glub and Boogle may be two facets of a single cosmic being or two separate, competing beings involved in some sort of cosmic battle—it's hard to be sure.

Be warned—the letters make pretty depressing and sickening reading. Still, they do usefully reveal just how manipulative and scheming *some* people can be. Thank goodness such deliberate charlatans are few and far between.

Stephen Law
Oxford
August 19, 2010

The Bodgers Centre
Newcastle
January 2, 2008

My Dear Woodworm,

How pleased I was to hear of your graduation from our guru training college—and with a distinction too. Great things are expected of you, as I'm sure you've made aware. I see you have been assigned to one of our newest recruitment centres—in Oxford. That is also excellent news. There's plenty of fodder there. But you now need to prove yourself. And that is where I come in. As you know, our Leader prefers Juniors to be mentored by a Senior they know well. As I am your aunt, I have been asked to watch over you and provide assistance wherever I can.

I cannot be there in person, I'm afraid. We are having something of a crisis here at Bodgers—one of our Juniors was caught indulging in some questionable activity with a couple of young recruits, and we're having a hard time keeping a lid on it. It's all hands to the pump at Bodgers, at least for the next few months. Still, I can correspond with you and advise wherever I can. Just send me regular progress reports, if you will.

After your intensive training, you will be intimately acquainted with both our aims and methods. And you now possess your own copy of the *Handbook* (which, I need hardly add, you must guard with your life—it must *never* fall into the hands of a recruit). We have spent thousands of pounds and a year of our time honing your skills, so you won't be surprised to hear we now expect results.

Our aim is to ensnare human minds, to make them true and faithful servants of our teaching. Let me focus your attention on our Leader's opening remarks in the *Handbook*:

Our aim must be to instil in our patients such patterns of thought that their minds become wholly ours—so that they become impregnable fortresses to anyone else who might try to

*prise their way in. But we must do this while all the time main-
taining the illusion that these ways of thinking are perfectly
"rational" and "reasonable."*

Creating that illusion, Woodworm, is the clincher, the *real*
trick. We must make minds that are fortresses to those outside
and prisons to their occupants. We must forge minds in which we
have succeeded in entrenching such effective mental roadblocks
and self-perpetuating habits of thought that their owners will
never be able to think their way free again. For then they will be
our willing servants. But our "patients," as our Leader likes to
call them, must never suspect. The faithful must fall for the illusion that they are the ones whose minds have been set free and
that it is everyone else who remains mentally imprisoned!

To become the jailer of another's mind—what a prospect! An
impossible task? By no means. Difficult, yes. But armed with your
training, the *Handbook*, and a firm determination to succeed, let
me assure you that you *will* succeed! I have converted literally
hundreds of doobs over the last few years, and I am confident
that you will do better still.

Which brings me to our movement's current Achilles' heel,
and my sternest word of warning. As I say, the key to success lies
in maintaining an illusion—your patients must not suspect, not
even for a second, that you are deliberately deceiving and manip-
ulating them, that you intend to become their mental jailer. We
have one very obvious disadvantage compared to the promoters
of most other self-sealing bubbles of belief. We *know* we are
deceivers. We know exactly what we are doing as we pull our
patients' strings. Your local religious minister may use many of
the same techniques as you, but he really believes the doctrines he
promotes. He is quite convinced he is doing nothing more than
opening people's eyes to the truth—setting them free. Which
means he does not need to fake anything. His voice conveys real
warmth. His eyes glisten with genuine fervour. The same is true
of the political zealot peddling her leaflets on the street corner. At

least she believes the claptrap she peddles. She doesn't have to pretend.

We, the first generation of Followers, know that the beliefs we are selling are an ingenious fiction concocted by our Leader. While we plan that future generations will be sincere devotees, we, the First Wave, must unfortunately learn to fake that brand of misty-eyed enthusiasm. Take it from me, it's an illusion difficult to sustain for any length of time.

Knowing you as I do, I think this is what you will find most difficult, the challenge you will have to work hardest to overcome. As that unfortunate incident involving your father's car made clear, you are not a good liar. And you are prone to over-intellectualize. That might have proved an advantage in the academic world of our college, but out there in the real world, it produces pitfalls.

True, because we *know* we are deceivers, we have a great advantage over our sincere counterparts in other cults. We have studied the techniques necessary to enslave minds coldly and dispassionately—even *scientifically*—and have thus became far more knowledgeable and skillful than our competitors in their application. But do not underestimate the advantage our counterparts have over us—an advantage that will become quickly apparent to you as you embark on your first project. The truth is, it is only *later* that the intellectual traps and snares come into play. You will doubtless be eager to apply the bogus arguments, seductive fallacies, and other intellectual sleights of hand that you have mastered so well. But *patience, patience*! Take that route *too* quickly, and your victim will smell a rat.

The first step in ensnaring any mind is to focus on your patient's *emotions*. Emotion is the unlocked door on which we need only gently push to gain initial entry. Your patient must be seduced into feeling comfortable with you, liking you, admiring you. You must appear to exude warmth and compassion. You must seem to possess both depth and sincerity. You must be able to touch their sleeve, look into their eyes, and make that *special* connection. If they suspect, even for a second, that you're a fake, the game is up. Their critical defences will come crashing down, and your job will be one hundred times as hard. Fake sincerity—that's the thing. If only we could bottle it.

Here's my suggestion. Focus on one patient to begin with. That's a far more effective way of sharpening your technique. But how to find your first recruit?

My advice is to join some clubs: chess, model making, hiking, dance, acting, that sort of thing. It doesn't matter what, just so long as there's plenty of opportunity for one-to-one or small group chat. Strike up conversations with people in cafés and bars. Keep returning to the same places, so that you become a familiar presence. Slowly, you will build a circle of acquaintances. Appear confident and positive. Be fun to be around. And remember—no mumbling into your coffee. Be direct. Above all, *make eye contact*. Then, without appearing to pry, begin to ask them about themselves. They'll be more eager to tell than you might imagine. Slowly build up a picture of their emotional life, of their hopes and fears, of what they most care about. Pretend to open up to them, you'll find that they will then open up even more. The more they come to trust you, the more vulnerable to your wiles they will become. Then, slowly and carefully, begin to draw up your plans.

Good hunting!

Your affectionate aunt,
Tapescrew

The Bodgers Centre
Newcastle
March 4, 2008

Dear Woodworm,

My congratulations! You have assembled an impressive collection of "friends," built up a picture of their emotional vulnerabilities, and even selected your first patient. A thirty-two-year-old woman somewhat unhappy at work, few close friends, feeling a little lonely, still waiting, with increasing anxiety, for that "special someone" to come along and fill her life with love and meaning. She looks an excellent prospect. You have even let her half imagine that the special someone might be you!

The idea of the dinner party was a masterstroke, Woodworm. A small, intimate setting in which the conversation can be steered gently in the direction you desire without anyone becoming particularly suspicious. Just you, your patient, and two other Juniors playing the role of "friends." I have no idea why, but sharing food with someone always helps create a special bond. A little wine to lower the inhibitions, just the right questions asked, seemingly in a casual, offhand way: "Do you think that when you're dead, that's it?" I *particularly* approve of "I used to worry about where my life was headed."

You say your little fake confession of earlier torment caused a tear to appear in her eye. Luckily, you didn't overdo it. You gave just a hint that perhaps you had a deep secret, a source of inner contentment and security, of which she had managed to catch a momentary glimpse. And, once her curiosity was fired, *you* changed the subject, so she got not even a whiff of the fact that she's the fish on your hook. She was intrigued and left wanting to know more.

Most important of all, she left feeling good. She thought she'd communicated in a special way. She felt she had really been given a rare opportunity to address things that had been gnawing away at her. That feeling, Woodworm, that emotion you caused her to have, is our Archimedean point—the fulcrum on which our whole enterprise now turns.

In a few weeks, you will invite her to the Retreat. But not yet. I want to hear you have made real progress in the meantime. First, she must want to know more about that "inner strength" you seem to exude, that quiet certainty you have. Get her wondering where it comes from? If *she* could acquire it too? Leave clues. But no details just yet.

Why not? The truth is that the core beliefs of almost any cult or religion, if written down in unvarnished prose on the back of an envelope, will strike anyone unfamiliar with them as ridiculous. "You believe *that*?" they'll say, dumbfounded. "Why on earth do believe *that*?!"

That is precisely the reaction you'll get from this doob if you play your hand too soon. "If *only* . . ." I often find myself thinking. If *only* we had access to them when they are children, when their intellectual and emotional defences are so much weaker, while they exhibit such uncritical, sponge-like eagerness to accept whatever a grown-up tells them. One day, I hope, we will have our own schools. Portraits of *our* Leader will beam serenely down from *our* classroom walls. Each day will begin with the singing of one of *our* enervating anthems. The curriculum will devote time every day to the study of *our* Leader's inspiring words. Think of the opportunity such institutions will give us! But it's early days. We don't have them yet.

What such schools are after, of course, is usually *not*, as some of you novices seem to think, the opportunity to churn out mindless automata uncritically devoted to the cause. No, no. Desirable though that would be, it is an entirely unrealistic expectation given the unfortunate fact that the little darlings are exposed to so many rival ideas and pressures outside the school gates. Such ideas and pressures have a powerfully corrosive effect on those in which they're indoctrinated inside school.

No, it's impossible for a school to achieve a high degree of mindless acceptance without, say, the assistance of a family with very tight control over to whom their children speak and to what ideas they are exposed, a family that reinforces the indoctrination with further psychological manipulation both inside and outside the home, including subtle or not so subtle threats of complete social ostracism should the child ever leave the faith. This is the kind of assistance most faith schools don't have.

Today's post-Enlightenment, secular culture is wonderful in that it offers new movements such as our own a voice in the marketplace of ideas. It thus gives us a chance to enslave the minds of the unwitting. But, at the same time, it puts pressure on us to sign up to certain liberal ideals that are, in truth, a great obstacle to our mission—ideals such as that people should be encouraged to *think and question*, should make their *own* judgements, should *not* to be heavily psychologically manipulated as children, and so on. Which is why we have to pretend that we want only to give young people an "opportunity to explore their spiritual side" and other such nonsense.

Mindless followers are, I repeat, *not* what the schools of the mainstream religions usually aim for (though some do). They aim merely to till the soil and sow the seeds of faith, seeds that they hope may one day bloom.

Here's the *real* secret, Woodworm—gain access to the mind of a child, and you can apply *the anaesthetic of familiarity*, enough to last a lifetime. To a child, the barmy doesn't seem barmy. Get the child to feel that our beliefs are actually perfectly natural and sensible and then, when the child grows up, the harsh, barmy edges of doctrine will no longer stand out like a sore thumb. Our thoughts will seem comfortably familiar, particularly if they have been endlessly associated with powerful emotional experiences and rites of passage—weddings, funerals, bar mitzvahs, and so on. For such an adult, ludicrous beliefs no longer seem particularly ludicrous. In fact, such beliefs can feel like "coming home."

But I digress, Woodworm. Our own schools remain a fantasy for the time being. I mention them only to flag up a further advantage the mainstream religions have over us on the emotional front. Their schools may not churn out true believers. But they do produce minds that have at least been tilled and prepared, that are at least not entirely unreceptive to their doctrines. Indeed, their belief systems have in many cases successfully been woven into the fabric of the societies they occupy. To nonbelievers raised in such a society, accepting even a ludicrous set of beliefs can seem remarkably "natural."

The harsh edges of our nuttiest doctrines, by contrast, would be blindingly obvious to our patients to begin with, were we to reveal them—which is why you must keep them under wraps for the time being. Our patient is not yet ready. The emotional soil must first be tilled.

But it's not all bad news, Woodworm. We do have at least some advantages over many of our competitors. Remember that, unlike that of the mainstream religions, our own teaching will seem alien and exciting. While we lack the advantage of our patients having been previously anaesthetized to the utter barminess of what we teach, we do at least have the advantage that our doctrines, presented in the right way, can seem exotic and new.

So let's proceed slowly with your patient. Don't reveal too much. Otherwise the frankly ridiculous character of some of the beliefs we peddle will be detected and she'll be off. But we *do* want to convey a sense of the exciting and exotic.

Here's what I suggest. Randomly drop feel-good words like "peace," "contentment," "spiritual," and "moral," into your conversation rather more often than might be expected. Keep working on exuding that sense of inner strength and certainty that you have been faking so effectively. Radiate warmth. Touch her sleeve. Find some excuse to mention, seemingly only in passing, that you meditate. For goodness sake don't use the word "pray"—that's far too familiar and fuddy-duddy. "Meditate" will sound far more exotic, far more *mystical*, to her naive ears.

We want her to sense that there's something exhilaratingly *different* hidden away inside you—that provides you with a source of inner strength and contentment. Something that, perhaps, she could have too.

The questions will come. . . .

Your affectionate aunt,
Agatha Tapescrew

The Bodgers Centre
Newcastle
August 23, 2008

My Dear Woodworm,

Yes, as you say, she is hooked. She has heard you speak the name of our movement, and she has not flinched. Most importantly, she has agreed to accompany you to the Retreat to "explore her spiritual side." Fear not—our people at the Retreat know what they are doing.

The key, of course, is to produce a feeling. I once saw a bishop engaged in a debate on whether Jesus was "the way, the truth and the life." The bishop, along with a Christian philosopher, was up against a couple of atheists. The atheists were clearly getting the better of the argument, and many of the Christians in the audience were beginning to look uncomfortable. In one or two cases, doubt was creeping in. You could see it in their eyes.

The bishop, as last to speak, was masterful. He forgot about reason and argument and all the trappings of "winning" by intellectual means. He lowered his voice and appealed instead to personal experience—an experience relating to what he called "the meaning of life."

I've seen this done before, but the bishop was particularly good at it. He started with jokes, but then gradually began to speak more softly and with feeling. In our quietest moments, he said, each one of us—yes, even a cynical atheist—is aware, deep down, of a light. It's an awareness of something fundamentally good, of a yearning to be something better than we are. This something is . . .

. . . *Jesus*!

There was much sombre nodding from the Christian Union contingent. I noticed their eyes were now strangely lit up. When the bishop sat down, there was moment of quiet, reflective calm before the applause broke out.

Now, at the time, I made the dreadful mistake of thinking that the bishop had lost the debate. The arguments had all gone against him. Only much later did I realize that the bishop had won—spectacularly so, in fact. The truth is that the bishop was not out looking for new recruits that day. His real aim was to shore up the faith of waverers—to ensure that the application of reason didn't result in the raising of significant doubt. And in that he succeeded.

How? By invoking a *feeling*. It all begins with a feeling. No one really comes to sincere belief in religious doctrines on the basis of an argument. They come because of how they feel deep down inside.

Different cults rely on different feelings. Some focus on anger and resentment, others on feelings of helplessness, insignificance, or submission. But more often than not, the feelings that really do the trick are hope and, most importantly, joy.

The bishop reminded his Christian brethren of a feeling. It didn't really matter what it was. It could be a sense of loss or disappointment. Of a "hole" in their life. A sense of justice, or injustice. It might even be something as tacky and sentimental as "the strength to carry on" that Mariah Carey sings about in the song "Hero."

Of course, the Muslims and Jews in the audience had such feelings too. But when *they* looked deep inside, *they* found Allah, or Yahweh or whatever. And the atheists, puzzled, could find nothing more than a feeling. I could see them sitting there, scratching their heads, wondering what on earth the bishop was on about.

But of course the bishop wasn't interested in *them*. His concern was with only the Christians in the audience. The bishop spoke softly and with sincerity and conjured up a feeling—and then reminded the assembled Christians of what *they* already knew in their hearts—that this inner light is Jesus. And why did this work? Because calling such feelings "Jesus" is such a familiar part of their cultural landscape. They have so often felt such feelings and had it suggested to them that they are experiencing Jesus, that, when they have such a feeling right now, well, that's just how it seems to them. They *know* it's Jesus. They can just *see* him there, deep down at the bottom of their soul, glimmering. Nothing could be more obvious to them.

That, my boy, is how the bishop won. At the Retreat, your patient will be isolated and disorientated. Her mind will be messed with. She will be taught a little about Glub. But, much more importantly, we will ensure that she has *feelings*. The fasting, music, chanting, incense, meditation, ritual, the sense of community, of belonging, of that special, felt connection with others that is so rare nowadays—all these things will combine to produce powerful and unusual feelings in her, particularly feelings of *hope*, and above all, *joy*. Then, when she is deep in a reverie of such emotion, you will take our patient by the hand, look deep into her eyes and say, in a calm, steady voice, "My dear, in your quietest moments you're aware of something, aren't you? You might try to deny it, but you know there's something down there, at the bottom of your soul, don't you? It's a light, isn't it? A small, still light. Can you see it there, glimmering, like the evening star? Look closer. . . . Closer still . . . See . . . ? Can you see what it is yet . . . ?

It's *Glub*, isn't it?"

And as she looks more and more closely, the recognition will finally break over her: "Oh, my gosh! Yes . . . yes. . . . it *really is Glub*!"

Once she knows through personal experience the truth and reality of Glub, she will very probably be ours forever. No mere *argument* will ever be able to loosen our grip on her. For whenever any such intellectual threat pops up, we need only gently remind her of what she already *knows* deep in her heart! When critics present her with rational challenges to her belief, she will quietly and confidently reply with the words of Blaise Pascal: "The heart has its reasons of which reason knows nothing."

Of course, I am simplifying. The recipe we cook up at the Retreat is a complex and heady brew into which is mixed many other important ingredients.

For example, the patient will be shown the good works our Followers do—the compassion they exhibit, helping out in their local community, providing food to the homeless, and so on. That will further lower her guard. "These are *good* people!" she will think. "So much *more* generous and caring than the people I have spent my life with up to now."

And then we will repeatedly ask her the question: "But what if this teaching were *true*? How *wonderful* would that be! What a prospect! And you have *nothing to lose*, do you? So *why not* make the bet? Why not at least *give it a try*? Go on, *take the plunge*!"

Chances are, she will take the plunge, particularly if she's surrounded by others whom she sees joyously jumping in. Who wants to be the sad, solitary frump standing at the poolside when everyone else is in there splashing about in delight? She'll jump. And then we're in!

But as, I say, it is above all the cultivation of the *feeling* that we must focus on. Without the feeling, she may only take a quick dip. What we require is a lifetime's immersion.

Your affectionate aunt,
Tapescrew

The Bodgers Centre
Newcastle
October 4, 2008

My Dear Woodworm,

Everything appears to be going swimmingly. The Retreat has worked its magic. Your patient has a new circle of friends and is becoming immersed in the new, structured lifestyle that we had created for her—the endless round of meditation classes, talks, socials, and so on.

As we planned, the patient believes she is finding value, meaning, and purpose within the social, intellectual, and moral framework into which she has now firmly been plugged. She has entered what must seem to her to be an enchanted garden. Of course, the enchantment will eventually wear off somewhat. She will begin to see that it's not *all* wonderful inside this cosy world we have created for her. Which is why we must now begin to cultivate another emotion: *fear*. Even if she comes to see that not everything inside the garden is entirely rosy, she must learn to fear what lies outside its walls. She must eventually become so emotionally dependent upon our garden that the prospect of leaving it must appear to her to be a truly terrible thing. While joy may be what brings them in, it is often fear that keeps them here. Our patient must feel that to leave would be to fall from the light back into darkness—into the cold, lonely, meaningless oblivion from which we have rescued her.

But now to a more specific concern of mine. You write in your last letter of how you have been *reasoning* with the patient, thereby convincing her of the truth of some of our doctrines. Well, you are a gifted and able thinker. I don't doubt that this naive doob, entirely untrained in philosophy and the dark arts of persuasion, is putty in your hands. But you are making a terrible mistake if you place too much emphasis there.

Don't misunderstand me. Yes, it is desirable that she believes reason is largely *consistent* with our doctrines, perhaps even supports our doctrines to *some* extent. But don't go beyond that. For then she may end up supposing our doctrines *rely* on reason for their acceptability.

Which, reading between the lines, seems to be precisely what you have been suggesting to her, you fool. Once she believes that it's *only* reasonable to believe such things because they *are* reasonable, well, then we are in big trouble. The next time some smart aleck doob comes along able to pick apart these dainty confections of intellectual bullshit you have been serving up to her, her faith will crumble in a minute!

You have been teaching her *unqualified respect for reason.* That is *not* the right attitude to instil. A better attitude is fear. She should *fear* applying reason, particularly on her own, unsupervised by an appropriate authority such as yourself who can set her back on track should she err. At the very least, she should made to feel uncomfortable or guilty about "going it alone" with reason.

I don't mean she should be concerned about applying reason *generally*, of course. There's no reason for her to think twice about applying reason when filling in her tax return, calculating how many tiles she needs for her bathroom, or any other mundane matter. There's no harm, either, in her respecting the role of reason in science. At least up to a point. But get her to acknowledge that there are *limits* to what reason can reveal. Quote Shakespeare at her—"There are more things in heaven and earth that are dreamt of in your philosophy, Horatio." That sort of thing. But also imply something further. Imply not just that reason *cannot* properly be applied beyond a certain boundary, but also that *it is wrong even to try.* It is *arrogant* and *sinful* to attempt to exercise reason and freedom of thought beyond a certain point.

Take a leaf out of this book written by these two Jewish scholars, for example:

> We have been commanded not to exercise freedom of thought
> to the point of holding views opposed to those expressed in the

Torah; rather, we must limit our thought by setting up a boundary where it must stop, and that boundary is the commandments and the instructions of the Torah. . . . if a person feels that the pursuit of a particular argument is seriously threatening his or her belief in what is clearly a cardinal principle of Judaism, there exists an obligation to take the intellectual equivalent of a cold shower.[1]

Note this idea of setting up a *boundary* in the patient's mind. She must feel that, as she approaches this boundary armed with reason, warning bells are going off and red lights are flashing. She must feel that reason, fine in everyday contexts, is downright dangerous when applied to matters of faith.

Remember those Bible Belt church signs that read "A freethinker is Satan's slave"? Preachers erect those signs to encourage the belief that, when it comes to thinking freely about matters of faith, Satan will be at our elbow in a moment, leading us away from the Truth. Such preachers want their followers to suppose that, when it comes to *their* religion (it doesn't matter about other religions, of course) a freethinker is a fool whose arrogance will lead him to hell. A simple, trusting faith must prevail.

True, we have no Satan or hell with which to threaten our Followers. But we do have the reverse side of Glub: Boogle. Talk about Boogle to her. But remember, fear works best when aimed at something hidden and mysterious. Once the monster in the sci-fi film is seen, its terrifying qualities are inevitably diminished. Monsters from your own Id are always far more terrifying. Boogle must remain a cipher in the shadows. Hint at the existence of Boogle, but be vague. That way, her imagination can take over. Boogle will become her own *Room 101*.

Actually, none of this is to say that the patient should suppose her powers of reason can *never* be applied to our doctrines. They can be used, but only *in the service of* those doctrines, to deepen our understanding of them, *not* to challenge them! Given the tiresome, post-Enlightenment respect for this overrated thing called "freedom of thought," people will eventually accuse us of thought control—"You want to enslave minds, even children's minds. You want to *turn off* their ability to think and reason." To this, we can truthfully, if very misleadingly, reply: "No, we *want* individuals to be able to reason and think well! In fact, we *encourage* them to question! Come along to one of our sessions, and you'll see." What we don't mention, of course, is *the boundary*: the boundary that we have set up in the minds of our Followers, the boundary that is marked by a sign that reads: "By all means think as freely and as often as you want, but up to here and *no further*!"

And of course, having officially signed up to the virtues of reason and freedom of thought, we have the perfect excuse to endlessly fire off at our opponents what our Leader describes as the *Blunderbuss*. "Look!" we can say to our new recruits as we let off salvo after salvo of irrelevant or invented "problems" at the unbelievers. "See how *they* struggle to answer *our* questions! Their respect for 'reason' is ironic, don't you think, when they cannot use it to answer us? You see, in the final analysis, both our belief systems are faith positions. Both require a leap of faith!"

Let our opponents try to dig themselves out from under *that* load of ordure.

Your affectionate aunt,
Tapescrew

The Bodgers Centre
Newcastle
February 12, 2009

Dear Woodworm,

Your last letter is a source of serious concern. Her brother is visiting for a week, you say. Bad news indeed. And not just because our patient will be reminded of positive features of her old life, her old habits, her old ways of thinking.

The brother is clearly aware that we're up to something. He is not a religious man. And he has been asking questions, you say. Questions rather more direct and to the point than we usually get.

This man clearly fails to pay the kind of respect that's usually accorded any sort of "spiritual belief." The impertinence. This is a critical time for us. Even now the patient could escape our clutches. The arrival on the scene of someone our patient clearly likes and respects, someone who treats our teaching as if it were just *a set of beliefs like any other*, could wreak havoc.

The brother must be disarmed. You say you have been invited round for dinner to meet him? Here is your opportunity.

As that first glass of wine is poured, he will probably say, ever so innocently, something like this: "So, *you* are the person that has introduced my sister to these new beliefs she has been telling me so much about?" If you are not forthcoming with any details, he will eventually follow this up with a series of simple, straightforward questions, apparently expecting straightforward answers.

Do not, under any circumstances, give them. Our patient is not yet so caught up in our mindset that she will be entirely immune to the patent absurdity that a succinct and unvarnished statement of our teaching is likely to reveal. Yes, we have cast our spell over her, but the magic has not yet fully set.

I suggest you employ the strategy that our Leader calls *Moving the Semantic Goalposts*. Turn to the *Handbook* and reread that section with care. Whenever the brother matter-of-factly asks, "So you believe *such-and-such*, do you?" Suggest, slightly condescendingly, that he has misunderstood our teaching. For example, you might say, "Oh, dear! You appear to have taken us literally. *That's* not what we mean." Do not, however, edify him. Do not tell him clearly and succinctly what we *do* mean. That's for us to know, and him to find out!

If he tries yet again, just continue to move the goalposts around some more, "Ah, I see you have *again* misunderstood." Perhaps add, "Of course, you must remember we are using the language of metaphor and analogy—it's rather foolish to take such language at face value, you know."

If he asks exactly what the analogy is, waffle. Use words like "spiritual," "transcendent" and "ultimate" a lot. Wave your arms around in a vague way and look up, as if you are have some profound insight and are searching for just the right words to convey it, but you can't quite succeed.

In this way, you can endlessly give the brother the runaround. True, in some contexts, that you are employing such a sleight of hand with words would quickly become clear. However, some things really are difficult to express properly, aren't they? Our subjective experiences, for example, can be difficult to articulate. How we feel about something can often be communicated to others only in a rather fumbling and imprecise way, which allows much scope for misunderstanding. There's no denying that saying, "Ah, but that's not quite what I meant," is *sometimes* an entirely reasonable response to a criticism.

Use this to your advantage. Your patient believes she has had an experience of the transcendent, of the "other." You must stress that our access to what lies beyond is inevitably restricted. We can at best catch only glimpses. It's all very much "through a glass darkly." Admit that it's hard to capture using our everyday vocabulary. And of course, because what she had was a *feeling*, it very probably *is* very hard for her to put it into words! So your excuse will look plausible.

If any picture you paint of what lies "beyond" is inevitably vague and impressionistic, then it will inevitably be vulnerable to misinterpretation. But then any criticism of what we teach about what lies beyond can conveniently be put down to some misunderstanding on the part of our opponents.

Indeed, try saying this: "You see, what we ultimately believe is ineffable, is beyond the ability of language to express."

Trust me—this works. I have applied this same wheeze over an extended period of time without it ever dawning on my opponents what I was really up to. Do the same!

A little character assassination can enhance the effectiveness of *Moving the Semantic Goalposts*. Remember to imply at every opportunity that her brother is being terribly crude and unsophisticated in his ham-fisted attempts to characterize and criticize what we believe. Notice I said "imply"! Your patient no doubt loves her brother and may not respond well to a direct accusation. So never *explicitly* accuse her brother of being an unsophisticated, unspiritual twit. Rather, adopt an air of calm intellectual and spiritual superiority. Be just a little bit condescending. But—and here's the key—even while adopting that air of superiority, it's important to keep reminding them both how terribly *humble* you are. Admit that you cannot articulate the essence of that in which you believe, that you are struggling vainly to express in mere human language what you nevertheless know in your heart to be true.

Your humility will be sure to impress the patient, and the contrast between your calmness and the brother's mounting anger and frustration as you endlessly shift the goalposts about will become more and more obvious to her. You will seem humble and open-minded. The brother will increasingly appear dogmatic, unspiritual, and, I very much hope, aggressive.

This exercise in character assassination will be nicely rounded off with a suggestion of arrogance—get the patient thinking that her brother is being arrogantly dismissive of things that *he doesn't even properly understand*. Remind them both that there are "more things in heaven and earth" than are dreamed of in *his* philosophy. Shouldn't her brother be showing a little humility?

Notice the delightful switcheroo we pull here. We are the ones claiming certainty, yet *we* end up appearing humble while he is portrayed as the arrogant know-it-all! You'll enjoy the delicious irony! But remember—don't be caught savouring it.

There is a second strategy that will also prove invaluable in dealing with the brother—the *Way of Questions*. Look it up in the *Handbook* and study it well. Don't let the brother be *your* interrogator. You must become *his*. For every question he asks you, ask him three back. Get him on the back foot.

Of course, you must not come across as inquisitorial. Pretend your questions are merely for "clarification"—you just want to understand more clearly where the brother is coming from, so you can properly address his concerns. But here's what you actually do: *hit him with a series of thorny philosophical puzzles with which he'll inevitably struggle*. I recommend two in particular:

1. Ask him why he supposes the universe exists. Why there is something rather than nothing.
2. Ask him how he is able to know right from wrong. How is he in a position to say that something truly heinous, such as slavery, is wrong? Or, better still, the Holocaust?

If the brother is an atheist or agnostic, he's not going to have pat answers to these Big Questions. As you will know from that training in moral and religious philosophy we gave you, there are awfully deep and difficult questions to which there are no simple, easy answers (one of the reasons we provided that training is precisely so you can use it to tie people like this irksome brother up in knots).

The fact is, we don't have good answers to these questions either. But we *pretend* we do. We say, *Glub* is the explanation for why there is anything at all. We say, *Glub* provides us with our moral compass in this otherwise treacherously uncertain and increasingly morally depraved world.

Our patient will be impressed by the fact that, while her

brother struggles with such tricky moral and metaphysical questions, we do not. We offer quiet, calm, simple certainty. As your patient looks back and forth between—on the one hand—your serene, wise, and confident expression and—on the other hand—the look of exasperation creeping across her brother's face as he struggles and fails to provide an adequate justification for condemning the Holocaust, your job will be more than half done. Indeed, the thought might even cross your patient's mind that her brother is *morally rudderless*!

Even if the brother manages to deal successfully with your first round of questions (which, he almost certainly won't), you can just ask another "clarificatory" question, and then another: "Ah, I see. But then let me ask you this. . . ." "Hmm, that's interesting, but what do you mean by. . . ." This will tie him up in knots, very probably leaving your patient with the impression that you are the winner in this little intellectual exchange. The truth, of course, is that you never dealt with *his* penetrating questions. But the chances are your patient won't even notice this or even remember what his questions were, after half an hour or so of the Way of Questions!

At the very least, if you combine these two techniques, the patient will be left with the impression that the debate between you and her brother is all square—that neither side can be said to have achieved a decisive victory. And that is all the space we need in which to operate.

Your affectionate aunt,
Tapescrew

The Bodgers Centre
Newcastle
June 28, 2009

Dear Woodworm,

I have not heard from you for a while. Gibbons tells me (yes, I have my spies in Oxford) that you haven't been into our Oxford centre much over the last few weeks. I very much hope that is because you are beavering away with your patient, whose brother, I anticipate, has now been dispatched?

Let us hope so. If you suspect the patient is having doubts, and if the other techniques I recommended are not proving effective enough to allay them, then let me share with some further thoughts passed on to a select group of us Seniors at one of our Leader's training sessions held in the South of France last week.

First of all, our Leader says he wants us to focus attention more on *morality*. He believes we have been missing a trick there. We must get our patients thinking, first of all, that *morality depends on religion*. That's to say, get them thinking people won't be good without religion, that religion provides us with our only moral compass. Take that compass away, and society will eventually slide into moral degeneracy.

Of course, that morality depends on religion is something your patient probably believes already. That is because the mainstream religions hijacked morality long ago. They created the myth that morality is their invention. They took the basic universal prohibitions against stealing, lying, murder, and so on, rigidly codified them, added a few idiosyncratic prohibitions of their own (typically concerning sexual practices and foodstuffs), and said, "Voilà! Religion has *created* morality! Without us, *there is no morality!*"

Never mind that there's growing scientific evidence that our morality is in large part a product of our evolutionary history. Never mind that the least religious Western democracies—

Sweden, for example—are in many respects the most socially and morally healthy. Never mind that in traditional Chinese society—in which the dominant cultural force was not religion but a secular ethical doctrine, Confucianism—levels of ordinary morality have been much the same as in parts of the world dominated by transcendental religion. Because "morality depends on religion" has been endlessly repeated by religious folk—it is the one mantra they all share—it has, in many corners of the world, become a factoid, an unquestioned part of the cultural landscape. No one really thinks about it. They just accept it. Even many atheists (some of whom, while not religious, nevertheless suppose religious belief is therefore desirable *in others*—especially those lower down the socioeconomic ladder, who might otherwise burgle their house).

Take advantage of this widespread myth. Say, "Yes, morality *does* indeed depend on religion." Then add, "But of course, it has to be the *right* religion, doesn't it?"

As I endlessly repeat to you—the key to recruitment is not reason but emotion. However, the fact is that the emotions on which we rely change. As I have already mentioned, we seduce new recruits with joy, but, as they begin to mature into seasoned Followers, we must increasingly come to rely on fear. Fear of loss of friends. Fear of loss of meaning and purpose. Now our Leader wants us to add another fear to the mix—fear of *moral oblivion*. Get our Followers holding tightly onto nurse, for fear of finding something worse. Our Leader wants our movement to achieve official status. He wants the state to recognise it as an important moral beacon—providing moral guidance to young people who might otherwise fall into degeneracy and sin. This way, we may even receive government funds. Certainly, there will no longer be any official resistance to our starting our own schools.

At the conference (which, I must say, was lavishly catered for—never have I tasted such smoked salmon), our Leader spoke of something else too. What we ultimately want, he forcefully and inspiringly reminded us, is what he calls the *Vision Thing*.

The vision of which our Leader spoke, is not, of course, *a* vision—of heaven, or a religious figure descending, or anything like that. No, no. Not that there's anything wrong with our Followers having that sort of vision, of course. Sometimes they do. But our Leader meant something much less trivial. He was speaking of the all-encompassing mindset. He gave us various examples.

Sometimes a conspiracy theorist will become so enmeshed in their theory that they can just "see" that it is true. Wherever they look, they find their theory *fits*. Of course, what they are really doing is finding a way to *make it* fit. They interpret whatever they experience in such a way that it "makes sense" on their worldview. They also develop no end of moves to explain away anything that might look like a rational threat to their belief system. Anything that might seem not to fit—that the conspiracy theorist can't fully make sense of—is put down to the powerful and sometimes mysterious and inscrutable forces and plans of the conspirators. The conspiracy theorist supposes that he is the one whose eyes have been opened to what the rest of us cannot see. He turns on his TV of an evening, and discovers that each news item only further confirms his worst fears about the spread of the Conspiracy. He looks out the window and sees agents of evil spying on him from that parked car across the street. Eventually, the Conspiracy becomes *so* obvious to him that he is astonished the rest of us can't "see it" too, especially after he has pointed it out to us in some detail. So he supposes that we must be part of the Conspiracy. Either that, or our minds have been "got to" somehow. By *them*.

The Vision Thing is not uncommon in the political sphere, of course. Witness the Marxist who, wherever she looks, finds that Marx's theories account for what happens. It all *fits*. It all *makes sense*. So obvious does it become to our Marxist, in the end, that she's astonished we cannot see what's going on in front of our eyes. Have we somehow been blinded by the forces of capitalism? Perhaps our senses have been dulled by the opiate of the masses?

The religious person, too, can achieve such an all-encompassing vision. Indeed, people often say that religious faith is something like a perspective on the world, a way of viewing it. We fling open our curtains in the morning and see sunlight. They fling open their curtains and see the glory of God flooding into their room. It's so obvious to them, they wonder why we can't see it too. They suppose we must be defective. "Perhaps," they think, "it is because they have been corrupted by sin? Or *led astray by devils?*"

The Vision Thing can be produced in all sorts of ways. Sometimes it is a product of long immersion in a political ideology or some Internet-based conspiracy theory mindset. Sometimes it is a result of drug abuse. Sometimes it is caused by a mental illness. Sometimes it happens quite spontaneously. Occasionally, people look at the world and suddenly, apparently for no reason at all, just "see" that it is imbued with a kind of cosmic radiance.

Of course, others look and are suddenly consumed by a very different vision—a vision, say, of the world as the product of some awful cosmic malignancy. Those who have the latter sort of experience—and they are more common than you might imagine—tend to be put on medication. Those who have the former sort of experience tend to put on a dog collar. Had we the advantage of being one of the established, mainstream religions, many of those spontaneously having the first sort of experience would walk in through our doors, already converts!

What we are after with every patient is, our Leader helpfully reminded us, the Vision Thing. Our patients must come to *see*—with their hearts, if not their eyes—that our teaching is the Truth—that it accords in every last detail with everything they have ever experienced. They must find that it ultimately *makes sense* of everything.

I am concerned by the lack of communication, Woodworm. Get in touch. Now.

Your aunt,
Tapescrew

The Bodgers Centre
Newcastle
September 14, 2009

Woodworm,

Finally, a missive from you. But I would rather not have received it. The brother, it turns out, is a skeptic—someone who insists on subjecting claims of a supernatural or extraordinary nature to close critical scrutiny before accepting them? And the patient shows signs of becoming one too? She has even signed up for a class in critical thinking and taken out a subscription to *Skeptical Inquirer*? How could you have let this happen, you oaf? Now we discover why you have been so quiet of late. You have failed catastrophically. You have allowed him to throw her the lifeline of reason, and she has used it to pull herself free!

Had I been forewarned that the brother is one of these irritatingly persistent and clear-headed free-thought types, well, we could have made plans. We could have at least prepared to *Go Nuclear*. But now it is too late.

Remember, at the end of the day, all we have got is a collection of extraordinary claims for which we can provide scarcely a shred of evidence. Other than that *we say they are true*. That's it!

Of course, all other cults and religions are in the same boat, yet that has not stopped *them* from flourishing, sometimes spectacularly so. How do *they* achieve such extraordinary success? Rule Number One is this: They manage, by one means or another, to obscure the fact that the evidence for what they believe is simply *that they say it's true*. Either that, or they succeed in neutralizing this fact by making it seem unimportant. They insist that the truth of what they say is known, not on the basis of *evidence*, oh, no, but in some other, *deeper* way—"with the heart," or some other codswallop with which they fob off their respective followers.

Ultimately, you had one simple, basic job to do: to deal with the otherwise obvious thought that the only real reason our patient has got to believe any of this twaddle is that *we say it is true*. Which is hardly much of a reason, is it? That, Woodworm, is the one thought that, above all, you should have suppressed or neutralized. Yet that is the one thought you have allowed to pop—nay, *explode*—in the patient's head, and with devastating consequences!

You say she is now doubting even the "experience" we worked so carefully to cultivate at the Retreat? You say she thinks we have been playing with her mind? She supposes she may merely have felt certain powerful emotions that she *mistook* to be some sort of revelation? Good grief. We are sunk.

How on earth is our cult to expand if it has to rely on gurus as incompetent as yourself? The consequences of such an error will be serious, my boy. Our Leader does not forgive failure. You were warned.

Your bitterly disappointed aunt,
Tapescrew

Notes

INTRODUCTION

1. See Harry Frankfurt, *On Bullshit* (Princeton, NJ: Princeton University Press, 2005), p. 56.

2. Justin Barrett, *Why Would Anyone Believe in God?* (Lanham, MD: Altamira Press, 2004).

3. Daniel D. Wegner, *The Illusion of Conscious Will* (Cambridge, MA: MIT Press, 2002), p. 113.

4. John Polkinghorne and Nicholas Beale, *Questions of Truth* (Louisville, KY: Westminster John Knox Press, 2009), p. 17.

5. See my paper "The Evil God Challenge," *Religious Studies* 46 (2010): 353–73.

6. http://richarddawkins.net/articles/5481-believe-it-or-not (accessed September 27, 2010).

7. Broadcast by Premier Christian Radio on May 1, 2010, http://media.premier.org.uk/unbelievable/3ad5f46f-e8c4–4ef5–85c8–37429f399c86.mp3 (accessed September 27, 2010).

CHAPTER 1

1. G. W. F. Hegel, *Lectures on the Philosophy of Religion*, vol. 1, *Introduction and Concept of Religion*, edited by Peter C. Hodgson (Berkeley: University of California Press, 1994), p. 258.

2. Quoted in John Woodcock and Jennifer Hill, "Crystal Healing All in the Mind," *Scotsman*, March 29, 2001, http://www.rickross.com/reference/general/general369.html (accessed September 27, 2010).

3. http://recursed.blogspot.com/2006/05/debunking-crystal-healing.html (accessed September 27, 2010).

4. As the owner of the blog, Jeffrey Shallit, points out.

5. *Journal of Applied Social Psychology* 40, no. 3 (2010): 579–600.

6. Martin Rees, "Other Universes: A Scientific Perspective," in *God and Design: The Teleological Argument and Modern Science*, edited by Neil A. Manson (London: Routledge, 2003), pp. 211–20.

7. John Polkinghorne, *Questions of Truth* (Louisville, KY: Westminster John Knox Press, 2009), p. 45.

8. Paul Davies, *The Goldilocks Enigma* (London: Penguin, 2007).

9. Richard Dawkins, *The God Delusion* (London: Black Swan, 2007), p. 136.

10. Published in the *Times* (London), February 10, 2007.

11. Dawkins, *God Delusion*, p. 80.

12. Ibid.

13. Ibid.

14. Ibid.

15. Alister McGrath, *The Dawkins Delusion* (London: SPCK, 2007), p. 14.

16. Quoted in Hales "You *Can* Prove a Negative," *THINK* 10 (2005): 109.

17. Ibid., pp. 109–12.

18. Quentin Smith, *Two Ways to Defend Atheism*. Speech presented to the Atheist Alliance convention in Minneapolis, Minnesota, on April 6, 1996.

19. Stephen Wykstra, "The Humean Objection to Evidential Arguments from Suffering: On Avoiding the Evils of 'Appearance,'" *International Journal for Philosophy of Religion* 16 (1984): 91.

CHAPTER 2

1. See, for example, the Gallup report "Evolution, Creationism, Intelligent Design," http://www.gallup.com/poll/21814/evolution-creationism-intelligent-design.aspx (accessed September 30, 2010).

2. H. M. Morris, *The Remarkable Birth of Planet Earth* (San Diego: Creation-Life Publishers, 1972), p. 75.

3. See, e.g., Richard E. Lenski, "Evolution: Fact and Theory," http://www.actionbioscience.org/evolution/lenski.html (accessed September 30, 2010).

4. http://ldolphin.org/cisflood.html (accessed September 30, 2010).

5. http://creation.com/were-dinosaurs-on-noahs-ark (accessed September 30, 2010).

6. Ibid.

7. http://ldolphin.org/cisflood.html (accessed September 30, 2010).

8. http://www.answersingenesis.org/articles/nab/really-a-flood-and-ark (accessed September 30, 2010).

9. Ibid.

10. Douglas Theobald, "29+ Evidences for Macro-evolution Part 1: The Unique Universal Phylogenetic Tree," http://www.talkorigins.org/faqs/comdesc/section1.html (accessed September 30, 2010).

11. See, for example, ibid.

12. "Science as Falsification," http://www.stephenjaygould.org/ctrl/popper_falsification.html (accessed September 30, 2010).

13. Ibid.

14. Quoted in Martin Gardner, "Fads and Fallacies in the Name of Science (New York: Courier Dover Publications, 1957), p. 126.

15. Robin Pharoah, Tamara Hale, and Becky Rowe, *Doubting Darwin: Creationism and Evolution Scepticism in Britain Today*, pp. 138–39, http://campaigndirector.moodia.com/Client/Theos/Files/Theos DoubtingDarwin.pdf (accessed September 30, 2010).

16. http://www.answersingenesis.org/home/area/the-lie/chapter4.asp (accessed September 30, 2010).

17. http://www.answersingenesis.org/docs/206.asp (accessed September 30, 2010).

18. Bodie Hodge, "Why Don't We Find Human and Dinosaur Fossils Together?" http://www.answersingenesis.org/publicstore/pdfs/samplechapter/10–2-267.pdf (accessed September 30, 2010).

19. http://www.apologeticspress.org/articles/184 (accessed September 30, 2010).

20. "Science as Falsification," http://www.stephenjaygould.org/ctrl/popper_falsification.html (accessed September 30, 2010).

21. http://www.answersingenesis.org/home/area/the-lie/chapter4.asp (accessed September 30, 2010).

CHAPTER 3

1. Quoted in Solomon Schimmel, *The Tenacity of Unreasonable Beliefs* (Oxford: Oxford University Press, 2008), p. 66 (quoting Samuel Heilman, H-JUDAIC Discussion group, January 15, 1997).

2. In a comment on my blog post at http://stephenlaw.blogspot.com/2008/08/sye-latest-twist.html (accessed September 20, 2010).

3. MacLaine quote taken from Theodore Schick and Lewis Vaughn, eds., *How to Think about Weird Things*, 5th ed. (New York: McGraw-Hill, 2007), p. 310.

4. http://www.psychicbutsane.com/intuition/how-to-discern-what-is-true (accessed September 20, 2010).

5. Allan Bloom, *The Closing of the American Mind* (New York: Touchstone, 1987), p. 25.

6. Quotation is the first line of "On Truth," available at http://www.personal.psu.edu/jxm22/browseread/bacontruth.html.

CHAPTER 4

1. http://elizaphanian.blogspot.com/2008/06/meaning-suffering-and-integrity.html (accessed October 2, 2010).

2. Karen Armstrong, *The Case for God* (London: Bodley Head, 2009), p. 293.

3. Ibid., p. 307.

4. Ibid.

5. Ibid., p. 246.

6. Ibid., p. 34—also see p. 314.

7. Denys Turner, "How to Be an Atheist" in his *Faith Seeking* (Cambridge: Cambridge University Press, 2002), p. 10.

8. Ibid., p. 13.

9. Ibid.

10. Ibid., p. 19.

11. See A. J. Ayer, *Language, Truth and Logic* (Harmondsworth, UK: Penguin, 1971).

12. Nicholas Lash, "The Impossibility of Atheism" in his *Theology for Pilgrims* (London: Darton, Longman and Todd, 2008), p. 34.

13. Lash, incidentally, then goes on to argue that the latter sort of atheism is *impossible*, as "effective refusal to have anything to do with God can only mean self-destruction, annihilation, return to the *nihil* from which all things came" (p. 35). Lash's argument for the impossibility of this kind of atheism contains two obvious flaws: (1) Lash here just *assumes* that there is a God from which all things came, and (2) in case Lash muddles up two senses of "refusal to have anything to do with." I can refuse to have anything to with my mother in the sense that I can ignore her, etc., but of course I still have *something* to do with her, and indeed do so necessarily: it remains true that if she had not existed, then neither would I. Atheists might similarly refuse to have anything to do with God even if there is, as Lash here just assumes, a God on which their existence depends.

14. Lash, "The Impossibility of Atheism," p. 34.

15. Ibid., p. 35.

16. Ibid., p. 26.

17. Ibid., p. 15.

CHAPTER 5

1. Charles E. Miller, "Intuitive Policing," in *FBI Law Enforcement Bulletin*, February 1, 2004. Also see Malcolm Gladwell's book *Blink* (London: Penguin, 2006) for other examples.

2. Rich Proctor, "The Bush Style: Going on His Fabled Gut," *CounterPunch*, February 22, 2003, http://www.counterpunch.org/procter02222003.html (accessed October 5, 2010).

3. Ron Suskind, "Faith, Certainty and the Presidency of George W. Bush," *New York Times Magazine*, October 17, 2004, http://www.nytimes.com/2004/10/17/magazine/17BUSH.html (accessed October 5, 2010).

4. Clifford's paper "The Ethics of Belief" is currently in print in W. K. Clifford, *The Ethics of Belief and Other Essays* (Amherst, NY: Prometheus Books, 1999).

5. Richard Dawkins, *A Devil's Chaplain* (London: Weidenfeld & Nicolson, 2003), p. 248.

6. For a brief overview of Plantinga's view, see his entry "Reformed Epistemology" in *A Companion to the Philosophy of Religion*, edited by Philip L. Quinn and Charles Taliaferro (Oxford: Blackwell, 1997), pp. 383–89.

7. Alvin Plantinga, *Warranted Christian Belief* (Oxford: Oxford University Press, 2000), p. 214.

8. My thanks to Tim Mawson for this nice way of making the point.

9. Karen Armstrong, *The Case for God* (London: Bodley Head, 2009), p. 305.

10. Ibid., p. 316.

11. Ibid., p. 34.

12. Ibid., p. 314.

13. In his book *Why Gods Persist*, biologist and psychologist Professor Robert Hinde, having surveyed the scientific literature on religious and certain sorts of nonreligious experience, also tentatively concludes that the two sets of experiences are remarkably similar, differing largely only in how they are interpreted:

> It is difficult to draw a line between experience that is clearly religious and experiences of a more secular nature. The emotions aroused in many secular gatherings are not clearly different from those involved in religious ones, and aesthetic experience would seem to have much in common with religious experience. The view tentatively suggested here . . . is that the experiences are essentially the same, and it is primarily the interpretations put on them that differ. (Robert A. Hinde, *Why Gods Persist: A Scientific Approach to Religion*, 2nd ed. [Abingdon, UK: Routledge, 2000], p. 205)

Hinde adds the caveat that the nature of the experience, once it is interpreted religiously, may change as a result.

14. http://www.answers2prayer.org/bible_questions/Answers/prayer/speaking.html (accessed October 5, 2010).

CHAPTER 6

1. In a speech to the American Atheists Institution conference in 2009, http://www.youtube.com/watch?v=D_9w8JougLQ (accessed October 2, 2010).

2. Borrowed from the website http://www.parables.com (accessed October 2, 2010).

3. Maxwell's inaugural lecture at Cambridge University, 1871.

4. Quoted in Alan Sokal and Jean Bricmont, *Intellectual Impostures* (London: Profile Books, 1998), pp. 156–57.

5. Ibid., p. 156.

6. Ibid., p. 143.

7. Richard Dawkins, "Postmodernism Disrobed," http://richard dawkins.net/articles/824-postmodernism-disrobed (accessed October 2, 2010). Published as "Postmodernism Disrobed" in *Nature* 394 (1998): 141–43.

CHAPTER 7

1. Quoted in "Hidden Messages and the Bible Code" by David E. Thomas, which is published in Committee for the Scientific Investigation of Claims of the Paranormal, *Bizarre Cases* (Amherst, NY: 2000), p. 124.

2. Ibid., p. 127.

3. Philip J. Klass, *UFOs: The Public Deceived* (Amherst, NY: Prometheus Books, 1983), p. 83.

4. H. K. Beecher, "The Powerful Placebo," *Journal of the American Medical Association* 159, no. 17 (1955): 1602–1606.

5. Jean Piaget, *Plays, Dreams and Imitation in Childhood* (New York: Norton, 1962), pp. 187–88.

6. See S. J. Lynn, T. Lock, E. F. Loftus, E. Krackow, and S. O. Lilienfeld, "The Remembrance of Things Past: Problematic Memory Recovery Techniques in Psychotherapy," in *Science and Pseudoscience in Clinical Psychology*, edited by S. O. Lilienfeld, S. J. Lynn, and J. M. Lohr (New York: Guilford, 2003). Also see E. F. Loftus, "The Reality of Repressed Memories," *American Psychologist* 48 (1993): 518–37; E. F. Loftus and

K. Ketcham, *The Myth of Repressed Memory: False Memories and Accusations of Sexual Abuse* (New York: St. Martin's Press, 1994).

7. Margaretta Fox Kane, quoted in R. B. Davenport, *The Deathblow to Spiritualism* (New York: Richardson, 2009), p. 76.

8. Harry Houdini, *A Magician among the Spirits* (New York: Arno Press, 1972), p. 8.

9. From "Defence of Bloodletting," http://www.archive.org/stream/medicalinquiries04rush/medicalinquiries04rush_djvu.txt (accessed September 28, 2010).

10. Simon Singh and Edzard Ernst, *Trick or Treatment* (London: Bantam, 2009), p. 172.

11. H. Benson et al., "Study of the Therapeutic Effects of Intercessionary Prayer (STEP) in Cardiac Bypass Patients: A Multicenter Randomized Trial of Uncertainty and Certainty of Receiving Intercessionary Prayer," *American Heart Journal* 151 (2006): 934–42.

12. M. W. Krucoff et al., "Music, Imagery, Touch, and Prayer as Adjuncts to Interventional Cardiac Care: The Monitoring and Actualization of Noetic Trainings (MANTRA) II Randomized Study," *Lancet* 366 (2005): 211–17.

13. Quoted in Richard Dawkins, *The God Delusion* (London: Black Swan, 2006), p. 90.

14. Caroline Fraser, *God's Perfect Child* (New York: Metropolitan Books, 1999), p. 417.

15. Quoted in ibid., p. 421.

16. Quoted in ibid., p. 425.

17. R. W. England, "Some Aspects of Christian Science as Reflected in Letters of Testimony," *American Journal of Sociology* 59 (1954): 542. Quoted in Fraser, *God's Perfect Child*, pp. 432–33.

18. England, "Some Aspects of Christian Science," p. 451, quoted in Fraser, *God's Perfect Child*, p. 432.

19. Richard Feynman, *The Meaning of It All* (London: Penguin, 2007), p. 93.

CHAPTER 8

1. Solomon Asch's conformity experiments revealed people are prone to denying the evidence of their own eyes if it brings them into

disagreement with others (although admittedly this is not quite the same thing as changing what one believes in order to conform). See S. E. Asch, "Effects of Group Pressure upon the Modification and Distortion of Judgment" in *Groups, Leadership and Men*, edited by H. Guetzkow (Pittsburgh: Carnegie Press, 1951).

2. *Times* (London), July 20, 2005, p. 25.

3. George Orwell, *Nineteen Eighty-Four* (Harmondsworth, UK: Penguin, 1954), p. 265.

4. Kathleen Taylor, "Thought Crime," *Guardian*, October 8, 2005, p. 23.

5. Kathleen Taylor, *Brainwashing: The Science of Thought Control* (Oxford: Oxford University Press, 2004), p. 23.

6. Edward Hunter, *Brainwashing: The Story of Men Who Defied It* (New York: Farrar, Strauss, and Cudahy, 1956), p. 309.

CONCLUSION

1. Erich von Däniken, *Chariots of the Gods?* (London: Souvenir Press, 1990).

2. Róisín Ingle, "Where No Angels Fear to Tread," *Irish Times*, May 28, 2008. http://www.lornabyrne.com/TheIrishTimes28may2008 .pdf (accessed October 4, 2010).

3. Entry on "Nostradamus" at http://www.skepdic.com/ nostrada.html (accessed October 4, 2010). This article is the source of the other quotes in this section.

4. This example is taken from p. 127 of "Hidden Messages and the Bible Code" by David E. Thomas, published in Committee for the Scientific Investigation of Claims of the Paranormal, *Bizarre Cases* (Amherst, NY: CSICOP, 2000).

THE TAPESCREW LETTERS

1. Jewish scholars quoted in Solomon Schimmel, *The Tenacity of Unreasonable Belief* (Oxford: Oxford University Press, 2008), p. 47.

Index